THE SACRED LITERATURE SERIES

Edited by Kerry Brown and Sima Sharma

WARLPIRI DREAMINGS AND HISTORIES

*The Sacred Literature Series of
the International Sacred Literature Trust
in association with HarperCollins*

Other titles in the series

BUDDHISM
The Words of My Perfect Teacher
◆

INDIAN TRADITIONS
In the Dark of the Heart: Hymns of Meera
◆

JAINISM
*That Which Is: A Manual for Understanding the
True Nature of Reality*
◆

JUDAISM
Gates of Light
◆

TAOISM
Lao-tzu's Treatise on the Response of the Tao

Further titles are in preparation

YIMIKIRLI

Warlpiri Dreamings and Histories

Collected and translated by
Peggy Rockman Napaljarri and Lee Cataldi

SPONSORED BY THE AUSTRALIAN INSTITUTE OF ABORIGINAL
AND TORRES STRAIT ISLANDER STUDIES

HarperCollins*Publishers*

For more information about the ISLT,
please write to the ISLT at:
23 Darley Avenue
Manchester, M20 8ZD
United Kingdom

HarperCollins Publishers
1160 Battery Street, San Francisco 94111
United States of America
77-85 Fulham Palace Road, London W6 8JB
Great Britain
25 Ryde Road, Pymble, NSW 2073
Australia

Proofread by Anne Hegerty
Photoset in Linotron Sabon by Northern Phototypesetting
Company Limited, Bolton, U. K.

Library of Congress Cataloging-in-Publication Data
Warlpiri dreamings and histories = Yimikirli / collected and translated by
Peggy Rockman Napaljarri and Lee Cataldi. — 1st ed.
p. cm. — (Sacred literature series)
"Sponsored by the Australian Institute of Aboriginal and
Torres Strait Islander Studies."
ISBN 0-06-066125-9 (alk. paper)
1. Warlpiri (Australian people)—Folklore. 2. Warlpiri (Australian people)—Religion. 3. Warlpiri (Australian people)—Social life and customs. I. Napaljarri, Peggy Rockman. II. Cataldi, Lee. III. Australian Institute of Aboriginal and Torres Strait Islander Studies. IV. Title: Yimikirli. V. Series.
GR366.W35W35 1994
398'.0899915—dc20   93-34863
                                                              CIP

94 95 96 97 98 RRD(H) 10 9 8 7 6 5 4 3 2 1

The two drew close to each other in order to make peace

INTERNATIONAL
SACRED
LITERATURE
TRUST

The International Sacred Literature Trust was established to promote understanding and open discussion between and within faiths and to give voice in today's world to the wisdom that speaks across time and traditions.

What resources do the sacred traditions of the world possess to respond to the great global threats of poverty, war, ecological disaster and spiritual despair?

Our starting point is the sacred texts with their vision of a higher truth and their deep insights into the nature of humanity and the universe we inhabit. The translation programme is planned so that each faith community articulates its own teachings with the intention of enhancing its self-understanding as well as the understanding of those of other faiths and those of no faith.

The Trust particularly encourages faiths to make available texts which are needed in translation for their own communities, and texts which are little known outside the tradition but which have the power to inspire, console, enlighten and transform. These sources from the past become resources for the present and future when we make inspired use of them to guide us in shaping the contemporary world.

Our religious traditions are diverse but, as with the natural environment, we are discovering the global interdependence of human hearts and minds. The Trust invites all to participate in the modern experience of interfaith encounter and exchange which marks a new phase in the human quest to discover our full humanity.

Contents

CONTENTS

Contributors

D. M. Jakamarra
Henry Cook Jakamarra
Jacko Ross Jakamarra
Joe Jangala
Popeye Jangala
Ted Egan Jangala
Tiger Japaljarri
Jimmy Jungarrayi
Liddy Nelson Nakamarra
Uni Nampijinpa
Peggy Rockman Napaljarri
Kajingarra Napangardi
Mary O'Keefe Napurrurla
Molly Tasman Napurrurla
Ngarlinjiya Mary Robertson Nungarrayi

Preface

At the beginning, some time ago, Napaljarri [Lee Cataldi] and I talked about how people tell these stories, these really true stories about the law.

At first we went around Lajamanu. We collected stories from people in their homes, one by one. We went around collecting them. Some people said to us, "No, we do not know any!" But from many other people we were able to record their stories.

We also recorded stories when we took people hunting as well as when they were in their homes at Lajamanu. They spoke Warlpiri really well. These Warlpiri people let us record their stories, old men, middle-aged people, and some younger adults as well. However, some people became too nervous to talk.

Then we travelled to other places, Napaljarri and I. In these places, people also spoke to us really well. Some of the stories they told were very long, long stories. After we had collected these stories, we asked many other people. Sometimes they could not tell us anything.

"I don't know. I can only tell little stories, I only know a little about telling stories." So they just told very brief stories. Then we asked other people.

"Could you tell us a story?"

"Yes, I can tell you the story of my own dreaming, belonging to my father."

These people were able to speak for a long time, which was very good. They told the really important stories. Then we went and asked other people. "I don't know," others said. We went to ask many other people. These people then would be able to tell really true stories, ones belonging to their fathers' country, to the law, from the Dreaming. That is how we collected them.

The stories in this book are the sorts of things that people tell. These stories are really good. When we went around collecting them, many people wanted to tell them to us. With some, we were not sure what to do. This is because they were in other languages such as Kukaja, Walmajarri or Kurinji. This made some people rather shy.

However, the people of Yuendumu spoke to us in very strong

Warlpiri, either Ngaliya or Warnayaka Warlpiri. They spoke really well. They told us many important stories. They recorded the stories that belonged to themselves and their country.

People in Willowra also spoke in the same way. They speak very well about their country, and the things that belong to it. They also speak very strong Warlpiri. These stories are very good, very important.

In Nyirrpi, there lives a Japaljarri, a very good storyteller, and he too tells his own stories very well.

In different places, other people were unable to speak. Perhaps they do not know their own dreamings or about their own country.

At Alekarenge, many people spoke really well, especially women. One Jangala also spoke very well. The people there really wanted to record their stories. This made us very pleased.

This is the way we travelled around, talking with people. Some of them spoke really well, but others unfortunately became frightened and nervous. They became ashamed. This may be because they do not know all the things they should, because maybe their fathers and mothers or their grandparents have not taught them properly and have not told them all the stories that belong to them. So they are ignorant and cannot speak.

This is what I wish to say about our project.

Peggy Rockman Napaljarri

Translators' Acknowledgments

We wish to acknowledge the assistance of the following institutions and people without whose help this collection would not have been possible:

The Australian Institute of Aboriginal and Torres Strait Islander Studies for the grant to Peggy Rockman Napaljarri and Lee Cataldi for the project Yimikirli in 1990 during which these narratives were collected, transcribed and translated;

Mary Laughren, linguist with the Northern Territory Department of Education, for her hospitality, assistance, information, advice and, not least, for proofreading the Warlpiri texts;

Christine Nicholls when principal, Lajamanu School, for her assistance, advice, cups of tea, and for taping the narrative Wapurtarlikirli with Liddy Nakamarra;

Jenni Mandersloot, teacher-linguist, Willowra School, for her assistance and hospitality;

Valda Shannon when assistant principal, Alekarenge School, for her assistance and hospitality;

The staff of Nyirrpi School and Nyirrpi Store for their help;

Robert Durand, then literature production supervisor at Yuendumu, for his assistance and hospitality;

June Granites Napanangka for transcribing Popeye Jangala's "The Two Dogs", Warren Williams Japanangka for help in transcribing Uni Nampijinpa's "What Happened at the Place of Fire", Elizabeth Ross Nungarrayi for help in transcribing Peggy Rockman's "The Man from Wawarlja"; and, finally, all the Warlpiri people whose stories are not in this book because we had to select a small and, we hope, representative number, but who so generously gave their narratives to the project and therefore to the tape collections in all the Warlpiri schools, for their children and their children's children to hear and learn.

ISLT's Acknowledgments

We acknowledge and thank:

Quentin Smith, L.K. Sharma, Doreen Mantle and Shashwati Sharma for their ideas and constant support;

Josephine Edwards for her diligence and helpfulness in administering the Trust;

Oliver Caldecott, Mark Cohen, Ivan Hattingh, Jack Hogbin, Martin Palmer, Aubrey Rose and the International Consultancy on Religion, Education and Culture for their time and commitment in the founding years of the ISLT;

Dr Howard Morphy at the Pitt Rivers Museum in Oxford and Dr David Nash at the Australian Institute of Aboriginal and Torres Strait Islander Studies (AIATSIS) for the trouble they took to introduce us to the people who could provide the first book in our series of Australian Aboriginal traditions;

Lee Cataldi and Peggy Rockman Napaljarri for enduring the more tedious chores involved in the preparation of their exceptional manuscript, made more tedious by the great distance between us and them and between them and the storytellers across the central region of Australia where they all live;

The Australian Institute of Aboriginal and Torres Strait Islander Studies for funding the collection and translation of the narratives.

We especially thank the Warlpiri people for sharing their great heritage with us.

Introduction

Warlpiri Land and Religion

It is well known that for Australian Aboriginal people religious beliefs are inseparable from the land to which the different language groups, families and individuals belong. Thus the narratives in this book which describe the travels of ancestral figures from place to place also describe actions which caused the natural features of the land, particularly water, rock formations and trees, to come into being. The ancestral figures are often also food, either vegetable or meat. The narrative is simultaneously an account of the creation of the places in the story, an account of the mythical but human behaviour of the ancestral figures, and a mnemonic map of the country with its important, life-giving features for the purpose of instructing a younger listener. These elements make up Warlpiri Jukurrpa, commonly translated as the Dreaming. The Jukurrpa or Dreaming is Warlpiri culture and law. It is the time of the creation of the world which continues to exist as an eternal present embodied in songs, stories, dances and places. It is always there, although people may forget or abandon it. While the Jukurrpa or Dreaming is a universal, each person and place also has their own particular dreamings.

The major ceremonial event of Warlpiri life is the kurdiji, when young men just reaching puberty are initiated into the first stage of the education of a Warlpiri man (see "The Travels of the Witi Poles", pp.73–91). The kurdiji ceremony is the initiate's entry into manhood and also marriage; during the ceremony, the arrangements for the provision of the girl or even baby who is to be his promised wife are put in place. Thus the key social bonds for a Warlpiri person are entered into here – the man's set of binding and reciprocal relations with the men who are the key functionaries at the ceremony, and his relations with his new set of in-laws. The ceremony also reinforces the ties between families created by the giving of children in marriage.

The other distinguishing characteristic of this system of beliefs is its integration. At the kurdiji ceremony the bonds between the various agents are also links between the various parts of the country, as mapped by the travels of the different Jukurrpa figures whose actions are precisely the content of the singing, the dancing, the sand and body designs, and often the deliberations of those taking part. Warlpiri people have a very refined and elaborate system of hand-signs, a complete language. These signs, with their specific and precise meanings, are also the gestures used in the dances that re-enact the actions of the Jukurrpa beings. Thus, song, narrative, painting and dance all embody the same meaningful events.[1] To these, Warlpiri people have recently added the medium of acrylic paint on canvas to provide yet another way of expressing the true events of the Jukurrpa. Examples of this are in this book.

The narratives of the Jukurrpa, the gestures, the songs,[2] the dances and the designs which are painted on sand, wooden implements or human skin, form the record of the beliefs of the Warlpiri people, and despite all the breaches and interruptions caused by the intrusion of Europeans into Warlpiri country, the Warlpiri have succeeded in handing them down to the present generation of middle-aged people as a complete and living system. Of course, many people are very concerned about whether this will continue, and the recording enterprise which led to this book (one of several like projects in these areas) is part of an effort now being made to supplement oral traditions with paper and tape.

Warlpiri social arrangements are based on what is described in English as the "skin system". This is how Tess Ross Napaljarri describes it:

People bear the following names:

Napaljarri	Napangardi	Nakamarra	Nungarrayi
Japaljarri	Japangardi	Jakamarra	Jungarrayi
Napurrurla	Nangala	Napanangka	Nampijinpa
Jupurrurla	Jangala	Japanangka	Jampijinpa

---

[1] Often at the end or even during a narrative, a character is described as "going in". This means that the being returns to its normal or rightful place in the earth.
[2] Another type of singing pertains to the use of healing power or sorcery, and is a very specialized activity.

The names that begin with "J" are used for men and the names that begin with "N" are what women call themselves. If you say "Napaljarri", then it is a woman; if you say "Japaljarri", then it is a man, and "Jakamarra" is a man and "Nakamarra" is a woman, "Jangala" is a man and "Nangala" is a woman. Everyone has one of these names. The people who have these names are related to each other. For example, I am Napaljarri and my mother is Nangala and my father is Jungarrayi and my husband is Jakamarra and our child is Jupurrurla if it is a boy and Napurrurla if it is a girl. Then, Japanangka marries my daughter and my son marries Napanangka, Japanangka's sister. These people are some of my family. This has been the way since the beginning and people inherited it from their ancestors.[3]

This kinship system relates the people to each other, but its central importance for the Warlpiri world view is that it also relates the people to the Jukurrpa and the land. That is, for Warlpiri people the relationship between each person and the world is mediated by their kinship subsection. Each jukurrpa, and each place, belongs to one (or possibly two) of four pairs, Jupurrurla-Jakamarra, Jungarryi-Japaljarri, Jangala-Jampijinpa, Japangardi-Japanangka, and the female counterparts. These pairs also mark the relationship of father and son. That is, through their particular subsection, each person is related to other people, to their jukurrpa ancestors, to the places they own and are responsible for, to the narratives and songs concerning the places and ancestors, and to the gestures, dances and designs that belong to the places.

In Warlpiri religious beliefs and practices, each person is responsible for the nurturing of the places they own from their father, and reciprocally for the good conduct of the other owners for the places in which they have an interest inherited from their mother. Knowledge and respect are gained through participation and learning, and also good sense. Thus the most respected elders are those who have exerted themselves the most. Traditional responsibilities are inherited, rights are earned.

---

[3] Tess Ross Napaljarri, "The People and their Home", *Kuruwarri: Yuendumu Doors*, pp. 7–9.

The Warlpiri People after the Arrival of the Europeans

For Warlpiri people, the coming of the Europeans was "the end of the Jukurrpa". When Rosie Napurrurla said this at Lajamanu, she explained that this did not mean there was now nothing to be learned from the Jukurrpa but that, from that time, Warlpiri people have no longer been living in it. It seems that Rosie Napurrurla and many others are very aware that the intrusion into their lives and land of the dominating, metropolitan culture of the West meant the end of the Jukurrpa as a world view, as a single, total explanation of the universe. It is apparent that many Warlpiri people are much more clearly aware of the nature of cultural conflict and the nature of the two cultures than Europeans are. Such awareness is the privilege of the loser in this kind of conflict.

By 1862, the European spread across Australia reached into the Warlpiri region in the central north of the continent. From the initial explorations through to the gold rushes of 1910 and 1932, and the beginning of pastoral settlement in the east in 1917, the encroachment was slow by our criteria. However, for timescales established in the steady and orderly progress of generations measuring the growth of populations and the expansion of resources across tens of thousands of years of Aboriginal settlement on the continent (estimated at 40,000–100,000 years), these arrivals and the changes they brought must have been frighteningly rapid and violent.

At first, families continued to live on their own lands in their own way, paying occasional visits to white encampments, out of curiosity and also drawn by the attractions of the goods the whites had – steel implements, food and particularly tobacco. A number of violent clashes are recorded, but open conflict, reprisals and massacres such as that at Coniston (see "The Events at Yurrkuru", pp.161–171) did not occur until the arrival of the cattle and eventually a drought that precipitated the inevitable and desperate conflict over water. With this open conflict, the systematic eviction of Warlpiri families from their lands began, in the areas to the east around the Lander river, and also to the north-west in the area around Yaruman.

A number of factors – the presence of starving and dispossessed people at the stations along the telegraph line to the east of Warlpiri country, where the Stuart Highway now runs, the known brutality of some of the miners and pastoralists, and the increasing pressure coming from interested European anthropologists, particularly Olive Pink (see "Taking Care of Miss Pink", pp. 173–179), and missionary bodies – led to the establishment of government settlements for Warlpiri people, first at the Tanami in 1945, and then at Yuendumu in 1946, followed by another settlement at Lajamanu in 1952.

Warlpiri people still live at Lajamanu and Yuendumu, and these are now communities in which the social system and many financial and economic arrangements are dominated by Warlpiri people. This is also true of Willowra, the lease of which was transferred to the Warlpiri families living there in 1973 thanks to the efforts of Edgar Parkinson who owned the lease and the persistence of the Warlpiri people. Willowra (Wirliyajarrayi) in particular is a society created by Warlpiri people.

Currently, the Warlpiri people live in a number of different communities and outstations. The largest community is Yuendumu with a population of approximately 1000 people. Lajamanu has a population of approximately 700 people, Willowra approximately 300 people, Nyirrpi approximately 150 people. Many Warlpiri people live at Alekarenge (with Kayeteje, Warrumungu and Alyawarra people). Others live with other Aboriginal people in the Balgo, Yaruman, Kurrurrungku, Yakayaka, Areyonga, Dagaragu, Pupanya, Mount Allen and Turkey Creek communities.

The outstation or homelands movement is a new development, and is the realization of the desire many Aboriginal people have had since white settlement removed them from their traditional lands to return to those lands. Under the Land Rights Act for the Northern Territory, the families claim their traditional land and establish themselves there with government assistance for a bore, windmill, small houses and even a small school with a local Aboriginal teacher. These outstations are not full settlements but rely on a large settlement nearby for food, health, education visits and so on. There are Warlpiri people living in the outstations of Jiwarranpa, Munkurrurpa, Wayililinpa, Jila, Yumurrpa and Kulurrngalinypa. Other places are visited regularly, and new outstations are being established all the time.

There are also sizeable Warlpiri groups living in the towns of Tennant Creek, Alice Springs, Katherine, Hall's Creek and Darwin.

Although it is true that Warlpiri people no longer live within the logic and constraints of the world view known as the Jukurrpa, it is also the case that, like other traditional Aboriginal people, they have succeeded in creating for themselves a way of life which is unique and distinctive, nothing like the European culture with which they have to live. We hope that something of the spirit of this social creation is communicated by the translations and the narratives in this book.[4]

Warlpiri Perspectives on Past and Present

A group of trainee teachers at Lajamanu School gives a recent history of the area:

In the early days, Lajamanu was called Hooker Creek. It was Gurinji land once but the Warlpiri people fought the Gurinji people and so they had to go to another place and live there. Our people used to walk in those days and they were good at it.

The white people came and they started to build houses and roads and other things. Then more Aboriginal people came on big trucks from Yuendumu settlement because at that time Yuendumu was crowded with people. Some Warlpiri people were shifted to Willowra, Warrabri [previous name of Alekarenge] and Hooker Creek. A few years later they changed it to a new name called Lajamanu. . . .

We call white people "kardiya" and we call ourselves "yapa" which means a black Aboriginal person. In the '50s and '60s, we were living in humpies [huts] and windbreaks but now most of the people live in houses the same as European people. There are still a few old people who are living in humpies, and there are some at the top camp out of the settlement. . . .

At Lajamanu, the yapa council runs everything in this community. At Lajamanu, the yapa people are very happy because they

---

[4] Some of the material in this section is derived from the Warlpiri and the Warlpiri-Warlmanpa-Warrumungu Land Claim documents, and is reproduced here with the permission of the Central Land Council.

are running it themselves. Lajamanu is the first self-governing community. . . . This community is run by the council and they want to fight for this community because they have lived here for long enough.

There are about 700 people living in Lajamanu, and we are all of the Warlpiri tribe.[5]

Tess Ross Napaljarri describes contemporary Yuendumu:

Yuendumu is north-west of Alice Springs, in the middle of the Centre, a big place. There are many Warlpiri people living there. I am a Warlpiri living at Yuendumu.

The types of game that we hunt and kill are: emus, kangaroos, wild cats, bush turkeys, blue-tongue lizards, skinks, goannas, birds, snakes and perenties. For vegetable foods, there are little seeds which fall from trees and onto the ground. These are ground with stone and prepared for seedcakes. Some of the seeds are from pig-weed, grasses, mulgas, witchetty grub trees, and bean trees. From the flat country and sandy ground, we dig up bush potatoes, bush yams and bush onions. For sweet things, we chop down sugar bag [honey] from the tops of trees. . . .

The country here is good, with sand hills, rocks, creeks, trees and flat country. There are water soakages lying some distance apart through the spinifex country. There are rockholes in the hills. The names of some of the rockholes and soakages are Mirijarra, Wakurlpu, Yakurrukaji, Yurntumulyu, and so on. It is only after there has been a lot of rain that the rockholes get water. When there was no water, the people would walk around from place to place, from one water soakage to another, from one rockhole to another. This was the way the people brought up their children. Today, people are still walking around and are going back to the country of their ancestors where they grew up. They know that they want to live there forever now that the Europeans have given them back their land. . . .

[5] The Lajamanu RATE students 1986, "Lajamanu School Prospectus", Lajamanu, 1987, pp 2–5.

The name of this place is "Yurntumulyu", which was the name of a Dreamtime Woman. Today everyone calls it Yurntumu (Yuendumu). However, Yurntumu is over there, to the east, where we pass on the road to Alice Springs, beside the hills. Yakurrukaji is the name of the place where the houses stand, where the soakage is. This is the land where we live. Yuendumu people have been living here for a long time and, as the children grow up, this land will become theirs.

This is the land of Honey Ant Dreaming for Napanangka, Japanangka, Napangardi, Japangardi, Napaljarri, Japaljarri, Nungarrayi, and Jungarrayi. It comes under and across from Papunya, then the Honey Ant emerges east, on this side of Mt Allen. There are many other dreamings – Water, Snake, Possum, Kangaroo, Budgerigar, Big and Small Yam, Goanna, and many others. These have belonged to our ancestors and they hold no lies.[6]

Lee Cataldi
Peggy Rockman Napaljarri

---

[6] Tess Ross Napaljarri, "The People and their Home".

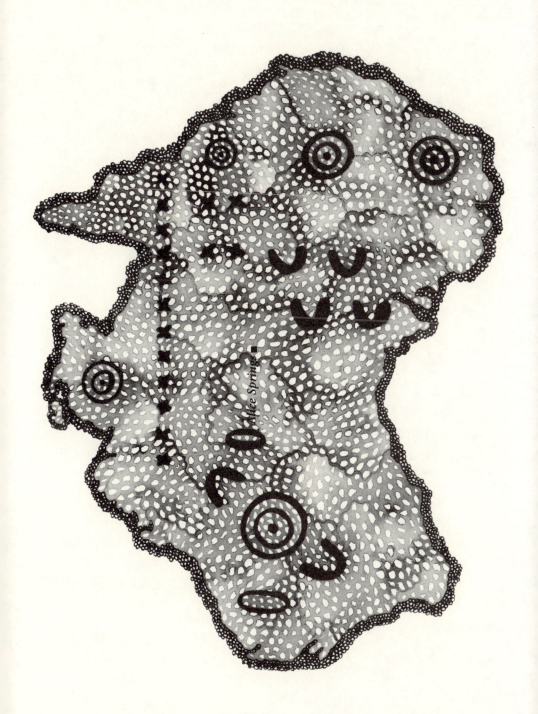

JAJIRDIKIRLI

The Spotted Cat

TOLD BY

Molly Tasman Napurrurla

Parnkajarla ngajukupalangukuju kirdanakuju. Nyampungurlu pardija wurnturuwangu. Kunjuwunjungurlu nyampungurlu jajirdiji yanu. Parnkaja. Ngarrkakurla wapal-pardija. Yanu-uu, yanu yati kurlirrapurda karlumparrarnuwiyi, nyampuwiyi yanu, nyampungurlujala Kunjuwunjungurlu. Yanu murra. Warru parnkaja, yanu. Nyampurlakulparla business-rlangulpalu, business-karirlalpa jinjirri-nyangu. Business-karirlalpa yanu.

"Aaa, mayalkujukurna kujajuku waja yani."

Yanulpa kujapurdawiyijiki. Yanu-uu. Walkujuku. Wartardirlajuku warru-nyangu. Business-ikari, business-ikari nyangulpa. Walku.

"Aaa, kukurna, kukurna yani maralpajuku kujajuku."

Yanulpa. Warru-jurruly-wantija. Walku. Wurnturulkurla purda-nyangu, yinyangurlurla purda-nyangu nyanungurlu jajirdirliji.

Mantarra wapanjakurra kinkikiji. Not kinki, yapa-ngarnuku, ngari, kinkikilarla, mantarra wapanjakurrarla purda-nyangu kujarlangurlu.

"Aaa, waraa, ngarraju kurdu-kurdu marda jajarni!" wangkaja. Jupu-karrija kujarlalkujuku, yinyarlalkuju, jupu-karrija. Purda-nyangulpa.

"Kukurna, kukurna yalipurdakiji-jarri waja. Ngarrajulu kurdu-kurdu, kalakaju kurdu-kurdurlu marlajarra-mani, ngarraju kurdu-kurdurlu!" kujajulpa wangkaja jajirdiji, "Ngarraju marlajarra-mani!"

Yirdi nyampulpalu Kunjuwunjurla nyinaja, ngati, kurdupatu. Nyanungumipa yanu. Kulpa-jarrija kakarrara. Kakarraralpa ngarrirninjinanu. "Nati, nati warlulku puralyarralya-jirrika! Ngulakulangalirla nyinpakuju riwarri-maninjinani kakarrararlu. Walku! Kulanpa rikarl-pardi, walku. Ngarrangku muku-pakarni ngarrangali!" wangkajalpa. Ya! Warla-pajurnulpa warlukujaku, pupakujaku yingkirninjawangu, walku.

Parnkajalpa. Kulkurrujarrajukulpa parnkaja. Not-i jardalpa ngunaja. Parnkajalpa, parnkajalpa.

"Awu, nyiyakuju punkungku?"

Kulpari-manu waja. "Ngayirna kujajuku maralpajuku yani. Ngunaju mantarlarlangu waja, ngunaju yaparlangu malurnpa waja mantarla. Four-iji kala mantarla yapa kanjaku, marnkurrpamalku.

He ran to my parent, my father. He had come from Kunjuwunju, not far away. The spotted cat had been travelling around. He had been looking about him for another initiated man. He went, he went south, first going along the west side, this way he went first, from here, from Kunjuwunju. He went on. He travelled to different places, attending different ceremonies, but leaving those he could not attend and going on to others.

"Ah, then I will have to keep on travelling like this."

He continued to travel in the same direction. Still no companion. He had to be careful not to blunder into secret ceremonies. He saw another ceremony. The people there were all occupied with these activities.

"Ah, well, I will just have to travel alone."

He went on. Then he turned back. The spotted cat heard messages about something, still a long way off, but coming from there towards where he was.

"It walks along making a booming noise with its feet on the ground, the monster, no, not a monster exactly, a man-eater, while it walks along beating the ground." This is what he heard about, making its way in his direction.

"Ah, alas, it has probably devoured all my children," he said. He stopped there, in that place he stopped. He listened. "If I, if I could only get back to my home. Otherwise I am going to lose all my children, all my children!" So the spotted cat declared. "I am going to lose them all!"

All these people were at a place called Kunjuwunju, the mother, and all the children. Only the cat went. He left and went back the way he had come, towards the east. He went eastwards telling people the news and advising them what to do. "Do not, do not light any fires! That one is going around in the east destroying everything that we hold dear. Do not let anyone wander away, lest he kill us all!" he said. He prevented them from lighting any fires at all.

He ran, he ran through the centre of the country. He did not stop to sleep, but ran on and on.

"For what reason does that evil thing do this?"

He turned to go back. "I am still travelling alone. If only I could find another person, a companion, to come with me. It would be much

3

Kukurna marlpaju kulpari-yani," wangkajalpa.

Ngunajalpa jintaku. Nyangulpajana yangkalpa pupayi yungkurnu yapangku. Aaa! Parnkajalpa muljukurra. "Aaa, nati pupaku yingkirninjaku! Ngula ka kutulku yaninjinani!"

"Nyarrpara? Nyuntujuku mayi kanpa purda-nyanyi?"

"Shh! Nati wangkanjaku! Wangkanjawangu, ngayi, wurulypa nyinaka! Ngari marnangkajuku nganja kuyuju, marnangkajuku yangkaju jungunyparlangu nganja. Mininirlangu nganja, jungunypa marnangkarlujuku."

"Nyangurla yingkirninjaku?"

"Walku, yingkirninjwangurlu waja nganja. Ngurrangku pardu-pardu-manu yinyarlu wurntururlulku waja yapa-ngarnurlu. Yapaku karla riwarri-maninjarla wapa, punkungku. Riwarri-maninjarla waja ka wapa. Walku, kulakarla jinta rikarl-pardi, walku. Riwarri-manirra nyanungurlujuku. Kulaka parnkamirra kurdu, jajinyanupardu, ngatinyanupardu jintakumarrarnijiki. Yuwayi ka walkurra-mani!"

"Yuwa!"

"Kala kurdu-kurdu yirdija wakurnjirla nyampurla kangu, nyampurla. Marliyarra-marliyarra nyampurla wirrijirla kala kangu, wiri-wirimanji nyampurla kala ranjarra-kangu, pirltirrkanyayirni nyampurla kala kangu yapangarnurlu. Kutu nyampu Warlakurla kakarrara ka nyanunguju karrimi, nyampulkuju ngapaji. Karrimi ka ngulangka wirijarlunyayirni, like a river-piya. Yuwa, witawangu ngayi ka karri."

Parnkaja-aa, yangka Granite-rla karlarrapurda Yarturlu-yarturlurla. Yangka Wilawana karlipa kuja kankarlarra parnka, ngulangka kujarninginti ngunajarni. Ngarnurnu, ngapa punu-ngarninjarla ngulangka ngunaja. Jukurra pardija. Yangka Yurlpuwarnurla kakarrarni kuja, kuja ka nguna, yaliwana parnkajarni wajilijiki. Wirliyawanajuku nyanungunyanguwana yanurnu. Kujapurda kuja yangka yanurnu.

"Waa, ngamarlangu! Walkulku marda karna ngari nyanungukarilki yapuntarlalku, karnarlajinta karri, aa, murrkuntarniki," wangkajalpa jajirdiji, "Murrkuntarniki karnarlajinta walkungkalku karrimi ngamarlangujarraku nyurru wayiji marlajarra-manku! Nyiyawangurlangu karna maralpajuku yani?"

better if I could persuade three or even four people to accompany me. However, I will just have to return home alone," he said.

He lay down on his own. He saw the other people make a fire. He rushed towards the soak, "No, no, do not light that fire. That thing is coming closer and closer!"

"Where? Can you hear it?"

"Shh! Don't talk! Stay as quietly as you can, without talking. Just try to eat mice and other small animals that you can catch in the grass, just mice and other little things."

"When? After lighting the fire?'

"No, eat them without lighting a fire. Don't think that that thing over there would not be only too happy to catch sight of you. That evil thing is a cannibal which is moving through the country destroying all the people it can catch. Stay in the one place without moving about. It really destroys people. Don't let the children run around, and keep all the fathers and mothers together. Yes, it will leave nothing!"

"Yes!"

"I believe it has carried around the bodies of children hanging from its armbands, and the bodies of older boys hanging from its belt. It has also carried around many bodies of fully grown adults, and also tiny babies. It is a terrible man-eater. At present it is near here to the east at Warlaku, at the water there, which is flowing, like a river. Yes, over there at that big stretch of water."

He ran on, to that place further west, to the Granites. We run with him up past Wila, which lies in this direction. There he drank, he bent down and quickly drank from the water which is there. The next day dawned. He ran on to Yurlpuwarnu which is just there in the east. He ran rapidly past there. He returned following the same path by which he had left. He went back the same way, and arrived home.

"Ah, mother and child! I was so afraid that I would be left a father without a family, that I would have lost my little boy," said the spotted cat. "I was so afraid that I would be left without my little boy, that I would have lost my wife and children. Why must I continue to journey alone without a companion?"

He went, he went away again. He reached that other country and he ran far inside it. He ran right to the east past Yurlpuwarnu, he ran along the west side past Wardalya. He went right inside that area. He

Yanu, yanurra, rdakurl-pungurra, tarda-rdakurl-pungu kaninjarra.
Yurlpuwarnuwana kakarrumpayi parnkaja. Wardalyawana
karlumparra parnkaja. Kaninjarra yukajarni. Warrpirnpawana
karlumparra parnkaja yangkaju Kunjuwunjukurra. Kurdu-
kurdujulurla wara-parnpija, "Taati! Taati!"

"Yawu, taatipuraji karnanyarra yanirra, taatipuraji karnanyarra
yanirra. Kalakankulu ngulangka wurulypa-nyina. Wurdungu waja
kajikankulu nyina."

"Nyiyarla?"

"Wurulypa-jarriyalu, wurulypalu nyinaka waja!"

"Yuwa, nyiyarlangu nganja kuja," wangkajarla
ngapujunyanukuju, "Yuwa, nyiyarlanpa wiyarrpa kulpari-jarrija?"

"Yuwa, ngarralungalpa muku-ngarningalpa ngulangkukula
kakarrarni nyiyawangu punkungku kulinyparlu."

Jungarniwarnulku majarnu-majarnu-manu warlaljarlaju
nyanungu ngurrangkaju. Kunjuwunjurlajunyanu manu, yii,
manunyanu nganayirla. Manunjunurra. Majarnu, majarnu, majarnu.

"Wurajijiki, wurajijiki karna pardi. Wankaruku ngari yingaju
nyanungurlujala wapirdi-pakarni kulinyparluju. Kalajana kurdu-
kurdukuju nyampurlajuku nguru-mardaka. Yardajana yampinja-
yanu." Jingi-jingirlijiki ngapujunyanurluju ngarrurnurra ngayi.

Kakarrara-pardija. Yangkarlipa Yinapaka nyangu, ngulaju
kujajuku, kala kulkurrujarra, kujajuku yanu nyanunguju yinya
yatujukari yilyampuruwana. Yarnkaja kakarrara yilyampurulku.
Jungarniwarnu ngarrirninja-yanu Jungarrayi, Japaljarri,
"Warluwangu wiyarrpa nyinaka-aa, wankaruku nyinaka-aa,
wankaruku waja nyinaka. Walkungka, ngulangka karla kutu
kurduku. Kutungkulku karla yangkurlu-maninjarla karla wapa,
yangkurlu-maninjarla karla wapa kutungkulku. Jungunypaji nganja
marnangkarluju. Wajili-pungka nyiyakantikanti ngulaju
marnangkarluju. Natili warlu yingkika, walku! Ngula kutu karla
mantarra-wapa."

"Nyuntujuku mayi kanpa pu —?"

"Wurulypalu, wangkanjawangurlangulu nyinaya!" wangkajalpa
kirrikarirla.

Tarda-yanulpa wurnturujuku. Ngukujulpa ngari ngarnunjunurra
ngari yaliji yapakurlangu. Wangkajalpajana, ngarnulpa ngapa,

ran along the west side past Warrpirnpa, and back to Kunjuwunju. As he returned, his children cried out when they saw him coming, "Father, father!"

"Yes, it is your father who is coming towards you. But please try to keep quiet, please be very good."

"Why?"

"Be quiet, please be quiet! Just eat this," he said to his wife.

"Yes, my dear. Why have you come back?"

"I am afraid that it is going to eat all of us. The evil thing is just to the east in a furious rage, and there seems to be nothing to stop it."

There in his own home with his family, he prepared many spears, straightening them. At Kunjuwunju he prepared his weapons, he collected and straightened them, he prepared them.

"I will leave in the afternoon. Let the ferocious thing strike at me from close by while we are still alive. I have been looking after my children here at home, and I have also left them from time to time." Their father then told them straight away what he was going to do.

He went east, towards the area around Yinapaka that we have seen, but he went straight across the centre. It was in this direction that he went, just to the north past the sandhills. He travelled east to the sandhill country. He went and spoke directly to Jungarrayi and Japaljarri, the owners of that country.

"Please remain without lighting any fires, in order, poor things, that you may remain alive. That thing is close by here, walking around taking every last child, closer and closer, taking every last child. Just eat the mice that you find in the grass. Chase all the little things that you find in the grass. Do not light any fires, no. It is travelling very close to here, snatching people away."

"What are you going to do?"

"Be quiet, do not talk!" he said, as he went from camp to camp.

He stopped later, a long way further on. He drank the water belonging to the people of that country. He spoke to them, he drank their water, he returned.

He decorated himself and he danced. He practised, and he practised, he practised the ceremony first. He placed his hands upon himself, like this, he placed them, he placed them, he placed his hands upon himself and changed himself, the spotted cat, the father.

kulparilpa yanu.

Yaku-jarrijalpa, yaku-jarrijalpa. Wala-parrurnulpanyanu, wala-parrurnulpanyanu, wala-parrurnulpanyanu. Yawulyuwiyilpanyanu wala-parrurnu. Rdakakulpanyanu kujapiyarlu yirrarnu, yirrarnu, yirrarnu, yirrarnu. Yirrarnulpanyanu nyanugurluju warri-warrirliji jajirdirliji.

"Nyiya-jarri japarna? Aaa, nganayirna jarriji? Ngarlu-ngarlurnpajarrirna? Kalakaju purrupardu-pakarni?" wankajalpa jinta.

"Purrupardu marda kalakaju nganayirli ngarlu-ngarlurnpaju pakarni? Aa, walku. Nama marda jarri ngarrarna, nama marda ngarrarna jarri? Kari namaju kalakaju purruparduyijala pakarni? Kalakarna marda kutangka jarri? Kari ngulaju kalakaju wiri nyanyi kakalaju pakarni," wangkaja. Jirringi-yirrarnulpa jintangku.

Nyiyakantikanti yalumpukula yirdi-manu. "Kalakaju pakarni waja!"

Wala-parrurnulpanyanu. Yalilpa jungunypapiya-jarrijawiyi nyanunguju jajirdi. Warrulpa parnkaja, juurl-juurl-juurl-juurl-pungulpa. "Kari, walku. Wiri karnaju nyanyi!" Malurnpalpanyanu nyangu. "Yama yangka kujaka yaninjarra-yani manu parnka kuja, kari wiri yaliji." Might be nganayi karlta-karltapiya-jarrija. Juurl-pungulpa, juurl-pungulpa different way-lki. "Walku. Yuwa, yuwa, marda yalipiyakula? Yinyapiya marda ngarrarna nyina? Ngarraju marda nyanungurlujala pakarni?" wangkajalpa.

Kulparilpa yapa-jarrija. Nyiyakantikantiwiyilpa wala-wala-parrurnu. Namapiyalpa yanu, nganayipiyalpa yanu, yangka ant-piya yangka kujaka yani through ngula, nama. "Ngula kalakaju waja pakarni purrupardu," kujalpa wangkaja.

Kulparilpa yapa-jarrija. Murrurnulpanyanu, murrurnulpanyanu, murrurnulpanyanu. Kurlardalpanyanu majarnu. Majarnulpa, majarnulpa kurlardalku, majarnulpa, majarnulpa. Yiri-manulpa-aa. Karrinja-pardijalpa yapalku.

"Yungurnarla," wangkajalpa, "Nyinaka, kujarlarlujuku marnangkarlu nganja kajirnarla jalangu jija."

Parnkajalpa. Yijardu wurnalku yarnkaja. Parnkajalpa-aa. Wuraji-wuraji-jarrijalpa, kirrikarikirralpa yukaja. Ngapakurralku jakatilpa-yirrarnu wurnturujuku, wurnturu nyanungurlujulpanyanu jakati-yirrarnu nganayiji jinpirri, nganayipiya mulyarripiya, mulyarripiya,

"What will I become? Will I change myself into a hornet? What if it brushes me away?" he said to himself. "If I was a hornet, what if it just brushed me away? Ahh, no. Maybe I should become an ant, but then it could just as easily kill me by swatting me. Perhaps I should change myself into a big rat? But if it sees something big, it will hit it," he said, thinking about this, by himself all the while.

He named many different things. "What if it hits me?"

He tried changing himself into different creatures. First that spotted cat became like a mouse. He ran around, he jumped about. "No, like this I am too big and it will see me!" He looked at his reflection in the water. "It has to go and rest in the shade. It has to find a big area of shade for itself." He might have become a honey ant. He jumped about, he jumped about, differently. "No! Well, like what then? What if I resembled that one over there? Would it be able to hit me? Would I be likely to be hit?" he asked himself.

Then he restored himself to the appearance of a man. He had practised becoming all kinds of things, he had become like an ant, a honey ant, and he had also changed into other kinds of ants, the ones that can travel underground. "But what if he just brushes me away?" he said. He changed back into a man. He rubbed out the designs he had painted on his body. He straightened his spears. He straightened them, he made them sharp. He stood up, as a man.

"If you all stay in one place, as I have said, if you all eat what you find in the grass, as I have indicated . . . ."

He ran off with his weapons on his shoulder. He did leave on a journey. He ran on. When it became late afternoon he arrived at another camp. He hid his spears in a place near the water some distance off, out of sight he hid his shovel-nosed spear, the spear with the broad head, the executioner's spear. He put the powerful implement down some distance away. Then he ran to the water, and knelt down and drank. He drank, and he washed himself.

"People, people, please do not light fires. The evil thing is coming close to you destroying everything that he finds!"

"Where is it doing this?"

"Please remain without talking, please try and be very quiet. Do not, do not light any fires! Stay alive! Guard the entrances to your homes!" he said, the spotted cat, their guardian. "While I am drinking this

milinyimpapiyalpa yirrarnu, nganayiji jinpirri nyampukuju. Yuwayi, yirrarnulpa wurnturujuku tarrukuju. Parnkajalpa. Ngapalpa turlamanu. Ngarnulpa. Yarlurnulpanyanu.

"Yapa-aa! Ngari nyinaka-aa pupawangunyayirni, nyinaka yapaju. Kutungkulkulparla riwarri-maninjarla wapa punkungku!"

"Nyarrpararla? Nyarrpararla?"

"Kuja wangkanjawangu ngari, wurulypa-nyinaka. Nati pupa yingkika! Wankaruku nyinaka, nguruku tarda-kijirninjaku!" wangkajalpa warri-warri jajirdiji. "Ngapa karna nyampuju ngarni, yalumpu. Ngarrarna jalangu kuja ngari ngarrarna nyanungurlujala ngarraju wapirdi-pakarni!" Ngarnulpa.

No-lpajana nyiyarlangu puntarnu, walku. Parnkajalpa, kulpari parnkaja. Luntu-kangulpa. Kujurnulpanyanu, kujurnulpanyanu, kujurnulpanyanu, kujurnulpanyanu, kujurnulpanyanu, kujurnulpanyanu, kujurnulpanyanu, kujurnulpanyanu. Ngulalpa yawurrpuru-jarrija.

"Ngarrarna jalanguju namapiya-jarri."

Kujajukulpa wangkanjinanu — kirrikari manu kirrikari. Walawala-parrurnulpanyanu-uu. Juurl-pungulpa, juurl-pungulpa. Malurnpalpanyanu yalijiki nyangu. Juurl-pungulpa, juurl-pungulpa. "Wiri marda ngarraju nyanjarla pakarni. Walku!" Walaparrirninjarla, yapa-jarrija kulpari. Riwi-pungulpa kurlardaju jinpirriji, riwi-pungulpa yarda-aa. Ngurrangkalpa ngunaja.

Yarnkajalpa. Kulkurru-kulkurrujukulpa ngunajarra. Parnkajalpa-aa. Kutukarikarrilki parnkanja-yanu. Nyurrujalalpa riwarrimaninjinanu.

"Ngarra, yukayarlarnikila nganayi side-i. Yinyaju Warlakuwana ngarrajana nganjarlalkukula kutungkulku. Nyampu kakarrara." Parnkajarra ngulawanalku. "Yuwa, wankarujukunya kanpa nyina, wankaruju." Yirrarnulpa jakati, parnkajalpa ngapakurra. "Yuwa, yapaju kanpa nyinpa-jarri, wankarujukunya?"

"Yuwa, kala nyiyarla? Kala nyiya ngulakula?"

"Ngulangku kutungkulku riwarri-maninjinani!"

"Waraa, wiyarrpa!"

"Jungunypaju nganja, mininiji nganja marnangkarlujuku. Pupa yingkirninjwangurlu, walku. Ngarra ngulakula pardu-pardurni maninja-yani pupakula. Nyanjarni-yani waja ka pupakula."

water, it is possible that the beast will come close to me and strike me."

He drank. It did not come for any of the people nearby. He ran off. He ran back. He decorated himself with ceremonial designs. Then he disappeared.

"Now I will turn myself into an ant."

From there he continued to take his message around to different places. He tried out different guises. He went to different places. He jumped, he jumped. He looked at himself in the still water. There he saw what he had become. He jumped again. "If I am big and he sees me he will hit me. No!" He tried again. He became a man again. He sharpened his big spear, he sharpened it again. Then he slept there.

He set off. He slept at different places on the way. He ran. He ran on, night after night. He kept sharpening his spear so that it was always ready.

"Perhaps it has gone into that country on that side, near Warlaku, where it is eating people, nearby, here, to the east." He ran past the place. "Yes, you are still here alive." He hid his spear, and ran to the water. "Yes, you people, are you all here still alive?"

"Yes. What's going on? What is all this about?"

"There is a creature which is devouring everybody and it's coming close to this place."

"How terrible, the poor things!"

"Just eat mice and little things that you find in the grass. Do not light any fires, none! It comes straight for a place where it sees a fire. It goes around looking for fires."

He ran off.

"This is what I have been telling everybody. I carry around this on my shoulder in case it gets close enough to try to kill me," he said. "It may speak to me, or try to kill me."

The spotted cat, the father, has fur the colours of the mantawajiwaji flower, like that if you have seen it.

He ran. He did not eat anything, nothing. He began to prepare himself by studying and thinking. He changed shape, he changed shape. He tried different forms, he tried different forms. He painted designs on himself. He disappeared. He jumped, he jumped. He looked at himself in the water, in the water he looked at his different reflections. He examined himself closely. Before deciding on the

11

Parnkajalpa.

"Nyampu, nyampujukurna wangkaja. Ngarrarnarla ngajujala jija, ngarraju wapirdi pakarni," wangkajalpa kuja. "Ngajujala ngarraju wangkami, pakarni."

Pirtipilawu ka nyanunguju jajirdi nyina, warri-warri kajilpanpa nyangkarla nyanunguju, yuwayi, nganayipiya nyangka mantawajiwajipiya, Pirtipilawu yangkaju ngaju kaju nyina nganayi yuwurna, ngulapiya yumurruju.

Parnkajalpa. Natilpa ngarnu nyiyakantikanti, walku, miirl-nyinanjakulparla rdujurnu. Yirrarnulpanyanu, yirrarnulpanyanu. Wala-parrurnulpanyanu, wala-parrurnulpanyanu, wala-parrurnulpanyanu, wala-parrurnulpanyanu. Yirrarnulpanyanu yawulyumipa. Yawurrpajilpa-jarrija. Juurl-pungulpa. Juurl-pungulpa. Wala-parrurnulpanyanu malurnpa. Yangka kalanyanu malurnpajuku nyangu. Warra-warra-kangu. Warra-warra-kangulpanyanu. "Kari wiri marda ngarraju. Yali karnaju?" Nyangu kalanyanu, "Ngarraju wiri marda, kurlurrpa wiri pakarni, warri-warri, ngarraju marda pakarni. Kala ngarrarna karlta-karltapiya-jarri. Ngarraju wiriyijala marda nyanyi, kalakaju kurlurrpa wiri pakarni. Might be pankiji-jarri, aa, marda, yali."

Wala-parrurnu kalanyanu yalilkijiki. Yii, kala tarda-yanulku. Yaparni-jarrija kala. Nyinaja. Kala riwi-pungurra, riwi-pungurra, riwi-pungurra. Kalanyanu wurra-manu, wurra-manu, wurra-manu, wurra-manu. Kala karrinja-pardija. Jinpirri kala manu. Yawirripilinjirli kala yarnkaja. Kutukurralku parnkaja-aa, kutulkurlapardu ngunajarra.

"Kutulku karla mantarra-wapa!"

Nyangulpa wurnturungurluju. Wurnturungurlulpa nyangu.

"Waa, wapiji no more witalpa ka kanja-yani, wapukurru nyanungurlu yinyarla kinkingki. Wapukurru yangka. Wayi wapiji yarturlu luwarnu kala yalirli wapukurru. Yangka japu-japu kujakalu pakarni ngulapiya wapukurru witawangu nyanungukuju. Wapiji no more kujapiya, wumarra!"

Ngulakurlurlu lajalingki karrinja-pardijarni nganayikirliji wapijikirli. Wapukurru manu. Yuwalimanjirla, yangka yapajilpa nyantarl-karlija. Wurnturungurlulpa nyangu, yangka yapajilpa yurdingirlilpa nyangu, wari-yanu. Nyangu-uu. Yanurni mantarra-

change he looked at his appearance, Napaljarri. He examined himself very closely.

"Maybe I should become something big. Like this?" He would look at himself. "But if I was big and had big balls and big genitals, then he would probably strike me dead. Rather I should become something like a honey ant. If he sees something with big balls, something big, he will flatten it. I should become a small stinging ant. That might be the one!"

He tried himself out in that shape. Then he sat down. He had become a man again. Then he stopped. He loaded his spear-thrower, he loaded his spear-thrower. He held himself ready, he held himself ready. He stood up. He had a big, broad-nosed spear. He set off loaded with weapons. He ran until nightfall. That night he slept.

"It is walking around very near here, its feet booming on the ground." He saw it from a long distance away, from a long distance away, he saw it. "Waa, it is carrying huge stones with that club, that monster. Look at that big club, look at the stones it hits with it. With those clubs they hit those big stones about like softballs. Those are big stones, not pebbles like this, but really big stones!"

Then it stood up, with the club on its shoulder, and with all the stones. The bodies of the dead people had been put up on a platform, the fat slowly dripping from them. He watched it from a distance, from the top of the tree, from where he could see all around. He watched it come towards him, with its heavy tread. It seemed to stand up and go toward the east. As it moved it slapped its thighs. It went, it moved along slapping its thighs, slapping its thighs. Behind it, the man followed.

It carried the bodies of people about with it, their fat dripping from them. It carried around the bodies of people like us. Here and there it put them up on top of bough shelters.

He set off, he set off. Before moving on, he saw the other, to the east. As he moved, he hardly seemed to move at all, lifting his feet lightly like a cat. He ran. His two knees made marks in the ground. From there, from the east, he went to the water, and bent down to drink it quickly.

He went. He tried out his changes, he tried out his changes, he tried out these different things while keeping low down in the green bushes.

wapanjarla. Karrinjarra nganta pardija. Kakarrarapurda pardijarra. Kuja ngantarla ngurrngu-ngurrngu-wangkanja-yanta. Kula ngarralparla walyaju nyiya mantarra-wapaja. Yanulpa. Ngurrnguku, ngurrnguku, ngurrnguku, ngurrngukurra pardijarra. Nyanungu purdangirli rdakurl-pungu.

Yapamanjilpa warra-warra-kangu, wiyarrpa-aa, nyantarl-karlinjarlalpa, yapaju ngalipapiyaju, warra-warra-kangu-uu. Yuwalikari-yuwalikari ngurralparla karrija.

Pardija. Pardija. Kamparrurluyijala nyangu yali kuja, kuja yali kakarru. Jungarni yaninjawangu, ngayi yanurnu yantarn-yantarnpa. Parnkajarra. Mirdijarra kalarla yuljarr-pungu. Ngapaku kala kujangirli kakarrungirli turlurl-wantinjarla ngarnu.

Yanu. Wala-parrurnunyanu, wala-parrurnunyanu, yukakari-yukakarinyanu wala-parrurnu, wala-parrurnu, wala-parrurnu. Kanunjumparra yukangka yirrarnu nganayiji jinpirriji, yuurnpa. Nyangulparla. Pankiji-jarrija, pankiji wita, kulinypanyayirni. Tarnnga kajana nyanungurlu pajirni kurdu-kurdurlangu, yaparlangu kajana pajirni, tarnnga. Yarnma-mani ka pankijirliji. Well, nyanungu pankiji-jarrija, nyanungu. Nyanungu now pankiji-jarrija, nyanungu-piya-jarrija – ngula nyanunguju jajirdi warri-warri.

Nyinajalpa. Kutulku nyampukulalpa well ngapangkajuku yangkakula yuka karrinjarra-yanu ngapangka side. Ngulangkalpa nyinaja – wita – inside. Mantarrarni wapanja-yanu, yunpurrku-kujurnu nyampujangka kurdu-kurdu, yunpurrku-kujurnu, nyampujangka yunpurrku-kujurnu. Nyampujangka, yangka, yiriwarrajangka kurdu-kurdu, pirltirrka kujurnu, wartirlijangka kujurnu. Kala yapaju wiri-wiri kujakula yunpurrkurnu-kujurnu. Nganta ngukukurraju parnkaja. Parnkaja nyanunguju kinki. Nganayi kinki mantarrarni-wapanja-yanurla. Turlurl-wantija. Pirri-manu, pirri-manu yangka kujarlu kuja karlipa ngarni yangka, kujarlu, well, jarranturlu.

Jalangunya turlurl-wantija. Lirraju pujuly-pajurnujuku. Pujuly-pajurnu. Kulanganta nyiyarlu lintarr-yirrarnu. Julparra-pungu yalikarikirralku. Purlurr-pakarnunyanu. Yuwayi, purlurr-pakarnunyanu. Yarda turlurl-wantija. Kujarnilki jila yarda juurl-pungu. Pujuly-pajurnu. Juurl-pungu kujayijala.

"Awu, nyiyarlu?" purlurr-pakarnunyanu, "Awuu, nyiyarlulku

Then he put his big shovel spear down underneath the grass. He looked around him. Then he made himself into a tiny stinging ant, one that bites very severely. These are the ones that always bite children, and older people also they bite, and the bites make people very sick and thin. Well, he changed himself into a stinging ant, that spotted cat, the guardian.

Then he waited. He went into the grass growing near the water and hid underneath. There he hid, very tiny, underneath. It came along, its feet beating on the ground. It threw to the ground the bodies it had been carrying, the bodies of children and new-born babies. It threw down the babies hanging from its headband and its belt. It also threw down the bodies of adults. It went towards the water. It ran, that monster, it ran, thumping the ground with its feet. It bent down to drink. It sat down, as we do, with one leg folded under it.

It was at this moment it bent down to drink, he stung it on the lips, he stung it on the lips. It had no idea what had started to drive it crazy with pain and it gave a great leap away from the water. It started to beat at its arms and head. It started gouging great holes out of its own flesh. Again it bent down to the water to try to drink. Then it spun round, crashing to the ground again. He bit it again. Again, it leapt into the air.

"Oh, what is doing that?" it cried, beating itself about the head, "Oh, what is doing this to me, like nothing I have ever experienced before? What is it, then?"

It sat down again with its two legs doubled up underneath. When our hero saw this, he rushed at it and stung it again and again. Then this is what it did to itself – it gathered big stones from around about. It went and got the stones, then it ran back, it ran back and sat down again. It thrashed around, trying to get at the water, bashing at the water. It bent down again towards the water. It had the big stones it used with the club. It bent down to the water again. He stung it again, a little later. It took up a stone and started beating itself severely. Yes, it beat itself.

"What is doing this to me? This water used to be quite all right. It used to be good for drinking. It used to lie here quietly but now what is biting me?" It smashed the stone into its body. "Ahh, waa, ahh, no!"

Time passed. Still it had not had a drink. It still had not managed to

kaju? Nyiyarlulku kaju kujawangujala ngarralpa ngunaja? Ngulalpa yangka?"

Kujalpa nyampujarra mirdipijipiji-nyinaja. Ngulalpa yangka kujarlu kujalpa nyangu, tuurl-pajirninjarla parnkajarralpa. Kujarlu manulpanyanu yumpa! Yarturlukulku yarnkajarra, yarturlukulku manu wurrangku. Manunjunurra yarturlulku. Parnkajarni, parnkajarni, yarda tarda-yanu. Ngapajilparlajinta nganta wapal-wapal-pakarnu, wapal-pakarnu, wapal-pakarnu, wapal-pakarnulparlajinta ngapaji. Nganayi turlurl-wantija. Wapiji, ngari yarturlulpa mardarnu wapukurru. Turlurl-wantija. Ngalyalkulpa pujuly-pajurnu murnmajuku. Yarturlu manu, piirl-pakarnulpanyanu nyanungurlulku. Yuwayi! Pakarnulpanyanu.

"Nyarrparlu kaju nyampuju? Nyampuwiyi nyampuju ngapaju ngarra ngurrjujala. Nyinpajulpaju ngarra ngurrjujalalpaju ngarra. Ngunaja nyinpaju kala nyiyarlulku kaju pajirni?" wangkajalku. Piirl-pakarnulpanyanu! "Aaa, waa, aa!"

Wurra-jarrija. Purrakuju walku ngarninjawangu. Natilpa ngurrku-kujurnurlangu, walku. Yardalpa turlurl-wantija. Nyampukulpa pujuly-pajurnu yangka rduku-rdukuwana. "Awu!" pakarnulpanyanu wapijirliji, "Waraa, waraa, waranpalkurnaju pakarnu yaparnaju!"

Ngulalpa kujarlaji yardarni pujuly-pajurnunjunu. Yangka turlurl-wantija, yangkalpa yirri kujarlu nyangurra. Ngulalpa yaparr-pajirninjarla pajurnu. Jiralpanyanu pakarnu wapukurrurluju. Ngulajangka yardalpa turlurl-wantija. Kunalkulpa nyampu pajurnu, ngulalpanyanu kujarlu pakarnu. Ngulalpa yarda turlurl-wantija. Kunalkulpanyanu yardalpa pajurnu, kunakarilki. Ngulalpanyanu pakarnu.

"Walku! Nyarrpa-jarrijalkuju? Ngarralpaju ngurrjujala nyinpaju ngunaja. Warantaa! Walyuruwiyirna ngarni!" wangkajalpa. Yuwa, walyurukujala purraku-jarrijalku. Yangka nyampukarilki wapurr-pajurnu kujakurralpa kulanganta nyiyarlu pajurnu. Purlurr-pakarnunyanu nyampu. Well, putalku nyutukirdi-wapaja nyampukarilki, nyampukarilki. Yardarni pujuly-panturnu. Ngulajangka yardarni pulyurr-pakarnunyanu.

"Waraa, nyarrpa-jarrijalkirna? Nyarrpa-jarrijalkirna? Nyarrpa-jarrijalkirna?"

swallow even a drop. Again it bent down to the water, he stung it again, on the chest near the heart.

"Ohh!" It beat itself with the stones. "Ohh, ohh, ohh, I am beating myself!"

Then he stung it again. Again it bent down to the water, again it looked around trying to see what was tormenting it, again it started to pierce its flesh, again and again. It beat against its tendons with its own big club. Again it bent down to the water. It had cut itself right through to the guts. It had also beaten itself. Then it bent down again to the water. It stabbed itself in the guts again. Again it beat itself.

"Nothing! What has happened to me? This water I always found good. Ohh, ohh, I am really thirsty! If only I could drink!" it said. The evil thing had become desperately thirsty. It tried to brush away the invisible thing that was driving it mad. It beat at itself, breaking its flesh like cracking an egg. Doubled up in pain, it tried to walk away, but the other one, the other one stung it again, and again it started beating itself.

"Ohh, what will I do, what will I do, what will I do?"

And then this happened. He stung it in the balls, hard. Well, it hit the other testicle, very hard. It could not stop what was happening. It was losing control. Again our guardian, our father, sprang up, and bit him in the other ball. Then it began to run around frantically beating itself everywhere. It also stabbed itself repeatedly in the upper part of the body, where it had at first, so that bits of flesh were hanging off in strips, particularly where it had stabbed itself in the chest, which it had done with one of the stones it had sharpened earlier.

It was on the way out. It had completely lost its head, from being so long without water, from being for so long unable to drink or quench its raging thirst. So now it had stabbed itself all over the head and chest. It rushed in all directions, beating itself to death.

The hero became a man again. He sprang over to where he could grab the big spear. He speared it right through the body, leaving the spear in the trunk. Then he dragged the body away to where it had built a fire in a hole, to cook the people it had killed. He dragged it over to there and pushed it into the fire. That person, the hero, my father, my grandfather, won the fight.

Mourning for them, he covered up the bodies of all the people lying

Yangkalpa kujarlu nganayi-jarrija. Kurlurrpalkulpa pajurnu
nunjurnurni. Well-a, kurlurrpakarilkinyanu pakarnu-uu, jintakari.
Aa, walkulkulpa, wangamarralku. Yardalpa juurl-pungu warri-
warriji. Kurlurrpakarilki pajurnu. Ngulanyanu yarda riwirr-
pakarninjinanu jintawarlayilki. Kankarluwarnumanjilki pajurnu.
Nyampuwiyi pajurnu, that waliwiyi. Yangkalpa jiwinparra-pungu
nyampuwiyi. Rduku-rduku pajurnunjunurnu ngulanyanu wapijirliji
sharp-manu, wapukurrurluju.

Walkulku, now, wangamarra-wangamarralku, wangamarra-
wangamarralku, tarnngaju ngukuwangurlajuku, ngukuwanguju
ngarninjawangu, walyuruwangu. Ngulajangka yangka
kankarluwanalku marda kujarlajapa muku-pajurnu. Ngulalkunyanu
tarnngalku riwirrparni-pakarnu.

Yapalku wantijarra. Nyanungu juurlparra-pungu warri-warri,
tuurl-mardarnurla jinpirrkilki, jukarnirla yirrarnu, jukarnirla
yirrarnu, jukarnirla yirrarnu, juka-juka-yirrarnu. Wirlirlparra-manu.
Yangka yali kujalparlajinta rdakungka pupa jankaja yapaku,
ngulakurra wilil-kanjarla. Julyurl-kujurnu. Yapa, warri-warri,
ngajunyanguju kirdanaju kumunjayi-jarrija, warringiyiji. Yapakulku
nyinpakulku rdirri-yungu. Pangirninjarla, pangirninjarla,
pangirninjarla, pangirninjarlalpa muru-pungu. Muwa-manulpa
yapaju, yapalpa muwa-manu.

Nyanungujuku tarnngajulpa karrkurr-jankaja. Wapukurrurla
kujurnu. Wapiji karla marda marlaja-ngunajajukujala nyanungukuju
palkajala. Manu, warurnu. Manu, muku yungkurnu malurnpa
mapirri. Yuwa, ruyungku yungkurnu. Kulpari-pardija
warlaljakurrayijala yangkawanayijala. Pardija warlaljawanayijala,
wiyarrpa. Yanu, yanu. Wirrpiyilki parnkajarni kirrikarirla.

"Purrayarra! Yungkurla-jirrika-aa! Wiyarrparlungkurla yingkika
wajangkurla kuyukuju. Marnangkurla yingkika! Yingkikalkungkurla
nyanungukarirlalku. Nyurrurna, mukurna rdiji, ngari
nyanungurlujala wapirdi-pakarnu!"

Well-lpa ngurrangka ngunaja. Ngulajangkalpa yanu-uu
kirrikarikirralku. "Yingkikangkurla! Ngaringkirla purrayarra
yangkurla-jirrika wiyarrparlu ngayi nyanungurlalku!"

Yanulpa. Ngulakarilpa ngunaja. Nyanungurlurlangulpa
yingkirninjinanu. Ngayilkilpa yimi-ngarrirninjinanu. Ngayilpa

there. After digging a huge hole, he buried them all. He put them all in a grave and covered them up.

That other one stayed there burning until it disintegrated. He threw in the club. All the stones, however, he caused to lie there and there they are to this day. Then he gathered together everything the monster had left in that place, including the bough shelter, and made a fire. He made a great smoking fire with everything, including the bough shade, that had been left in that place.

Then he returned to this own country, to his relatives. He left to rejoin his relatives, the dear ones. He went, he went. He ran with the news from place to place. "Cook! Make a fire whenever you like! Rejoice that now you can make fires to cook your meat! Light fires in the grass, light them wherever you like! I have already lit one, for the one that used to kill whoever it approached!"

Well, he slept one night. Then he went on from place to place. "Light fires, everyone, and please cook whatever you need wherever you are."

He went on. He slept again. As he went he lit small fires. He went along spreading the news. He went along lighting fires. At the sandhill he lit a big fire. That is the one we can see. There he travelled across the centre. There he went, there he visited place after place.

"You may light fires again in all these places, you poor things, light them. Light them in the grass, cook whatever you want, light a fire and cook meat whenever you need!"

He had destroyed that thing in the east. Now he approached his home, speaking to people in places that were nearby. He approached. He stuck his spear in the ground and left it at a very sacred and secret place. This place, Pawurrinji, belongs to us, where the spear has been placed upright in the ground – the spear, the spear, the dear one, which our hero, our protector, left at Pawurrinji upright in the ground at that sacred place.

He went on to where he found his wife, the mother of his children, at Kunjuwunju. When he arrived he took his children in his arms.

He returned to his home forever, and there forever he went in.

TRANSLATORS' NOTE

The story of the jajirdi or spotted cat as told by Molly Napurrurla is one of the

yingkirninjinanu yangkakulaju yilyampuru, wiri yingkirninjarni-
yananya. Yangka nyampu kujakarlipa nyanyi, yuwa. Yananyarni
kulkurruwanajuku. Yananyarni-ii. Kirrikarikirra yukajarni,
"Yingkirni kankulurla-aa nyanungukarirlalku, wiyarrpakurla
yingkika! Marnajingkirla yingkika, purrayarra, yangkurla-jirrika
kuyukuju!"

Kuna yalikila kakarrara pakarnu. Ngulajangka yanurnu-uu,
kutulku wangkajarni. Yanurnu. Nyampuju jawarlarrarla jinpirriji
jaarr-jaarr-kujurnu. Nganimpanyangurla Pawurrinjirla jinpirriji,
jaarr-jaarr-kujurnu, nganayiji jinpirriji, wiyarrpa, jaarr-kujurnu
jawarlarrarla, nyanungurluju warri-warrirliji– Pawurrinjirla.

Yanulkurla ngatinyanukulku Kunjuwunjurla. Ngamirlji-manujana
yaninjarla kurdu-kurdu, ngapujunyanu.

Yukajalku tarnngalku, now. Yukajalku, wiyarrpa. Yuwayi,
tarnnga yukaja.

Recorded at Lajamanu, 29 April, 1990

most dramatic and exciting of Warlpiri narratives. It is also told in a most dramatic and vivid way. Much of the speaker's skill and passion in this style of narration is expressed in the acting out of what happens, in the different speaking voices the narrator imitates, and in the energy and emphasis of the narrator's voice in describing what is happening. Unfortunately, some of this cannot be transferred to paper.

The spotted cat is a culture hero who rescues the inhabitants of a large area from the depradations of a man-eating giant, a feat resembling others in myth, for example George and the dragon, Beowulf and Grendel or Odysseus and the cyclops. Indeed, the spotted cat has much in common with Odysseus because he kills the giant by cunning and learned skill rather than brute force.

The narrator maximizes the potential of the content of the myth – the hero defeats the giant by turning himself into an ant and stinging the monster every time it approaches water so that eventually thirst drives it mad. The style has an abundance of descriptive devices and an energy of genuinely epic proportions. It is among the tellers of these traditional oral narratives that we can still find living practitioners of the classical epic, an example of whose art we have here.

WARLUKURLANGU

What Happened at the Place of Fire

TOLD BY

Uni Nampijinpa

Warlukurlanguwardingki Jampijinpa purlka manu kajanyanujarra Jangalajarra. Wapaja, maju-majulpala watijarra, maju-majulpala watijarra wapaja kajanyanujarra. Jajinyanulpapalangu pardarnu yuntangka purlku. Wirlinyilpapala yanu. Kuyulpapalarla yinja-yanu, yinja-yanulpapalarla kuyu, Lungkardaku yirdijiji.

Warlukurlangurla maju-maju.

"Nyinakarla waja pulya nyampurlajuku muurlpa," kalapala ngarrirninja-yanu Jangalajarrarluju Jampijinpa purlkapardu milpaparnta. Pampa kala nyinaja.

Kalapalangu karrinja-pardinjarla nyangu. Parrarl-parrarl-nyangu kala milpangku. "Wurnturulku kapala yanirra ngajunyangujarraju kajajarraju. Kukurna mani waja kurlarda ngajunyangu. Kapirna wirlinyi waja jalanguju yani ngajulku."

Wirlinyirlirla kala panturnunjunu. Milya-pinjawangu kalapala kajanyanujarra nyinaja, lawa. Kulanganta pampakuju kalapalarla nyinaja.

Kalapala kulpajarni. Ngulakungarntijala kala yangka kuyuwiyi nyanungurlu purraja. Kala kanunjumparralku yirrarnu kuyuwanayijala, yangka linjiwana. Mungalyurruwarnu pirrarniwarnuwana kala kanunjumparra yirrarnu, wati yangka yinyajarrakujaku watijarrakujaku Jangalajarrakujaku. Ngulajangkaju, kalapalangu wapirdi-nyangu wurnturukurra. Yanurnu kalapala kuyukurlu yijalyikirli wirlinyijangka. Kala pampa-jarrijalku. Kutungkarnijiki kala nyinaja pampalku nganta.

Kalapalarla manngu-nyanja-yanu, kalapala yangka wirlinyijangkarlu,

"Wiyarrpa, marda ka pampa nyina purlkayijala ngurrangka ngurrju marda."

"Yuwayi, ngurrju ka nyina!"

Kala nganayilkijangka pampa-jarrija nganta — nyanjarla kutungkalku — watijarrakujaku, yinya kuja kalapala watijarra yanurnu, Jangalajarra, kajanyanujarra nyanungunyangujarra. Kalapalarla wara-parnpija.

"Ngajunyangujarranyanupala, ayi?"

"Yuwu, wirlinyijangka waja nyurrurlujarra yanurnu."

"Kuyukurlu, mayi waja?"

They had great difficulty in walking, those two men, they walked in great pain, the two sons. The father, the old man, waited for them at the windbreak where it was warm. The two went out hunting. They went about giving him meat, they went about giving meat to the one called Bluetongue [Lizard].

At Warlukurlangu, in great pain.

"Stay here in this place quietly and look after yourself," the two Jangala used to say to Jampijinpa, to the blind old man. He was blind.

Having stood up, however, he used to watch them go. He glanced around to see where they were, with his eyes. "They are going a long way off, my two sons. Now I am free to get my own spear. I will go hunting now, for myself."

He used to go hunting and spear game. His two sons knew nothing about this, nothing. They thought he was blind.

Eventually they would come back. He was ready for this, having already cooked his own meat. He used to bury it along with the dried meat left over from the morning or the day before, so that the two men, the two Jangala, did not know about it. Then he would watch them as they approached. Returning from hunting, they came towards him carrying pieces of meat. He pretended to be blind. When they were close he sat like a blind man.

As they returned from hunting, the two sons would think about their father.

"Poor thing. I hope all is well with the old blind man at the camp."

"Yes, he is well."

Well, after, you know, having watched the two men coming towards him, the two Jangala, his two sons, he appeared to be blind. But he knew where they were.

"My two sons, ayi?"

"Yes, here we are back from hunting."

"With meat I hope?"

"Yes, here is the meat."

He had already hidden his own meat.

Then, "Will you eat this meat, old man?"

"Yes, just give me a little." He seemed to only eat a little. "Could you put some meat for me up on the top so that while I am sitting here at home I can have something to eat, here at home?"

"Yuwayi, kuyu waja nyampurra."
Nyurrujukujala kala nyanungurlu wuruly-yirrarnu kuyuju.
Ngulajangkaju, "Kuyunpa ngarni purlka nyampu waja?"
"Yuwa, witajupala yungka!" Kala ngarnu wita nganta.
"Kuyujupala yurdingka yirraka waja yuwalirla yungujupala nguna,
yunguju nguna waja yantarliji yingarna ngarni yantarlirli."
"Yuwa purlka, nyampurla karlijarrangku kuyu yirrarni waja,
karnangku!" kala kukurnunyanu wangkaja.
Ngulajangkaju, ngulajangkaju, ngulajangkaju, ngunaja kalalu
ngurrangkalku. Kalalu ngunaja sleep-lki ngurrangkalku. Warlu
kalapalarla yarrpirninja-parnkaja yitipijarra kajanyanujarrarlu
nyanungunyangujarrarlu watijarrarlu yuntardijarrarlu
Jangalajarrarlu Warlukurlanguwardingkijarrarlu, yalumpurla
kujapala palka-jarrija, ngulajarrarlu.
Yakarra-pardija kalalu mungalyurru. Kalalu yangka kuyu
warlungka kardu-yungu maninjarla mungalyurrurlu. Nyampurlaju
kalu mangarriji, flour-lkujala ngarni, nyampurlaju kardiyarlaju. Kala
kardiyawangurlawiyiji kalalu ngarnu jukurrparluju nyurruwiyiji
mangarri puurdapinki, yumurnunjupinki, janmardapinki. Marlu
kalalu kuyu ngarnu, luwajirripinki.
Kalapalarla ngarrirninja-yanu, "Purlka nyinayarra. Nyampunya
mardakarra waja."
"Yirrakajupala warlurlangujupala waja. Marlurnparla jamulu-
yarrpika yungurna nyinami waja; kuyu yirna linji waja ngarni
purdangirlirli, kuyu wajarna ngarni purdangirlirli linji. Kajinpala
kuyukurlu yani waja papankurlangu." Kalapalangu ngarrurnu
kajanyanujarra nyanungunyangujarra kujapala yalumpurla palka-
jarrija Warlukurlangurla.
Kalapala yanu wirlinyi. Kalapala wapaja yinyakula karlarra
Jarlarripinkikirra. Jarlarri-yirrarnu kalapala. Kalapala warrulparni
kulpaja Warlukurlangukurra yangka, yalumpu kulkurrukurra, kuja
kapalangu rduyu-karri warlu jukurrpawarnu. Ngulangka kala
Lungkardaju nyinaja.
Kalapalangu yarda yirri-puraja. Milpa kala yakarra, milpa kala
tiirl-pardija milpa purdangirli. Kala yakarra-pardija. Karrinja-pardija
kala.
"Kari wurnturulku kapala yanirra ngajunyangujarraju

"Yes, old man. We are putting the meat here for you. I have put it right here for you," the younger brother used to say to him.

Then they all lay down in the camp and went to sleep. The two Jangala, the two sons, the two beautiful young men, the two from Warlukurlangu, the two who had been born there, those two ran and made fires on each side of the camp.

In the morning they awoke. In the morning after getting the meat, they warmed it on the fire. These days they eat bread and flour, in the days of the white man. But before the white man, in the time of the Jukurrpa [Dreaming], in the old days, they used to eat all kinds of big and small yams, and things like wild onions. They used to eat the meat of kangaroos and all kinds of goannas.

They left him saying, "Stay here, old man. Here, take this for yourself."

"Put some firewood here for me as well, and build me a shade so I can sit here, and later I can eat some of the dried meat. Later you, my two sons, will come back with fresh meat." This is what he used to say to his two sons who had been born there at Warlukurlangu.

They walked away from there towards the country near Jarlarri. At Jarlarri they used to start hunting. They would then circle back round towards Warlukurlangu, towards the centre, towards where the fire from the jukurrpa burns for them.

He used to watch where they went, with his awakened eyes. He used to open his eyes, after they had gone, he opened his eyes. Then he used to stand up.

"Ah well, they are going a long way, my two sons."

Then he would pick up his spear and spear-thrower. He too would set off to find meat. He would go and spear it. He used to cook it in great haste. Then he would cover it all up near the meat from before that the others had already left. He used to cook his own meat until it was dry. Then he used to bury it. Then with his eyes he would look around for the others.

"Well, there are my two sons approaching. They are coming this way loaded down with meat."

Then, "Old man, are you well?"

"Are you bringing meat?"

"Yes, meat."

kajanyanujarraju!" Kala kurlarda manu, pikirri kala manu. Kala
yarnkaja kuyukurrayijala. Kala panturnunjunu. Kala purraja yaruju-
yarujurlu. Kala muku jurrurr-yungu kuyungka yangka nyurruwarnu
kujapala kamparruwarnurlu yirrarnu. Kala linjikarda purraja
nyanungunyanguju. Kala yirrarnu kanunjumparra. Ngulajangkaju
kalapalangu wapalpa nyangu milpangkuwiyi,
    "Kari yinyapala rdipijarni waja ngajunyangujarraju kajajarraju.
Kuyukurlu kapala yanirni waja, wawurla-wawurla-yanirni yangka."
    Ngulajangkaju, "Purlka, ngurrjunya kanpa nyina?"
    "Yuwayi, ngurrju karna nyina. Kuyukurlu mayinkili rdipija?"
    "Yuwa, kuyu waja!"
    Kala, kalapalangu nyurruwiyi nyangu. Ngayi kala wangkaja.
Ngulajangkaju, kalapalarla kuyu yungu.
    "Kuyunpa ngarni!" Ngirntirlangu kalapalarla yungu kuyu marlu
nyampupiya. Kala ngarnu. Pakarninjarla kalapalarla yungu,
milpakurlukujala. Well, pampa-jarrija kala. Ngulajangkaju,
ngunajalku kalalu. Warlulku kalapalarla yarrpu-yarrpurnu. Ngunaja
kalalu. Kala ngunaja jajinyanu, kajanyanukari, kajanyanuyijala.
Jampijinpa kala ngunaja kulkurrujarraju, Lungkarda yirdiji. Kalapala
Jangalajarra ngunaja nyanungu-nyangujarra.
    Ngulajangkaju yanu, mungalyurru, yanupala watijarra
yangkajarraju. Yanupala. Well kala wati nyampuju yanu
purlkapardu. Kala wurnturu yangka nyinaja-aa.
    "Walykakurra karna yani waja. Yinya walykangka waja karna
nyina, yarlungka waja.
    "Ya, nyinaya waja!
    "Walykangka karnangkupala jurnta nyina waja nyampujuku,"
kala wangkaja purlkaparduju. "Yuwaw!"
    Kala marlu nyanungurluju kala purda-nyangu, kurdu yangka, kuja
kala yangka kirrkirr-manu yinyarla, Kirrkirrmanurla yirdingkaju,
nyanungunyangu maralypirla, mayi? Marlu kala witaju purda-
nyanguwiyi. Kala kujarlu yangka purda-nyangu. "Kari palkajuku
waja ka wangka."
    Kulpajarni kala ngunanjakulku.
    Ngulajangkaju, ngunajalkulpalu. Yanulkulpapala watijarra
wirlinyi. Ngulajangkaju, lawa-lawapala parnkaja kujarra, yangka
yungupala nyurruwiyi mukupungu Warlukurlangurla kutuju.

Although he had already seen them, he used to speak to them in this way. Then they would give him meat.

"Please eat this meat."

They would give him the tail of the kangaroo to eat. He ate it. After hunting the animal, they used to give him meat although he could see. However, in the camp he used to pretend to be blind. Then they would lie down to sleep. The two of them built him a fire. Then they would lie down. They would lie down, the father, one son, the other son. Jampijinpa whose name was Bluetongue slept in the middle. The two Jangala would sleep beside him.

Then in the morning the two men would leave. They went. Then the old man would leave. Sometimes he sat down some distance away.

"I'll just go over there to where it is cool. I will sit there where it is cool, in the open. There, sit down! I'll sit here in the cool away from you two," the old man used to say to himself. "Yes, indeed!"

Here he used to listen to his own kangaroo, a baby one which used to whimper in that place, the place called Kirrkirrmanu, which was very sacred to him. He always used to listen to the little kangaroo, before. He used to listen to it, saying to himself, "It is still here, the one that talks."

Then he would go back to the camp and lie down.

Then they slept. The two young men went out hunting. They ran in that direction, away from the camp, but found nothing, that is, in the area where before they had caught everything, near Warlukurlangu. So they continued along the south side towards the place called Kirrkirrmanu. It was in that place that an animal used to call out, that particular kangaroo. He used to listen to the little animal.

What did the old man do with it in that place? Did he turn it into a person? I do not know.

Well, the two of them speared and killed it, the one that was particularly sacred to him. They speared and killed it. They cooked it. They killed the little animal. Kirrkirrmanu is the place where the child kangaroo first hops around on its four legs, like that. It was a young kangaroo like that that the two sons, the two Jangala, killed. And then, to tell the truth, they cooked it. They took it back to their camp, back there to Warlukurlangu, nearby. Where they had their camp, that is where they took it.

Kurlirra side-lki kalapala yanu nganayikirra yirdikirraju
Kirrkirrmanukurra. Kuyu yalumpuju kuja kalapalangu kirrkirr-
manu, nganayi nyanungu marlu. Kala purda-nyangu kurdu.

Well, nyarrpa-mantarla marda watingkiji yinyarluju purlkangku?
Yapa-jarriyarla marda? Karijaju.

Well, jurntapalarla panturnu kajilpa nyinaja nyanungunyangu
yaliji maralypinyayirni. Jurntapalarla panturnu. Purrajalkulpapala.
Kurdupala pakarnu kurdukurlu. Warrulpa yangka Kirrkirrmanu
kujaka kurdurlangu warru yirrirlji-kanyi, ngulapiya.
Ngulapiyanyapalarla jurnta-panturnu Jangalajarrarluju
kajanyanujarrarlu. Yijardupala purraja. Kangupala ngurrakurra
yangka yinya nganayikirra Warlukurlangukurra, kutukurra.
Kujalpapala ngurrangka nyinaja, ngulakurrapala kangu.

Yungupalarla kuyu yirlara. Kulanganta yapakari, kulanganta
yapakari wurnturujangka, kala nyanungunyangu yinyaju kuyu
maralypirla, kujalpapalangu nyanungujarra nyanungukulparla
nyinajalku, yilparla kuyu. Kuyulpala nyinaja yapa marda, karija—
maralypirla.

Ngulajangkaju, mayajarrakurralkurla yanu,
"Ngurrjunyayirnirli kuja. Nyiya nyampuju ngurrjungku wajaju
kaaly-pungu kuyungku? Nyarrpara marlurlu?" Manngu-
nyangulkulpa, "Nyarrparawardingkiwiyiji nyampuju kuja kuyu
mayakurra yanu? Yangka kaaly-pungu ngurrjunyayirnirli."
Ngurrjunyayirni purda-nyangu kuyu. Nyampujarrakurrarla yanu,
mayajarrakurra yanu. "Ngurrju-manu yangka, nyampu
ngurrjunyayirni waja mirnimpaju. Nyarrparajangka kuyu kujajupala
kajanyanujarrarlu kangurnu waja?" Yirlarapalarla yungu wita.

Yanu. Wuraji-wuraji-jarrija. Wanta yukaja and munga-munga-
jarrijalku. Yarlukurralku yanu. Nyinajalpa purlkaparduju.
Ngulajangkaju, purda-nyangulparla. "Kari, lawajuku." Ngunajalpa
yangka kuja. Well, kuja kala ngunaja-yi, "Nyarrpara kujaka wangka?
Nyarrpara? Nyarrpa-manupala nyampujarrarlujuku waja-pala
pakarnunjunu. Pungupala nyampujarrarlujuku? Yangkajuku kujaju
waja ngurrjunyayirni mayakurra yanu, nyampujuku marda?"

Ngulajangkaju, wurra-jarrija. Ngunajalkulpalu. Ngulajangkaju
wirlinyikirralkupala yanu. Wirlinyilkipala yanu watijarraju.
Wirlinyipala yanu. Mungakarirlalkulpa yarda ngunaja. Kari

They gave him the meat, from the muscle. He thought it was meat from a different animal from much further away, but it was his own sacred animal, from there where the sacred animal which belonged to him alone had presented itself to the two men. It was meat from that animal.

Then he wanted to eat more.

"Very good! What is this meat which tastes so good to me? Where did this kangaroo come from?" He considered the matter. "From what particular place did this meat come from which makes me want to eat more? It tastes really wonderful." He found that the meat tasted very good. He went to the two of them and asked for more. "That was well done. That I found delicious. Where did my two sons get that meat?" They gave him a piece from a muscle, a small one.

He went. It became late afternoon. The sun set and it became dark. He went out into the open. The old man sat down. Then he listened for it. "Still nothing." He lay down there, he lay down in that place. "Where is the one who talks? Where? What have those two done with it? Have those two killed it? Have they hunted it? Was it that which was so good to eat that I wanted more, was it that meat?"

Then some time later, they all lay down to sleep. The two went hunting again. That night he lay down at that same place again. Still nothing, nothing at all. He listened for the call of the little kangaroo that used to call out for its mother, but he heard nothing.

Then he lay down on his own, alone. He returned to that open space. Still nothing. He began to grow very angry with the two men, his two sons. They went hunting. Still he could not find that animal. He looked into his own feelings. He began to feel hatred towards those two, his own two.

So he cut a stick. He began to concentrate his thoughts in the manner of a sorcerer, to harm them. He sent a fire to await them, like one you might light with a firestick, when they returned from hunting.

"Ayi, ayi."

They came along, coming back from hunting, from a long distance.

"Hey, perhaps that fire has burnt the old man, poor thing, the old man!"

The old man had concentrated his thoughts to harm those two. He had sent a sorcerer's fire by concentrating his thoughts precisely to

lawajuku, lawajuku. Wanjani karla kirrkirr-manu, yangka marluju
yirdija kala kirrkirr-manu, marlu wita-witaju ngati nyanunguku.
Lawajuku.

Ngulajangkaju jintakulku ngunajarni, jintakulku. Yarda yanu
yarlukurra. Ngulajangka yanu. Lawajuku. Jungajuku waja
miyalurlulkupalangu nyangu wati nyampujarraju kajanyanujarraju
nyanungunyangujarra. Yanupala wirlinyi. Ngulajangkaju, walkulku
nyangu yangkaju kuyu. Miyalulkunyanu nyangu. Maju-jarrijalku
miyalu – yangka nyanungunyangurlu.

"Nyampujarra nyampujuku waja."

Watiyalku pajurnu. Jangkardulkupalangu manngu-nyangu
juyurdukurlurlu. Warlulkupalangu jirriny-pungu nyampupiya ngiji,
jangunyu wirlinyijangkaku.

"Ayi! Ayi!"

Yaninja-yaninjarlalkupala yanu wurnturungurluju.

"Purlka marda ka kampa warlungku wiyarrpa, purlka marda!"

Purlkangkunyapalangu jangkardu juyurdu-manu.
Nganayikipalangu manngu-nyangu jangkardu juyurdulku warlu.
Nyurruwarnupaturlu kujalpalujana jangkardu manngu-nyangu
yangka juyurdukurlurlu. Ngulajangkaju, purlka-purlkarluju kalu
yangka nganayi mardarni juyurdu – yunparninjakurlangu.

Kuturnupala jarrija. Nyampu, "Purlka ka rduyu-karri! Purlka
marda kampaja warlungku purdangirli pampa."

Kala lawa. Nyanungujarrakulaku yinyaju yungkurnu. Kuturnupala
jarrija, kuturnupala jarrija. Warlumanji jankajarralku.
Wapirdipalangu wajili-pungu warlungku. Wajili-pungupalangu.
Palu-pungulpapala, palu-pungulpapala, palu-pungulpapala.
Lawajukulpapala palu-pungu parrkangku nyampurrapiyarlu. Ngula
lawajuku. Juyurdu yalumpuju. Puyurrparlu pungulpapalangu. Palu-
pungulpapala, palu-pungulpapala, palu-pungulpapala
yalumpuwardingkirli yantarlirli, palu-pungulpapala, palu-
pungulpapala, palu-pungulpapala.

Kurlirralkupala pardijarra tarnngalkujuku. Ngurra, ngurrangkalpa
wantija. Nyanungu palijalku. Kulanganta yijardu warluju.
Ngulajangka yakarralpapala pardija watijarra, Jangalajarra.
Nyanungulpa warlu yakarra-pardi-jarrijalku. Yarnkajalpalu
wurnalku. Kurlulumpayi-ii yarnkajalpalu. Palu-pinja-yanulpapala,

harm them. It is for purposes like these that old men have the powerful incantation that is used in singing.

They came closer. One of them said, "The old man is burning! Maybe the blind old man has been burnt by the fire."

But no. The fire had been lit for them. They came closer and closer. The trees were burning all around. The fire chased after them, coming nearer and nearer. It pursued them. They kept putting it out all around them, again and again. They kept extinguishing it with branches but to no avail. It continued to burn. It was a fire fuelled by sorcery. They could not breathe because of the smoke. The two who had been born in that place, in their own home, kept on putting it out and putting it out but it burnt on and on.

They travelled away for a long time to the south. When they camped overnight, it died away. They assumed it was a real fire. Then the two Jangala woke. The fire became active at the same time. They left on the journey. They travelled a long way to the south. As they walked they kept putting the fire out, again and again. As when we look at the top part of a big fire, where it pushes itself right up to the clouds, well, it was a fire like that. As the old man had imagined it, so he watched it rise right up, like the top of a fire.

Then they lay down again. The fire died down and stopped. They set out towards the east. They awoke and the two of them travelled a long way. The sorcerer's fire woke at the same time, always present, always present. The fire chased them away from here, always further off it chased them, and they became more and more badly burnt. As they put it out, it consumed their feet. It ate at their feet, their knees, their heads until their skin was covered in burns.

At this point in the journey, the story belongs to the Pitjatjantjara [people in the neighbouring country].

Then the fire sent them back. It brought them back. "This fire has burnt us from head to foot. It has burnt us all over. What shall we do? Shall we turn back towards home? Shall we go up into the sky? Shall we go under the earth?" they asked themselves. This is what they said, their skin covered in burns from the fire.

So they returned to this place, to the same place. They travelled and travelled, back to this place. As they walked along they still had to keep putting out the fire that burnt them. It continued to follow them,

palu-pinja-yanulpapala, palu-pinja-yanulpapala, palu-pinja-
yanulpapala, palu-pinja-yanulpapala, palu-pinja-yanulpapala, palu-
pinja-yanulpapala, palu-pinja-yanulpapala. Yangka kujakarlipa
lirranji warlu nyanyi, lirranji yangka mangkurdurlangu kujaka
yirrarni warlungka, kujaka wirijarlu warlu ngula yangkaju fire,
ngulangka. Kankarlumparralku yirrarnu lirranjilki milya-pinjarlalku
nyampurluju.
  Ngulajangkaju, still ngunajalpalu yarda. Warlulpa lawa-jarrija,
walku-jarrijalpa yalumpuju. Kakarraralpapala pardija.
Wurnturulkulpapala, yakarralpapala pardija nyanungulpapala.
Warlu yakarra-pardijayijala palkaju, palkayijala, juyurdujangarra.
Wajili-pungulpapalangu warlungkuju kujarrarlalku, maju-maju
wajili-pungulpapalangu kujarrarlalku, wurnturulku.
Wurnturulkupalangu wajili-pungu. Palu-pungulpapala warluju. Palu-
pinjarla nyampujarrajulpapalangu ngarnu. Ngarnulpapalangu
nyampujarraju mirdijijarra, jurru nyampujarra winyirl-winyirlpalku.
Ngarnulpapalangu.
  Ngulajangkaju, wurnturulku yinya yimikari kujakalu wangka –
Pija-pija kujakalu wangka.
  Ngulangkapalangu warlungkuju kulpari-kujurnu, kulpari-
manupalangu. "Karinganta warlungkungalingki waja nyampurluju
jurrupinki waja maju-manu. Mukungalingki kampaja! Nyarrparli
jarri? Warrulparli kulpa ngurrakurra waja? Nyarrpa-jarrirli?
Yalkiriwana japarli yani? Kanunjumparrajaparli yani?" manngu-
nyangulpapala. Wangkajalpapala nyampujarraju winyirl-
winyirlpalku warlujangkaju.
  Kulparirnipala yanu jurrkukurra ngurrakurra, nyampukurra.
Yanurnupala, yanurnupala, yanurnupala, yanurnupala, yanurnupala,
yanurnupala. Palu-pinjarlalpapala wapaja, kuja. Yangkapiyarlujala
kujapalangu kujapurdarlu puraja, ngulapiyarlujala. Yanurnupala,
yanurnupala. Lirranjiwanapala yanurnu. Ngulangkupala jiwin-
pungu, jiwin-pungu, jiwin-pungu. Yanurnupala.
Pakajumanuwanapala yanurnu. Mata-jarrijapala ngulangkajuku.
  Yalumpu ka karri watikirlangulku. Nganayilki maralypilki ka karri.
Mardukuja-yaninjawangu, lawa, watimipakurra.
  Ngulajukurna ngarrurnu.

Recorded at Yuendumu, May 25, 1990

always with them, always burning in the same way. They came back. They came back past Lirranji. They staggered along in agony, trying not to brush against the places where they had been burnt. They returned. They came past Pakajumanu.

There they stopped, exhausted. That place belongs to men. That is a sacred place. Women do not go there, only men.

That is all I have to tell.

TRANSLATORS' NOTE

This account of the Warlukurlangu (fire dreaming) story by Uni Nampijinpa is distinguished by its psychological realism, the detailed attention given to the characters and their feelings. The traditional story, very ancient, has great dramatic potential, describing as it does the persecution by the father, a figure of great magical power, of his two sons after they have broken a taboo of which they were not aware, ironically in order to satisfy him, and the subsequent painful deaths of the two young men.

In this version, the father, always deceitful, seems to take a delight in deceiving, and also in inflicting pain. The sons, always innocent, are also beautiful, young, open-hearted and generous. Thus, the way the boys die, driven for ever greater distances by a sorcerer's fire that seems to die out at night but each morning inexorably returns and, as exhaustion overtakes them, inflicts worse and worse burns, is beautifully and movingly described.

The activities of the father and the two sons in the area around Warlukurlangu and Kirrkirrmanu, and the flight of the two sons away from Warlukurlangu to the south and their return, map the locations of the important places in what one might describe as one of the Warlpiri heartlands. Thus, the story is a major Warlpiri jukurrpa, frequently performed as a dance, and also recorded in a number of large and important paintings.

YARMURNTURRNGUKURRA KARNA PINA KULPA NGURRAKURRA YAJARLUKURRA

To Yarmurnturrngu and How I Came Back to Yajarlu

TOLD BY

Jacko Ross Jakamarra

Tennani Creek ■

■ *Yarturlu-yarturlu*

■ *Willowra*

Yajarlu ■   ■ *Yuendumu*

Yarmurnturrngu ■

■ *Alice Springs*

Jukurrpa yilpa karrija Yajarlurla, rdakulpa pangurnu, rdaku. Pangurnulpa karntangku wulkumanurlu. Well-ilpa kurdu, kiripi-kangulpa – kankarlu. Wapajalpa. Kurdulparla kiripi-kangu, kiripi-kangulparla.

Well-ilpa jintakari yanurnu. Nyangu. "Ayi, kurdu ka nyampuju nyina, ngarlarrpa karla nyinami. Kurdu nyampu waja yuruju." Well-ilpa wurrangku yangka jawirri-nyangu. Warrulpa wapaja. "Aaa, jurnta-manirnarla! Jurntarnarla mani. Ngayirnarla jurnta-kanyi." Well-i kurdu nyanungunyangulkurla yirrarnu. Yirrarnurla.

Yanurnulpa. Wapalkurlu pangurnu kaninjarra. No nyangu. Nyanjawangurlu. Wapajalpa. No nyangu yalirli kaninjarrarlu.

"Well, nyanjawangujuku ka nyina nyampuju waja?" Nyanjawangujuku waja, nyampuju. "Kukurnarla kurdu nyampu jurnta-kanyi."

Jurntarla kangu. Manu, jurntarla kangu. Well, kurdu nyanunguju jintakarilkirla yirrarnu, yapakarilki nyampungurlu, Karnilpangurlu, Yarmurnturrngurla kutungurlu – kujangurlu. Pirli ka japiya nguna. Aa.

Yakarra-pardija. "Ayi, nyarrpara yanu nyampungurluju kurdu?" Lawa-nyangurla. Warrurnurla. "Nyiyangurlu nganangkuju jurnta-kangu? Kurdu nyampuju yapakarilki!" Lawalku. Nyarrpara warrurnu-uu, no wirliya. Wirliywangurlu – jurnta-kangurla. Marnawana yanu – kankarlu. Wali jurnta-kangurla. Aa, warrurnurla-aa, nyangurla. Nyangulparla. "Aa, nyampuwanajuku yanu. Yapa nyampuwanarlu jurnta-manu. Yanu, kurlirra. Aa, nyampuwana yanu. Karna yani maninjaku."

Yanu-uu. Nyangurla. "Nyarrpararla ka, nyarrpararla ka nyina? Nyarrpararla ka nyinami?"

Kurdu panukarilpa nyangu, yapakarilpa nyangu.

"Aa, nyampu nyanunguju nyinanya!" Manu. Kurdu jintakarirla yali pina-yirrarnu nyanungunyangu warlalja maninjarla kangu. Kulpaja yangkakurra ngurrakurra. Nyanungunyangukurralku yanu. Pina yanu ngurrakurra nyanungunyangukurra. Kulpaja.

Well, yalirlajukulpapala yanu. Nyinajalpapala tarnnga. Tarnn galkulpapala nyinaja, ngamardinyanu manu kurdu. No yapa, no yapa jintakari yanurnu, lawa. Jintangkulpa mardarnu kurduju – jin tangku. No-wu nyangu jintangku wirriyarlu. Karlarralpa nyinaja

This is about the dreaming that belongs to Yajarlu. There was a woman digging a big hole. It was a woman, digging, an old woman. Nearby there was a small child, crawling about. The woman emerged from the hole and she walked about nearby. The child was still crawling about, crawling about near her. Another woman arrived. She saw the child.

"Ahh, look at this child here! How beautiful it is! This child is truly lovely!" She looked at the child, but she left it alone. She went away, and walked around. "Ahh, I am going to take that child away with me. Indeed, I am going to carry it away." She put her own child down instead, and left it there.

The first woman had come back. Without noticing anything, she started digging again, down inside the hole. She saw nothing. She did not see what had happened while the other woman was walking about. From down inside the hole she could not see, and so, without noticing anything, she continued to dig.

The second woman asked herself, "Is she still there, I wonder?" She was unable to see anything. "I am free to take this child away without being noticed."

She took it away. She grabbed it and took it away. She put her own child down in the same place, a child belonging to other people from here, from Karnilpa near Yarmurnturrngu, from that place nearby. That mountain is a very important place.

Suddenly the woman who had been digging realized what was going on. "Hey, where has that child gone that was here?" She could not see it anywhere. She searched for it. "Why has someone taken it away? This child here belongs to someone else." Still nothing. She searched the area all around. No tracks. The child had been taken away without leaving any tracks. She searched everywhere, she looked for it everywhere.

Then she saw something. "Ahh, the woman came this way. The woman has carried the child away this way. She went south. She went this way. I am going to get the child back."

She went. As she went she looked everywhere. "Where is that child? Where is it sitting? Where can it be?"

She saw many other children belonging to other people. "Ahh, there is the one I was looking for, sitting there!" She picked it up. She put the

kutuyijala. Wirriyaju. Lawa, nyanjawangu.

Nyanjarla yilpa nyangu tarnngangku. Kulpari warru, yilpa warru nyangu yalirli jintakarirli Jupurrurlarlu. Nyangulpa yali kirraju. "Yaa, palkajuku kapala nyina yaliji, palkajuku kapala nyina!"

Nyanungulpa nyinaja yalumpurlajuku. Ngapangka nganayirla —Yajarlurlalpala nyinaja. Nyinajalpala. Purraku nyanungurlalpa kiripi-kangu kurdu nyanungu. Ngulalparla jurnta kiripi-kangu. Yuwayi.

Well-i yalirlajukupala lawa-jarrija, yalirlajukupala lawa-jarrija. Yukajapala. Tarnngajuku. Yuwayi, tarnngajukupala yukaja. Mm. No-pala pina wilypi-pardija.

Jintakarirlipalangu lawa-nyangu yapangku, watingki. "Aa, lawalku kala! Kari nyarrpa-jarrijapala?" Warrurnupalangu puta. Lawa. Pina kulpaja yalikirrajuku. Tarnngalpa nyinaja yalumpuwar dingki, purlka, nyanunguju Jupurrurla. Mm, purlkalpa nyinaja. Yuwayi. Tarnngalpa nyinaja yalirlajuku. Nguru.

Nyangulpajana yali warlu. Karlarra kuja. Warlulpajana nyangu. "Yali kalu yingkirni warluju! Yuwayi, warlu kalu yingkirni yali — yapangku. Yingarna ngaka yani nyanjaku. Yuwayi. Yani karnaja na ngaka nyanjaku. Winijirna nyanyi jukurrarlu. Jukurrarlu karna nyanyi, jukurrarlu karna nyanyi."

Yanu yakarra-pardinjarla. Yaninjarla nyangu. "Yuwa, nyarrpa rangurlu? Nyarrparangurlu?" "Nyampungurlu karna kakarrara wapami. Nyuntulkurnangku pardu-pardu-manurnu, nyunturnangku pardu-pardu-manurnu. Yii, kanpa mayi nyampurla yingkirni?"

"Yuwa, nyampurlaju karna nyina. Yuwayi, nyampurlaju karna nyina tarnnga."

"Ngayi! Kala panukari?"

"Yali kalu kurlirra nyina. Kurlirra kalu nyina, kurlirra. Kuja. Yatijarra karna kulpa. Yatijarra karna yani ngurrakurra." Kuja wangkaja. Kuja wangkajarra nyanungu, "Ngurrakurra karna yatijarra yani, jurrkukurra, warlaljakurra."

Ngulajuku. Kulpayalu! Yuwayi.

Recorded at Yuendumu, 25 May, 1990

other child down in its place. Picking up her own child, she took it away. She went back to her own home. She went back home. She and the child both went back together. There they remained for a long time. For a long time they stayed there, mother and child. No other people came that way. She looked after the child alone, on her own. Not even the boy saw the child. There was a boy living nearby, to the west, but he did not see the child.

However, one person had been looking in that direction for a long time. He, that other Jupurrurla, looked back there toward that place again and again. "Yes, two people are still living there, they are still there."

That person lived always in that place beside that waterhole. The other two both lived at Yajarlu. That is where they lived. The child crawled about on her own near the waterhole there.

Well, suddenly those two disappeared from there. They disappeared. They went in, forever. No, they did not come out again.

Later another person, another man came that way, but he did not see them. "Ahh, nothing here! I say, what happened to them?" He tried to find them. Then he went back to the other place where he was living. He lived there for a long time, the person who belonged to that place, an old man, Jupurrurla. The old man lived there for a long time, in his own country.

Then he saw the fires. In the west. He saw the fires. "They are lighting fires over there! Yes, people are lighting fires! Later I will go over to look at the burnt-out areas, yes, later I will go over and have a look. I will have a look at the burnt-out areas tomorrow. Tomorrow I will look at them, tomorrow."

When he woke the next morning he went. After he left, he looked around. "Yes. How did this happen? How did this happen? I have been walking eastwards from over there. I am just coming to pay you a little visit, just to pay you a little visit. Are you lighting these fires?"

"Yes, I live here. I have been living here for a long time."

"Indeed, what about the others?"

"They live over there to the south. In the south they live, they live in the south. There. I am going back north, I am going back to my home in the north." This is what he said to him. "I am returning to my home in the north, back to the same place, to join my relatives."

That is the end. Let them go back to their homes. Yes.

TRANSLATORS' NOTE

Jacko Ross Jakamarra is regarded by older Warlpiri people living at Yuendumu as one of the finest exponents of the traditional narrative. To the Western reader, his way of telling a story may seem strange, cryptic, allusive and apparently disconnected; characters and activities are introduced that do not seem to relate to the apparent plot, the matter of the abducted child.

However, as the title indicates, what is important is the return of the mother with the child to her home at Yajarlu. In fact what unifies the narrative is place, not character or a single strand of events. All the events in the narrative take place at or in relation to Yajarlu: the theft of the child, its return to its rightful home, the separate but always present concern of the old Jupurrurla for both the people, the mother and child, and the country, and who might be lighting fires. The narrative is about restoring things to their rightful state and position. In this way, at the close of the story, the traveller who is passing through on his way to his own home and relatives provides a coda elegantly emphasizing this central concern.

There are two other aspects of Jakamarra's narrative technique which should be noted. One is the allusiveness, which both compliments and teases the listeners by demanding they supply details they should know, for example, that the Jupurrurla is the owner of Yajarlu. The other is the humour of the dramatized exchanges, the words put into the mouths of the different characters, and also of course the way the narrator acts these out, the way the other woman considers taking the child and decides to do so, the panic of the mother when she discovers the substitution.

MARLUJARRAKURLU

The Two Kangaroos

TOLD BY

Henry Cook Jakamarra

Ngajunyangu marlujarrapala yananyarra nyampu
kakarrumparra, marlujarrapala yananyarra.
Yananyarrapala nganayi, yangkapala yanu nganayi –
nyarrparaku karnarla nguruku yalikila warrirni? Nganayiki
Parntarlarlaku. Parntarlarlalpala nyinaja. Ngulajupala pardijarra.
Nyinajalpala. Kujapala Lawarrikirralku yanurra. And nyinajalpapala
Lawarri. Nyinajalpala yalumpuwardingki, marlujarra yalumpujarra.
Nyinajalpa ngurrapatu, ngurrapatu kapalangu karri, Lawarri,
Parntarlarla, Parra kapalangu karri, ngurra, ngurraju, ngula
kapalangu karri. Pardijarrapala. Ngula ngurrara
yalumpuwardingkilpala nyinaja. Ngurra panu-manupala, mulju-
mulju, there, found out.

Nyinajalpala, pardijarrapala. Ngakarra-ngakarralkulpala
pardijarra, karrija, ngari nyurruwiyi. Jukurrpaju ngayilpala wapaja.
Yananyarra-aa, yananyarrapala-aa. Pardijarrapala kurlarra-aa
yangka Granite kuja karlumparra, Granite-wana, Yurlpuwarnu,
kakarrumpara Yurlpuwarnu, kakarrumparrakari. Granite-ngirlipala
yanu karlumparrakarijuku, Granite-ki-juku. Granite-ngirli yanupala-
aa.

"Yi karla puntarnilki marlu jintaju." Puntarnulkurla nganayirli
yapurnurlu. Puntarnurla, nyangulpa.

"Kari, nyampu karna jintalku kuja yani! Nyarrpa-jarrija? Kari
nganayi ngapangku puntarnuju, jurin-pungu ngapa, you know-lpa
nyinajanputinja."

Yapurnu, yapurnurlurla puntarnu. Puntarnurla-aa, jinta puntarnu.
Yalumpurlajuku yampinja-yanu, waja-waja-maninja-yanu. Jinta now
yanu, yananyarra jintalku, yanurra.

Nyangulpa. "Nyiya ka nyampuju nyina?" Yangka wita nganayi
wulyu-wulyu, little rat, jungunypaku-purdangka – wulyu-wulyujuku,
yirdiji wulyu-wulyu.

Yukaja, manulku, manulku. Mii-mii-nyangulpa kujarlu, "Ayi,
langajarrakurlu? Langajarrakurlu, kapu ngirntikirli,
wirliyajarrakurlu, ayi, ngirntikirli?" Nyangulpa mii-mii.
Ngirntikirlilpa mii-mii-nyangu.

"Nyarrpara-manurna nyampuju? Aaa, kanyirna, kanyirna!"
Kangurra kuja nganayikirra Mulyukurra. Mulyukurra kangurra.
Ngulangkalpa ngurrju-manu, ngurrju-manu muku, marlu-manu.

These are my two kangaroos. There they went, along the east side. The two kangaroos travelled along the east side. They went, where, where am I trying to remember? They went to Parntarla. They stayed at Parntarla. Then they departed. They stopped again. They went to Lawarri next. They stayed at Lawarri. There they stayed, the two kangaroos belonging to that place. These two places belong to them, Lawarri and Parntarla. These places belong to them both. They are the two who belong to these places. They brought many places into being, many soakages, in the surrounding area.

They stayed. Then they left. A little later on they set off, then they stopped. You know, in the old days they walked about during the Dreaming. There they were travelling, the two of them. They travelled south, along the west side to the Granites, then back along the east to Yurlpuwarnu, along the east side again. From the Granites they went along the west side again, near the Granites. Then they left the Granites.

Then one of the two kangaroos was taken away. He was carried away in a big flooded stretch of water. Thus he was taken away. The other looked for him all around.

"Now I will have to travel alone. What has happened? Maybe he was carried off by all that water? The water has been running everywhere, it has spread out everywhere. That lake, that lake has swallowed him up."

He was taken from there, one of the two was taken away. Then, from that place the one who was left, went away. He went off, and put the other one out of his mind.

He looked around. "What is this sitting here?"

It was a type of little mouse, a little rat, somewhat related to a mouse but slightly different, called a wulyu-wulyu. He approached it and picked it up. He looked at it closely.

"Ah, it has two ears, two ears and it has a tail, it has two feet, and it has a tail." He looked at it carefully. In particular he looked at its tail.

"What will I do with this creature? I'll take it with me, I'll take it along." He carried it to Mulyu, he carried it to Mulyu. There he remade it, he remade it completely. He made it into a kangaroo. Now that he was a kangaroo, he started to hop about. Where did he go? He went away. Now that he was a kangaroo, now that he had been

Marlulku now-lpa parlparu-kangu. Yuwa. Nyarrparapurda?
Yanurralpa, marlulkulpa yanurra, marlulku muku wurduju-manu,
marlulku now.

Marlujarralku now-lpapala nyinaja. Ngula Wulyu-wulyurla
yirdingka, Wulyu-wulyurla yirdingka. Marlujarralkupala nyinaja
yalumpuwardingki ngurrangkalku. Marlujarranya nyinajapala,
nyinajapala, nyinajapala.

"Ya! Wurnarna pardiy!"

"Yuwa."

Nyanungurla jintakari yangkaju, papardinyanu marda, I don't
know, papardinyanu marda. Yali yangka marlunyayirni, wulyu-
wulyujangkaju, yangka murlurn-nyinajalpa, that one, kiripi-
kangulkulpa. Yanu-uu, nyinaja, pardija.

"Wurnalkurna yani-wu. Wurnalkurna yani."

"Yuwayi, yuwayi, wurnalku, yawu!"

"Junga yangkaju kamparru-jarra kuja."

Kamparru-manu yangkaju wulyu-wulyujangka. Kamparrujarralpa
yaninja-yanu nyanungunyangu marlukari wapanjinanu
purdangirliwarnu. Wapanjinanulpala.

Aa, yardapala find him-manu ngurrakarilki, yirdi nganayi
Nyurijardu, Nyurijardu, Nyurijardulku, yalikila big place. Now-lpala
ngurrju-manu, yilpala nyinaja. Yalumpurlalkulpala nyinaja-aa.
Nyinajapala, nyinajapala. Yalumpuwardingkilpala nyinaja.
Ngurrakari-ngurrakarilkikipalangu karri kuja mulju-mulju, kurlarni.

Karlarrapala pardijarra Jalyirrparntakurra. Karlarrapala
pardijarra Jalyirrparntakurra. Ngulangkapala ngunaja.
Nyinajarrapala. Ngulajangkaju, pardijarrapala kurlarra,
pardijarrapala tarnngalku. Wurnakaripala yanu, muljukari
yalumpuju, kulkurrukari, nyarrpaku mayi karnarla yirdiki warrirni?
Jalyirrparntaju purdangirlilki. Yalikirla kulkurru karnarla warrirni
yirdiki, yirdiki, yirdiki nyanungu ka karri mulju. Warrarna, no,
Jupurrurla's father knows that. I never been longa that country.

Ngulangurlu pardimirra mayi nganayiki, muljukari – yalikila.
Ngunajarrapala Kuyujarraku, Kuyujarraku. I don't know another
mulju there, kurlarra-yatijarra. Kuyujarraku. Kuyujarrajangka
Yintawalyarriki, Yintawalyarriki. Yintawalyarrijangkaju-uu
Kulpiyanuku. Kulpiyanujangkaju, yanurrapala –

completely remade into a kangaroo, he went away.

Now there were two kangaroos. One had come from the little animal we call wulyu-wulyu. The two kangaroos stayed in that place for a considerable time, in that place which belongs to them. The two kangaroos stayed there for a long time.

"Let's go on a journey."

"Yes."

The one that had spoken was probably the older brother, I am not sure, probably the older brother. The other was now also a real kangaroo, the one that had been made from a little rat. At first it hopped around on all fours, on all four legs. It went. It stopped. It went on.

"I am going on a journey, I am going on a journey."

"Yes, yes, on a journey then, yes."

"All right, you go in front, like that."

He made the little one, the one made from the little rat, travel in front of him. The other one followed him. In this way, he went along. Then they found another place, called Nyurrijardu, which is a very important place. They created that place, the two of them, and there they stayed for a while. They stayed there at that place for quite a while. They were the two belonging to that place. In that southern part of the country there are all those places that belong to them, all those soaks, there in the south.

Then they travelled east to Jalyirrparnta. They slept there, they stayed out there. Then they went on into the south for a long time. They also visited a soak on the way. Now what is that name I am looking for? Somewhere behind Jalyirrparnta. Warrarna, Jupurrurla's father, knows that place. I have never visited that particular country.

From there they went to another soak, further away, to Kuyujarra, Kuyujarra. I do not know of another soak there, either to the south or the north. To Kuyujarra. From Kuyujarra to Yintawalyarri. From Yintawalyarri they went along the west side to Warnirriparnta. They went a long distance away, along the west side. There they encountered another dreaming. At that place, the Pirlarla dreaming follows the same path.

Then they arrived at Lirrawarnupatu. At Lirrawarnupatu, they mistakenly made contact with that other dreaming. From

49

Kulpiyanujangkajupala yarnkaja karlumparra kuja yanurrapala
nganayikirra Warnirriparntaku. Mirni, karlumparrakulu yanu. Ayi,
mm, ngulaku nganayiki, Pirlarlarlu kujanyanu puranja-yanu
nyarrpara yangka?

Yuwayi, ngula, ngulapala wapu-pungu Lirrawarnupatu,
Lirrawarnupatu, yali wrong-jarrija. Yanurrapala-aa
Lirrawarnupatujangkaju-uu. Yanurrapala Japiyajarrakurra.
Panujarlu mulju-mulju, panujarlu mulju-muljuju witawangujala ka
nguna kulkurru-kulkurruju yalumpurlaju. Kala ngayi karna, ngayi
witakari witakari karna milya-pinyi because you know-rna
yalumpurla. Karlumparra kala ngayi karna yirri-puranja-yanulku.
Ngarrirni yangka kajulu, yirri-pura yangka.

Yuwayi yanu. Yukajarrapala Japiyajarrakurra. Ngulangurlu now
yangka nganayirla ngurungkaju Yintaramurrurla kuja karlarra,
Yintaramurrurla. They call, you white fellow call him nganayi Mt
Singleton. Mt Singleton white fellow-irliji kalu ngarrirni. That area,
kuja karlarra. Ngulajangkaju ngula yanurrapala-aa. Miyilpala
ngayaki yirrarnu, ngayaki yangka jarlparrpapiyayijala.
Ngurrangkalpala yirrarnu, yirrarnupala.

Yanurnupala. Yarrpawangulku now ka junma karri, ngula
Yarrpawangu junma yangka, stone knife they call it. Ngulangkapala,
ngulangkapala mangarri ngarninjarla yarnkajarra. Jurntapalarla
yanu. Yanupalarla Yintaramurrukurra. To the place called Mt
Singleton, now.

Yintaramurru. Ngulajangkapala yanu-uu nganayikirralku, Butcher
Creek, Butcher Creek. Ngulangurlupala yanurra-aa, tarnngalkulpala
yanurra.

We let him go from there now Butcher Creek-jangkaju
nganayikirralku Yanjiwarrakurra, Yanjiwarrakurra.
Yanjiwarrarlulpalajana yunparnu kurdiji. Jalpijuku yanurra
yalijipala. Yanurrapala nganayikirra, Pikilyikirrapala warrkarnu
Yanjiwarrajangkaju. Pikilyikirrapala warrkarnu. That far we let him
go, Pikilyikirra.

Ngulajuku. Ngurrju mayi kujaju?

Recorded at Lajamanu, 18 April, 1990

Lirrawarnupatu they went to Japiyajarra. In that area, many, many soakages, some very big, lie across the basin there. I learned about those places when I was growing up, a little at a time. I can follow this dreaming as it goes along the west side, as it has been told to me, as it has been shown me.

The two kangaroos continued their journey. They went into Japiyajarra. From there, now, into another country, into Yintaramurru, which is in the west. White people call that place Mount Singleton. That country, in the west. They went away over there. There they put down bush tomato plants, the fruit which we call ngayaki which is like jarlparrpa as well. In that country they deposited the bush tomato plants.

They came back this way. At Yarrpawangu, there is a stone knife, a stone knife at Yarrpawangu. From there they went back to eat the bush tomatoes. They went back to Yintaramurru. From there they went on to Butcher Creek, Butcher Creek. And from there they went further still. They went away for a long time.

From there we will leave them as they go from Butcher Creek to Yanjiwarra. At Yanjiwarra those two sang the kurdiji [initiation] songs for others. Then they left there, just the two of them. They went away towards that place, they climbed up towards Pikilyi, from Yanjiwarra. They climbed up towards Pikilyi. That is as far as I will take the story, as far as Pikilyi.

That is all.

TRANSLATORS' NOTE

The myth of the two kangaroos is a major men's initiation myth, not only for the Warlpiri people but also for the Arrernte and Pintupi people in the area to the south, mentioned briefly by Jakamarra. This version of the story is one told for an audience of young people including children. Although the basic outline of the events of the myth is present, what is esoteric and secret is not. However, this is more than compensated for in the charm of the delivery for a young audience, in which the power of the kangaroos, creators of water places, is tempered with humour and an affectionate characterization.

The section of the narrative in which the kangaroo creates another kangaroo, a companion, out of the rat and then teaches it to hop properly, is an innocent and emblematic way of mirroring the much more serious matter of

51

the creation and education of a man in the course of his initiation. Thus, one of the features of Warlpiri traditional narrative becomes clear; as young people growing up are deemed ready to hear more and more powerful versions of central myths, so the narrators of these stories are able to select the material to include for a particular occasion, and also choose an appropriate style. The proliferation of parallel incidents in the myths also makes this possible.

MARLURLUKURLU

The Youth

TOLD BY

Kajingarra Napangardi

Ngatinyanurlu manu jajinyanurlu mardarnu witawangunyayirni, wiri, marlurlu. Wirinyayirni kalapala mardarnu, marlurlu. Kalalu yampirrirlaju panujarlu nyinaja. Ngamirninyanu, jajanyanu kalalu nyinaja, jajinyanu yangka, panukari nganayi Wiinywiinypa, Kirrkirlardi, ngula kalalu nyinaja and Kaarnka kala yangka nyinaja. Yampirrirla kalalpapala yurunju-nyinaja nyampujarrakula.

"Nguru-mardaka wajarla, kuyukurra kajirna yani." Kala jakuri-pungu kirda-nyanurlu. Kala yanu-uu. Warru-pungu kala kuyu. "Nyiya kuja kuyuju? Rdipirri? Mala?" Ngula kala warru-katurnu yangka. Kangurnu kala.

Kala marlurlu yangka nyinaja yinya kankarlarra panparlirla nganayirla yantaru pamarrparla. Ngukungka kala nyinaja. Kalajana yangka panukariki nyanguwiyi. Kalalu kangu-kangurnu yangka mungalyurrukaturlu panukarirliwiyi.

"Kuyuku, kuyuku, kuyuku, murrku, murrku, kuyuku!"

"Karija. Ngayili tiriyi-nyinaka. Ngatiki ngarirna pardarni, sleep-wangukariki. Kulinypari ka ngati, kapurnarla kuyukurluku waja nyinami. Nganjarra, tiriyirlalkurla nyina kuja." Ngarrurnujana, juwayi-ngarrurnunya. "Nganjarralku wajalu!"

Kala nyinaja. Yijardu kala riwi-nyangu ngatinyanu. Kirdanyanuwiyi, kirdanyanurluwiyikilajala ngayi kala kangurnu yangka. Ngula kalarla mara-purraja. Well, ngatinyanu kala yanurni jalpijala yinya, kala yirakarijangka, you know. Ngula marlurnparla kala warlaljakurra yanurni. Watingki kala nyanunguparntarlu purraja kujakuwiyi.

"Wati, kuyu mayinpa kangurni? Nyajangunpa katurnu?"

"Ngantarna wirrkardu kangurni. Jurnta kajulu kuja parnkami waja. Wilypi-pardinjarla kalu parnkami kuja."

"Jajipardukurla yanta waja kuyuku! Nyajangulku ka purra?"

"Karija. Kularnarla yanku jajiparduku, ngarnirra!" Yii, kala ngarnu-uu ngatinyanukurlangu, ngarnu-uu.

Jarda-jarrijalu ngayinya. Kala witangkarra kala ngunaja. Kalarla yangka kuyu ngarrurnu watiki kalinyanuku, "Kuyurla kuja manta! Ngamarlangurlupalanyanu kuyu manta!"

Kala winmarla-pungu. Kala yakarra-pardinjarla nyinaja.

"Nyarrparangku wangkaja ngati? Jajiparduju?"

Although the boy was no longer small, although he was quite big, a boy nearing initiation, his mother and father were still looking after him. They were still looking after this big boy. There were many other men living in the single men's camp. His uncles, his grandfathers were there, his fathers and many others, the Grey Falcon, the Whistling Eagle, they were there as was the Crow. These parents slept in a camp near the single men's camp.

"Look after the boy, would you, while I go and get some meat." So the father said good-bye. He went off and hunted for game in the area around about. "Now what animal is that? Rdipirri? Mala?" He killed them by stepping on them. He brought the meat back.

The boy would sit high up on a flat rock, high on a hill. He sat by the water. He would be the first to see many of the other people as they came home. They would come back that way carrying meat, even in the morning.

"Meat, meat. Boy, boy, do you want some meat?"

"No. Keep it for yourself. I am waiting for my mother. She is not half asleep all the time, she is a good hunter. I will sit here until she comes back with meat for me. You lot can keep your meat for yourselves." He spoke to these people very rudely, "Finish it yourselves!"

Then he waited. He would see his mother as she came back. Sometimes his father would come home first, with meat, and get the mother to cook it. Or his mother would come back by herself first, after hunting on her own. The family would go and sit by themselves in the shade. When they did so, the man, her husband, would cook the food.

"Husband, have you brought any meat? How many did you get?"

"I think I only have a few. They kept running away from me. After they emerged, they ran off."

"Go to your father for some meat. Ask him how many he is cooking."

"No. I will not go to my father. Let him eat them!" All he ate was the food his mother brought him.

Then they went to sleep. They slept for just a little. The husband would call his wife to come for some more meat. "Here, give some of this meat to him. Mother and son, come and get some meat."

The boy would wake up, but having woken up, he would sit there.

"Ngariji waja kuyu ngarrurnu."

"Manunpa yarungku, mayi manu."

"Yuw, yarungkunyayirnirna manunjunu kuja." Kalarla wangkaja ngatinyanuju. Kangurni. Pajirninjarla kalarla yungu, yangka ruwu-manurra. Kala wartirli-manu kuyu. Kalarla yungu. Ngarnu, ngarnu-uu.

"Kuyu karnalurla," kuja kalalu yangka wangkajalku, "Kuyu karnalurla puta ngarrirni ngulakuju kuja wita kurduku. Paniyamiparlu kanganpa nyanyi jamulu kuja. Walku, yirrikarri kalu."

Yii, kutukari-jarrijalku kala, wuuly-wuulypa-jarrija. Warlukari kala yirrarnu, fire-kari kala yirrarnu, pupakari kala yampija, pupakari kala yampija kalajarla. Nyanungu kala ngunaja. Kulkurrukurra kalapala yangka yirrarnu. "Nyampurla kuja kulkurruwana ngunaka." Kirdanyanu kala ngunaja, ngatinyanu kala ngunaja. Nyanunguju yangka ngatinyanu kala ngunaja, nyanungu kala ngunaja yitipiwana.

"Kala ngayilpanpa kuja nyampuwana ngunakarla?"

"Nguna karna nyampurlakirli."

"Yuwa, kala?"

Wati kala yakarra-pardija, "Yangka ngayi, warlurlanguku, yangka, turnu-maninjaku."

Nyanunguku yangka kala ngarlun-kujurnu. Kala yakarra-pardija. Yuwayi. "Yuwa! Nyiyarlu kangku nganayi-mani?"

"Nyiyarlujala ngayiji pajurnu? Yarlkurnujalaju? Namangku!" Ngula kala warlka-wangkaja. Yi, kala wati purlku ngunanjunu, mardukuja kala ngunaja.

"Kala, yay? Kala yangka jungukurra wajarli, jungu wajarli kuja nguna, yirdija kuja kalinyanu waja." Kuja kalarla wangkaja kalinyanuju.

"Nyarrpa kanparla wangka? Nyarrpa kanparla wangka? Karnangkupala purda-nyanyi waja," kalarla wangkaja.

"Malypakarra, malypakarra!" kalarla wangkaja. "Ngayilkirnarla kuja wangkaja, ngayilkirnarla kuja ngatipurajiki wangkaja kuja yilparlijarra ngurrangka ngunakarla ngajarra jintarlangurla."

"Lawa, ngatiji kaju ngunamirni. Jinta ngunakarra, ngatiji kaju nguna nyampurlakirli!"

"Who is that speaking to you, mother? My father?"

"Yes, he is telling me to come and get some meat."

"Go and bring it back quickly!"

"Yes, I'll go and bring it back quickly," his mother would say to him. She brought it back. After she had cut it up, and pulled it apart and divided it into pieces, she would give it to him. He would eat and eat.

"We tried," they used to say, "we always tried to tell that child to get some meat from us. Without coming near us, he would just sit and look at us. No, he does not really like other people."

Then night fell and it grew dark. The boy would build fires all around himself and his parents. He left these fires burning all around. They slept inside them. He would sleep there. They placed the boy in the middle. "Here, you sleep here, between us." The father slept, the mother slept. The boy's mother slept, over to the side.

"But why are you sleeping over there?"

"I am sleeping here."

"But why?"

The man had woken up. "Now I am just going to move these fires closer, to bring them together."

This woke the boy up quickly. He woke up. "What are you doing?"

"What has stung me? What has bitten me? Ants!" But he was lying. The man went and lay down in the warmth, and the mother lay down again.

"Why don't you come over here and join your husband? You are my wife, aren't you?" said the husband.

"What are you saying to her? What are you saying to her? I can hear you!" he said.

"Little pest, little pest," he said to the boy, "I have every right to talk to your mother, so that we two can sleep together."

"No, no, my mother is sleeping here beside me. You sleep by yourself. My mother is staying here."

True.

"No, now you can move," the man said, the unfortunate.

Then, "Look, there, there, there, a centipede, a centipede! Mother, Mother, Mother!"

"What? What? Where is it? Where is it?" She looked around

Yijardu.

"Ngari, kala yangka yungkayi," nganayi-manu wiyarrparlu yalikila ngari.

"Ngulangka, ngulangka, yirrinjirla, yirrinjirla, yirrinjirla, purlkulurla! Ngati! Ngati! Ngati!"

"Nyarrpara kuja? Nyarrpara? Nyarrpara?" kalanyanu muku-nyangu. Aa, riirlikirlirli kalarla nyangu.

"Wawaaa!"

Tapulpa-manulku, tapu-jarrijalku ngulaju wati yali. "Aa, jungakirli kaju walku yirrngirnngi-mani. Nyarrpa-manirnarla kuja ngatinyanuwiyi?"

Yangka kuyu kala ngarnu, ngarnu panukari. Parnkajarra kalalu yangka kuyuku wirlinyi. Kala yanurnu. Purraku kalanyanu ngatinyanurlu manunjunu. Purraku waja kalarla manunjunu wirlinyirla.

"Wirlinyirla kuja wayiji mantalku purrakuju."

Yijardu kalarla manu purraku. Yuwa, yungu kalarla kalinyanuku. Ngarnu kala. Yarnkaja. Nganayiki, now, yarnkaja jatakarranyayirnilki. Kuja yangka kala yanu mardukujaju. Nyanunguju kakarru yanu.

"Ngati, kajirnangku yurtururralku-puraja, kajirnalku nganayikirra? Ngukungka kapurna nyinami, ngukungka kapurna nyinami, ngarirri, yurltunyparla."

Ngarirrirla, yurltunyparla nyinaja, jalparlarla, you know. Yantaru kala nyinajayi ngulangka. Yanu warru ngatiji. Yananyarra, yananyarra, yananyarra, yananyarra, yananyarra. Yuwurrku rarra-jarrija. Nyanungurlu kala yangka yurturu-puraja ngati. Nyurruyijala yarda yanu, yangka yarliyipala.

Well-i, yala-yala-manu now-rla yali mardukujaku wiyarrpaku. Jangkardurla yunparnu. Watiya that. Kalinyanurlu tuurnkarrija. Jangkardurla nganayilparla watiya yunparnu. Jarlturu-yirrarni ka kuyungkuju, malangkuju, yintirdirlanya, watiyarla. Yangka maalypari-pinja-yanu, maalypari-pungurla, maalypari-pungu. Yantarnparrarla karrinja-yanu, karrinja-yanu mardukjaju-uu, yantarnparrarla karrinja-yanu.

Katurnu yangka, tarnnga mala-tarturn-manu nganayirliji, nyampuju, that-i yunparninjirli — yala-yala-manu watiya, watiyarla

everywhere. She would even get a torch to look.

"Waaahh!"

The man began to get really angry. "Truly this boy's jealousy is really interfering with my life! What am I going to do about this mother?"

The next morning they ate meat, they ate and ate. Many others went hunting. The woman came back. She had been to get water. She brought the water ready for the day's hunting.

"Give me some water before I go hunting."

She got him the water. He drank it. He left. He was furiously angry. The woman walked off toward the south. The man went east.

"Mother, I'll watch as you go. I will sit here by the water, here by the water." Near the cave in the hill, near the cave in the hill, he sat, on the flat rocks, where he always used to sit. The mother moved away. There she went, there she went, in among the trees. He watched all the way. She had set out hunting again, early in the morning.

Now the man began to punish the woman, poor thing, by singing in order to destroy her, using a special stick. Her husband cursed her. He sang in order to destroy her with the stick.

You know, those animals such as the hare wallaby make big holes near trees. She was walking from hole to hole, blocking them up to prevent the animals running away. She moved about making no noise. Then she stamped down hard and suddenly something pierced right up into her leg. It was that which had resulted from the singing, from the stick, when the man had made the curse. It pierced right up into the woman's leg forever. She thought it had resulted from a real accident. She stood there.

The man continued to walk toward the east, ashamed. He met up with the men at the single men's camp. He sat down. The boy was steadily watching the people as they came back. He watched the men returning first. He saw his father, he saw his father.

"Ah, there is my father over there. He has gone over to that other place in the shade."

His father invited him to come and have some meat, meat from a little wallaby. "Run over here, run over here and have some meat, some meat, which you can take back over there and eat."

"No. I am going to wait for my mother. She's not lazy. Eat it

yunparnu. Tarnnga mala-tarturn-manu yali mardukuja. Yalikila
ngantalpa yijardu karrija. Karrijalparla-aa!
    Nyanungu yangka watilpa kakarrulku yanu, kurntaju.
Jangkayikirralkujana yanumpa. Yii, nyinajalpa. Wurrangkulpajana
nyangu yangka panu, tarda-tarda-nyangu, tarda-tarda-nyangu,
tarda-tarda-nyangu, watiwiyi, watiwiyi. Jajinyanulku nyangu.
    "Waa, jajipardu yinyawana, yamakarikirralku yanurni."
    Yangka warilya-warilya kuyupardurla ngarrurnu, "Kuyuku, yuwa,
kuyuku, kuyu kuja parnkayarni-parnkayarni, maninjintarningki,
kuja yinpa nyanyi yalirlakula!"
    "Karija-aa. Ngaju ngarrarnarla ngatiki sleep-wangukariki
pardarni. Nganjarralku ngayili!" Yijardu kala nyinaja.
    Kala yanurni. Yangka nyampurlangurla kala maalypari-karrinja-
yanu. Maaly-pungu kala. Luurr-luurr-panturnu kala. Yi kala
malyarrparra yukaja nganayikirra, yurltunypakurra, yantarukurra.
Eagle-jala kalarla luurr-panturnu. Kala yukajarra kaninjarra.
Nyinaja. All right, ngaka wilypi-pardijarni. "Waraw!
Pinkangkalkurna kuja yani!"
    Yinya kujakirlija.
    "Ayi, ngatikiji karla wuraji-wuraji-jarri."
    Kurntakirlijala yinyaju yanumpa. Nyangulku jajinyanu, "Yii,
ngatikiji karla wuraji-wuraji-jarrija, yijardu, wuraji-wuraji-jarri,
yangka wuuly-wuuly-wantijalku." Kurntajala yinyaju tirinkin-
yukaja. Ngarrurnulpa jajinyanuju, yijardu. Nyangu. Yulajalpa.
Putalpalurla wangkaja yapaju, walku.
    "Ayi, nyarrparawanarlarni waja ka yula?"
    "Kurdukuju nyanungurla, no?"
    "Karija. Kuja wayi ngatinyanuju yankurra," kalinyanu wangkaja.
    Ngunaja, ngunajalpa yangkangkakirli jurrkungka ngurrangka –
marlurlulpa yali ngun ja-aa. Yakarra, yakarra-pardija. Purraku
ngarnu. Yarnkaja. Parnkamirra, parnkamirra jamanawana yangka
yesterday-warnu. Puramirra, puramirra, puramirra, puramirra,
puramirra, puramirra, puramirra jamanaju. "Kuja ngunami ngatiji?"
Yananyarra. Jungarnirli kalajana puraja. Yananyarra. Puranyarra,
puranyarra.
    Nyangurra yangka kulkurrurrarla. "Yinyangarraju ngatingkiji
nyanganyarni, yuwa-aa. Kukurnarla parnkamalku!" Wajilikirli

yourselves!"

So there he sat. It came towards him, a big bird with its wings slowly flapping. It hovered over him, stabbing at him with its beak. He took shelter in the cave, he scrambled under the rocks, into the cave. He went right inside and stayed there. The eagle continued to stab at him, but he was too far inside.

He came out again later. "If I could just get a bit further away." The bird continued to pursue him, in the same way.

"It is getting late in the afternoon. Where is my mother?"

The man had already gone across to the other camp, ashamed. The boy watched his father. "It is really getting very late for my mother to come back. It is so late it is getting dark." He started cursing his father and saying terrible things about him. He wept. Other people tried to speak to him, but he did not stop.

"Where is that person who is crying?"

"That child over there."

Her husband said, "I don't know. His mother is probably on her way home."

The boy slept there, in the same camp. He slept, he woke up. He drank some water. He set out. He ran off, he ran off, following the tracks from the day before. He followed the tracks, he followed them. "Is my mother there lying down?" There he went. There he followed the tracks, exactly. There he went, there he followed.

He saw it. He saw her standing in an open space. "Yes! My mother can see me. There she is looking at me! I can run to her!" He flew over the ground. She seemed to be standing there still alive. She seemed to be looking at him, still alive. But no. She was standing there, dead. She had been pierced in the leg by a stick, as big as a digging stick, which had killed her.

He ran, he ran. He saw her. "Ah!" He looked about him. "Yes, Mother, are you still alive?" He turned her around. He shook her. "Waraah! Mother! Who has killed my mother? My mother has been taken from me by that one who out of shame did not dare to come right to our camp." Weeping, he laid her down. Then he removed the stick from her leg. He laid her down, her body which had been held up by the stick.

"What will I do now?"

paarr-parnkaja. Kulanganta wankarukulparla karrinjakurraku.
Kulanganta kajilpa nyangurnukula wankarurlu, kulanganta. Kala
walku. Nyurnu ngayilpa karrijarnijiki. Tarnnga mala-tarturn-
manulku. Yirdija nganayi kanangurlu.

Parnkamirra, parnkamirra. Nyangulpa. "Aaa!" Warrulpa nyangu,
"Yuwayi, ngati, wankarunya?" Yurnku-yurnku-manu kuja. "Waraa,
ngati! Yuwa, nganangkuju tirnpa-manu? Yangkangkukulajalaju
kurntakirlijala?" Yaninjarla tarda-yanu. Ngunanja-yirrarnu
yulanjakarra-yulanjakarrarlu. Yangka nyangu, yuwayi, jamana.
Yurlukurl-wilypi-manu. Kujakurlulkujala ngari ngunanja-yirrarnu
ngatinyanumipa.

"Ayi, nyarrparna mani?"

Yarnkaja. Tirirl-pinja-yanu nganayi wurlampi, yangka white one.
Pajurnu, yirrarnu, tirirl-pinjawarnu. Kulpajarni. Yangka pajurnu
nyampu, nyampupiya, nyampu. Pajurnu-uu, yanu. Mukurlangu
nganayi yirrarnu wiyarrparlu. Tirnngi-yirrarnu nganawiyi,
watiyalparla kujurnu ngatinyanuku.

Wurrangkurla nganayi-manu, muku nganayi-manu
yulanjakarrarlu. Yananyarni. Yururrurliji parlu-pungu, yururrurliji
parlu-pungu. Warlarlu-yirrarnu nganayijulpa, nganayi-manu paniya
yangka kujakalu rurrpangkarla karri-karri, ngula, rurr-rurrpa.
Warlarlu yirrarnu yangka nyampurlu, lampurnurlu, ngapurlurlu.
Warlarlu yirrarnu kujakarilpa, kujakarilpa warlarlulpa yirrarnu.
Kulanganta nganayi mulyukuna, pirntina kulanganta kuyu, you
know. Warrulpa nganayi yirrarnu. Mukulpa nyanungujarralku-
jarrija. Mukulpa warlarlu yirrarnu, pirdikari, pirdikari, pirdikari,
pirdikari. Watiya pajurnu, kirrirdi. Witi-yungulpa.

"Aa, wapirrarlu yuka jajipardu, kapala kutulku mayi, kapala
pangirni. Yuwa, kuku kaninjarrarlalku yarujanyayirnirli." Parnkaja
walalku. Yanu yimikirlilki.

"Yuwa kuja?"

"Ngulakula yuwayi kari kakarrukarirlilkingalpa ramarri walangku
marda, kakarru kuja yarnkajarni. Warrurningalpa pungu."

"Yuwayi, rdipinjanyanparla kuja?"

"Karija. Wurna marda yanu. Yali wayi nganayiki jilangkaku ngayi
kanyanu manirra, kanyanu pirntinanpurturnjarlu, ngayi kanyanu
manirra! Rdajanyayirnirla. Karnangkupala pina kanyi jajipardujarra.

He went away. He made himself a stone knife. He cut it out and sharpened it. He went back. He cut off these, the mother's breasts. He cut them off. He went away. Out of pity he covered her body up. He threw branches over the body of his mother. There he went away, still weeping. Later he came upon a hole which had belonged to mice, a large mouse burrow.

He made tracks resembling those of a snake all around the hole, so that the tracks near the hole would make it seem there was a snake in the burrow. He made the tracks like the snake with the two breasts, the woman's two breasts. He made the tracks like the snake all around the burrow. They were made to look like those of a python, a carpet snake, the sort whose meat we can eat. He put these tracks all around, he made them everywhere, all over the ground in that place. They spread out from the hole in every direction. He cut himself a long stick and tested the depth of the hole.

"Ah, when my two fathers [father and father's brother] come close to here, they will both dig, and they will both be able to climb down inside. They will be able to get down in there very quickly. They will come this way very happily once they have heard my story."

He ran back again. He went to tell his story.

"Yes, what is that?"

"Yes, it is the boy, coming back this way, very happy. He is coming to the camp on this side, he is coming to the east side. He is coming to meet us."

"Did you meet your mother?"

"Not yet. Maybe she has gone off to stay a few nights. However, there is a python over there, which is racing around its burrow. It has been rushing everywhere over there! The hole is shallow. I can take you two, my fathers, both there. Truly."

They went to sleep. They went to sleep happy in the single men's camp. They woke up. They had something to eat.

"Bring a firestick!"

The two men got a firestick, ready for the meat. "Yes, take us back there and show us."

"Yes."

His mother had gone that way earlier, a long way. It was in the direction that his mother had gone that he took them .

Yijardu!"

Ngunajalu-uu. Walalku ngayilpalu ngunaja ngulaju jangkayirlalku.
Ngunaja. Yakarralku-pardija. Ngulalkulu ngarnu.

"Ngijipala manta!"

Ngijipala manurra kuyuku nyanungujarrarlu. "Yunganparla
yungu pina kangka!"

"Yuwayi!"

Nyampuwanakula ngatiji yananyarra pinka yanu. Yinyakurlurla
nyanungukupalangu kulpaja.

"Yinyajala yangka paya! Wurrkarli karrinyarni! Nyampukurra
wurrkarlikirra." Pina kangupalangu yijardu.

"Yi, yali rdaljakirli, isn't it? Yalikila? Rdaljanyayirni ngayi, ngurl-
ngurljirdijinpa ngula."

"Yijardu." Kulkurrurla rdirri-yungu. Warlaljarlu jajinyanu
warlaljarlu nyanungunyangurlu pangurnurra, pangurnurra.

"Nyarrpara nganta karna rdilypirr-yinyi kutuju?"

"Kari, walkujala."

"Ngulakirli, ngulakirli, ngulakirli!" Witi yilpa yungu.
Pangurnulpalarla, pangurnulpalarla, pangurnulparla
papardinyanurlu, papardinyanurlu, papardinyanurluwiyi.

"Nyarrpara nganta karna rdilypirr-yinyi?"

"Walku mayiji?"

"Wurrakirli. Kurlulu!"

Pangurnurra, pangurnurra, pangurnurra, pangurnurra,
pangurnurra, pangurnurra, pangurnurra, pangurnurra, pangurnurra.

"Ayi, walku nyampuju."

"Wurrarna warrurra yani."

"Kala mayirli kuja jutu-yani nyurrulkurla?"

"Ah, yijardu."

Kukurnunyanu kuja jitija. Pangurnurra, pangurnurra,
pangurnurra, pangurnurra, pangurnurra, pangurnurra, pangurnurra,
pangurnurra, pangurnurra, pangurnurra, pangurnurra, pangurnurra,
pangurnurra, pangurnurra, kaninjarranyayirnilki.

"Aaa, pujulkurna kuja pinyi, pujulkulpa yangkarna rdakukari-
rdakukarilki warru-yaninjakurlangu."

"Walku-uu. Jitinja-yanilki kuja, puntarninjaku kuja."

Yijardu, puntarninjarlalparlangu papardinyanurluju kujurnu.

"Look! Just over there where that bloodwood tree is standing, just over there near the bloodwood tree." He took them right back to that spot.

"That one? Shallow, isn't it? That one? That one is very shallow. I can already touch the bottom, really." But he started digging in the middle section. So his own father, of his own family, his own father started to dig. He dug and dug.

"Just where can I break through into the deeper part?"

"Maybe later."

"Here! Here! Here!" He pushed his stick through into the ground.

The two fathers dug away at the hole, the elder brother taking the lead, taking the lead.

"Where can I break through into the rest of this burrow?"

"Still nothing?"

"Hang on! Maybe over there, to the west."

They continued to dig.

"No, nothing here."

"Wait! I'll go around here."

"Perhaps you should climb right down into the hole?"

"Yes, you are right."

The younger brother climbed down. They continued to dig, going right down inside.

"Wait on while I cut some footholds. I'll just make some small holes for our feet, as we climb in and out."

"That's enough. Climb down now and pass the dirt up."

After pulling the earth out at the bottom, the elder brother threw it up, getting it from his younger brother. They were both right down inside the hole, excavating.

The boy ran off. He kicked at the spinifex bushes, and pulled them out and carried them back. He put them down. He brought more and more, and put it all into the top of the hole. He ran around collecting it. It was the hard dry spinifex from the desert that he put there. Then he lit the fire. He used a stick to push the burning spinifex right down into the hole. He burnt the two men, right down inside the hole, he burnt them. They flung themselves about, struggling in the flames.

"Aaahh!" They screamed, they screamed. Their screams could be heard from a long way off, but there was nothing there, nothing. They

Marlangu yalikila kukurnunyanulkulparla puntarnu,
kaninjarrakurra rawungkaku puntarnu.

Parnkajarralpa yangkaju marlurlu. Lukurl-pinjarlalpa yirrarnu.
Yuwa. Yukaja. Yirrarnulpa. Yirrarnulpa, yirrarnulpa. Yirrarninja-
parnkajalpa. Tarltarlpanu ngayilpa yuka yirrarnu. Rduul-yungu!
Watiyalpa wirnpangi-mardarnulku. Julyurl-kujurnupalangu, jalyurl-
kujurnu, kaninjarrakurra jalyurl-kujurnu. Ngayilkilpapalangu
kurinjikarra kangu.

"Aaaa . . ." purlajalpapala, purlajalpapala. Nyuwin-
nyuwinjardulku ngarilpapala purlajarra. Walku, walku, ngayilpapala
nyinaja yalirlalkukirli! Kaninjarra-manupalangu watiyarluju.
Tarlurrmirntipalangu kampaja kaninjarraju yalijarra yinyajuku.

Kujawiyi ngayilpanyanurla yirdi-manulpanyanurla yungunyanurla
nyanunguju marlurlurlu. Yi, yatijarrawarnu lukurl-pungu,
kakarrarawarnu lukurl-pungu, karlarrawarnu lukurl-pungu.

Yarnkajarra. Kujakarraju karrija tarnngalku. Jalyurlku, jamulu
jalyurl-kijirninjarla kurinjikarra kangkangku. Purdangirli ngayi
yinyalkulpajana ngayijana nyanjarra-yanu. Yanu kurntaju
tarnngalku. Yangkakujana yinya yapawatiki.

"Ayi, rdipijarni. Yuwayi Nyarrpara nganta kuyuju kuja?"

"Yangka wayipalarla pangirnilki yinyarla kala. Purraku-
jarrinjarlarnapalangu jurnta-yanu kuja. Purrakukurralkurna kuja
yanu. Yirrijijirliji kampaja. Ngayi, kutu kujarla kapala ngayi wurna-
wurnarrajala pangirninja-yani."

Ngula-yi, nyinajalu, nyinajalu, nyanjaku, nyanjaku. Yangka
panukarirli yalirlilpalupalangu nyangu.

"Yii, walku marda ka wangka. Marda kangalpa ruyu-wangka
ngulaju. Yii-ii, yii-ii, walkukirli. Walku marda kuja." Ngurrangkalu
wantija nyanjarla, nyanjarla.

"Yuwayi ngari yilpapala wangkaja, marda jukurrarlangujala
kapala yarnkamirni."

Kala walku. Ngayilpapalangu jalpingkijala ngayi yungu yimi.

"Awu, yanilkirlipa. Walku!"

"Jurntarliparla yani, waja?"

"Yungu nyinami nyampuju."

"Jurntarliparla yani."

Jurntalpalurla yanu. No yapakarirli jina-mardarnu, walku. No-rla

had to stay where they were. He pushed the men back down inside the hole with his stick. The fire burnt the two men to ashes, the two men right down inside the hole.

Before, while he was tearing up the spinifex, turning in each direction, north, east, west, the boy had cursed him, naming him.

Then he left that place, forever. He had set them alight there, burning them as they struggled. He left it behind him. However, as he left, he glanced backwards to where they were burning. Then he went away, ashamed. He returned to where the other people were. Yes, he came towards them.

"Yes? Where is that meat you were supposed to get?"

"Look, they are still digging over there. I have left them because I needed water. I came back because I was thirsty. The sun was burning me. While they dig, they are coming back in this direction."

The people sat for a long time, watching for the two men to return home.

"Maybe he was not telling us what really happened. Maybe that one was lying to us. No truth in what he said, perhaps." They all went to sleep in their camp. They continued to watch out for them.

"Yes," he said to them, "that is what they told me. Probably they will be coming back tomorrow."

But no. He had made up this story about them himself.

"They are not coming back! Let's go!"

"Are we going to go and leave him?"

"Let him stay here."

"Well, we will go and he can stay."

They went and they left him. There was no-one left to look after him. They left him there. He stayed on. He went back up to his place on the flat rocks. He sat up there. There he stayed. He ate the meat off old bones, rubbish. Then he left to go to another camp, some distance away. He went.

It plunged down upon him out of the sky. The eagle swooped down, right down on top of him, and stabbed him through the back of the neck. The blow killed him. He died. That was the end. In that way, his neck had been broken. Yes. Thus he died.

yapakarirla wuwurl-maninjarla kangu, walku. Yampinja-yanulu
ngulangkaju. Nyinajalpa. Nyinajalpa-aa. Yangkakurra panparlikirra
yanu. Nyinaja kala ngulangka. Nyinaja, nyinaja, nyinaja. Kuyu kala
yungkurnulku yangka ngarnu yapuntawati. Yanu waja kirri
yinyakula. Yangka yanu-uu.

Jiilyparnu-yirrarnu nganayirliji eagle-urlu, kulu jiilyparnu-
yirrarnu-uu. Kaninjarra nyanungukurra, nyampujuku luparl-
panturnu, tarnnga that one panturnu. Walku-jarrija. Ngulajuku.
Walku. Kula nyarrpalku nyampuju kakardajangarra tuurl-panturnu.
Pieces-manurra. Yuwayi, walku-jarrijalku.

Recorded at Lajamanu, December 9, 1990

70

PLATE 1: STORY: *Warlukurlangu: What Happened at the Place of Fire.*

Dreaming: Warlu (fire). Skin Group: Jampijinpa/Nampijinpa, Jangala/Nangala.
Artists: Judy Nampijinpa Granites, Peggy Nampijinpa Brown, Dolly Nampijinpa
Granites, Molly Nampijinpa Langdon, and Lucky Nampijinpa Martin.
(Warlukurlangu Artists/South Australia Museum)

PLATE 2: STORY: *Yarmurnturrngukurra Karna Pina Kulpa Ngurrakurra Yajarlukurra: To Yarmurnturrgnu and How I Came Back to Yajarlu.*
Dreaming: Pamapardu (flying ant). Skin Group: Jakamarra/Nakamarra, Jupurrurla/Napurrurla. Artist: Jacko Ross Jakamarra.
(Photographer: Michael Cook)

PLATE 3: STORY: *Witikirli: The Travels of the Witi Poles.*

Dreaming: Ngalyipi (vine species associated with the witi poles). Skin Group:
Japaljarri/Napaljarri, Jungarrayi/Nungarrayi. Artists: Paddy Sims Japaljarri,
Cookie Japaljarri Stewart, and Larry Jungarrayi Spencer (deceased artist).
(Warlukurlangu Artists/South Australia Museum)

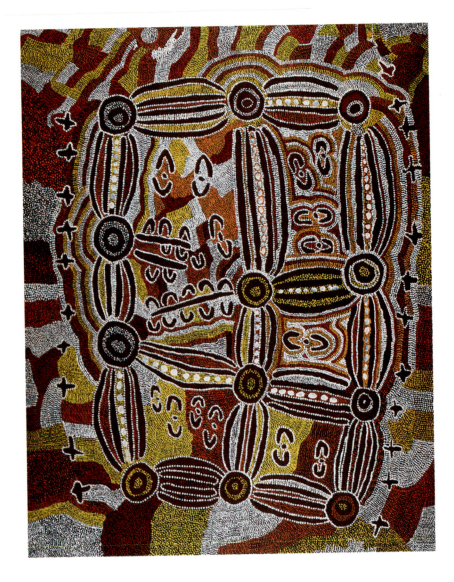

PLATE 4: STORY: *Patilirrikirli: About Patilirri.*

Dreaming: Ngatijirri (budgerigar). Skin Group: Jungarrayi/Japaljarri,
Nungarrayi/Napaljarri. Artist: Peggy Rockman Napaljarri.
(Photographer: Michael Cook)

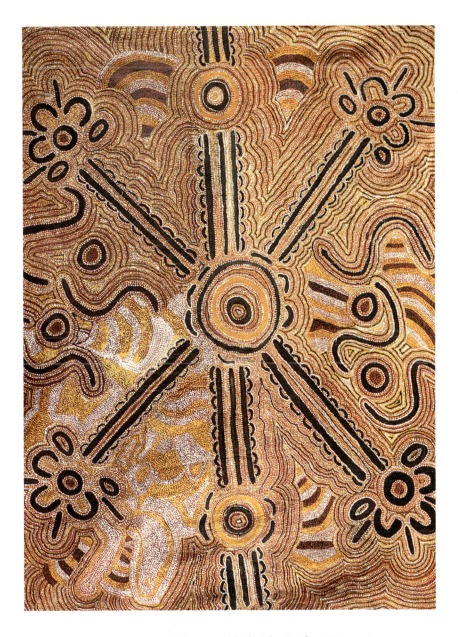

PLATE 5: STORY: *Warpurtarlikirli: The Battle at Yumurrpa.*
Dreaming: Wapirti (little yam). Skin Group: Jakamarra/Nakamarra,
Jupurrurla/Napurrurla. Artist: Liddy Nelson Nakamarra.
(Photographer: Outback Photographics)

PLATE 6: STORY: *Jarntujarrakurlu: The Two Dogs.*

Dreaming: Jarntujarra (two dogs). Skin Group: Jangala/Nangala,
Jampijinpa/Nampijinpa. Artist: Popeye Jangala. (Photographer: John Smith)

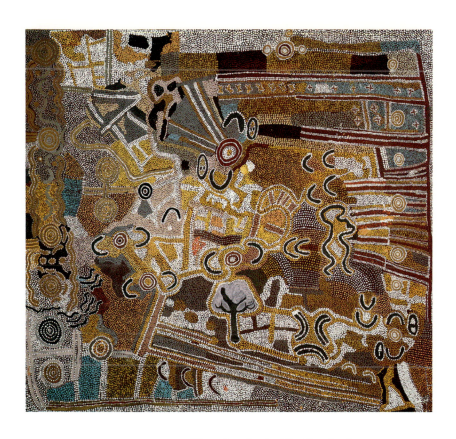

PLATE 7: STORY: *Warnajarrakurlu: The Two Snakes.*

Dreaming: Kunajarrayi (central place through which the witchetty grub associated with the snake, budgerigar, and women's dreamings passes). Skin Group: Japaljarri/Jungarrayi, Napaljarri/Nungarrayi. Artist: Paddy Sims Japaljarri. (Warlukurlangu Artists/Collection, the Art Gallery of Western Australia)

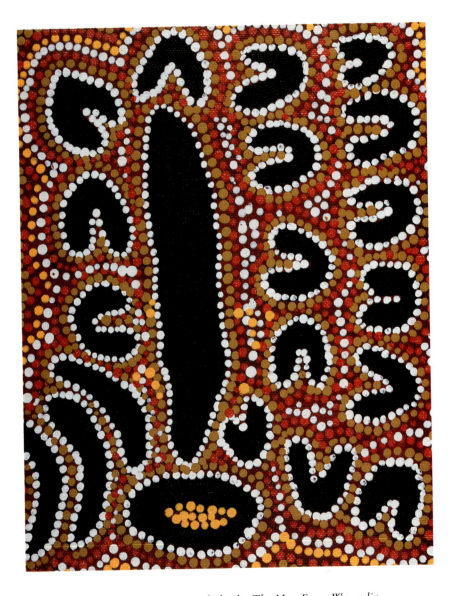

PLATE 8: STORY: *Wawarljakurlu: The Man From Wawarlja.*

Dreaming: Jungarrayi (the man from Wawarlja). Skin Group:
Japaljarri/Jungarrayi, Napaljarri/Nungarrayi. Artist: Peggy Rockman Napaljarri.
(Photographer: John Smith)

TRANSLATORS' NOTE

The story of the marlurlu, a boy old enough to be an initiate, is an intense family drama, one with tragic consequences which, in this version, narrator Kajingarra Napangardi has been able to make very clear. She has added to the plot both a dramatic intensification of the psychological conflict and a depth of dramatic irony other versions of the story do not have. The boldest addition is her introduction of the vengeful fury-like bird before the boy commits his awful but necessary crime, prefiguring and ironically pointing to the hideous and tragic logic of the conclusion when the boy, who refused all food except what his mother gave him, is finally forced by hunger to leave the shelter of the cave. Outside the eagle is poised and retribution follows.

The other section in which irony is used to great effect is that pathetic and moving moment in which the boy coming upon his mother, whom the audience know to be dead, at first thinks she is alive and cries out with joy. This is beautifully told, a performance of great art.

The jukurrpa itself contains elements familiar to many from the family dramas of the Greek tragedians: an incestuous conflict between son and father for the attentions of the mother in which a fundamental balance is upset by the inappropriate victory of the son, and the consequences – rage, death, a necessary sequence of acts of revenge – before the social universe is cleansed and restored. A major imperative in Warlpiri social life is that offences must be met by the appropriate restitution, known as "kunka" or "pay-back", even if in extreme cases the hero necessarily exposes himself or herself to a fatal penalty in turn. In this way, the tragic loss of the marlurlu story is set in motion and moves on to its inevitable conclusion.

WITIKIRLI

The Travels of the Witi Poles

TOLD BY

Ngarlinjiya Mary Robertson Nungarrayi

Lajamanu ■

■ Kurlurrngalinypa

■ Yururlyariparnta

■ Kirriwarrangi

Willowra ■

Purrparlarla ■

■ Purayilpalpa

Yanjilypiri ■

■ Yuendumu

Alice Springs ■

Yatijarrapurdarna yitaki-manaw. Yinya pinarna kulpari mani.
Nyampu kujalu, kujalu kurdu kangu yatijarrapurda
Yanjilypiriwardingkiwiyi. Ngulawiyi karna kulpari-mani.
Ngalipanyangukurraju karna yirri-purami yalumpukurra. Yuwa.
Warringiyikirlangu, warringiyijilpa nganimpaku kujalpanganpa
nyinaja Jungarrayiji, Marlku yalumpujuku
Ngarrkakurlanguwardingki jukurrpa, jukurrpajalpa, jukurrpakula
nyinaja kala jukurrpajuwarnu karna yirri-purami nyampu.
Yatijarrapurdalku kangu Yanjilypiriwardingki. Kangulu.
Karntawungukupalangu kangu.

Ngulajangkaju-uu right up-lu kangu-uu nganayikirra Kuurrinji,
Kuurrinjkirralku, Kuurrinjipurukurralku kangu, walyakurra.
Kujalpalu mardarnu nganayiwardingki Yanjilypiriwardingki.
Ngulajangkaju, mardarnulu, mardarnulu. Ngulajangkaju, pinarnili
kulpari-manu ngula nganayikirralku Kurlurrngalinypakurra ngulalu
pina kulpari-manu. Witajala karnanyarra yirri-puranjini yatijarra.
Pinarnili kulpari-manu pupuwatirlilki.

Ngularlajinta Kartangarurru yukaja – ngarri-ngarri –
Kurlurrngalinypakurraju. Ngulakurralu yurrpurnu. Ngulangkarla
jarnturlurlu-karrija. Kujarnikirlirlajinta Wakayarlajinta yukaja
Kuurrinjiki, Kartangarurrurlajinta yukaja, Wakaya-side-rlajinta
yukaja kakarrumparrawarnu – jintakurra Kurlurrngalinypakurra.
Wakaya-side-ji. Kartangarurrurlajinta ngarri-ngarri yukaja.

Ngayi karna Kurlurrngalinypaji yirdi-mani nyanjawangurlu.
Ngulajangkaju, yuwayi, ngulangkajukulurla wirntijalku.
Yulpurrujulurla jarnturlurlu-karrija. Minyiralkurla yirrarnulparla
Nangalarlu – nguru Jingalku-wardingkirli. Yirrarnulpalu – ngarri-
ngarrirli marrkarinyanuku. Wakurnjinganajarrarla yirrarnu,
jurrungkarla yirrarnu, waninjanganarla yirrarnu. Wali,
ngunajalkulpa wantakurra. Yirrarnulu. Ngunajalpa nyanunguju
kurdu.

Ngulajangkaju, wali manu. Ngulangkarla jarrarlarl-karrija
wurnakurralkuju. Ngula kanalyurl-pardijalku nyanungu wati.
Manulku ngulapururluju.

"Nyampuju karna manilki waja. Nganayi marrapinti karna mani
jirdawarnu waja." Kuja wangkaja Nangalaju.

Ngulajangkaju-uu, jakururlalu karrija-aa. Kanalyurl-pardijalku

I have followed this story to the north. And from there I can relate it as it comes back. It was at this point that they first took the child, the one from Yanjilypiri, into the north. From this first point, I can relate it as they journey towards there, towards that place belonging to us. Yes, this story belongs to my father's father, to our father's father, that Jungarrayi called Marlku, the one belonging to the story of the initiated men. He was the one who knew this same story which he used to tell.

They took the boy from Yanjilypiri into the north. They took him and they took a woman to look after him. They took him right up into Kurinji country, into that country belonging to other people. By these means, they cared for and instructed the boy from Yanjilypiri. They cared for him, they cared for him. Then they brought him back to Kurlurrngalinypa, they brought him back. I can only tell you a little about the north. The young men brought him back.

Then all together with the Katarngarruru people, all under the guidance of the elders, they entered Kurlurrngalinypa. They took him in there. There they danced together. So together, the Wakaya speakers and the Kartangarruru people together from the east side entered Kurinji country going into Kurlurrngalinypa on the Wakaya side, all together. Still following the orders of the elders, the Wakaya and the Kartangarruru went into Kurlurrngalinypa. I can name Kurlurrngalinypa although I have not seen it. Then they danced. All the mothers and the aunts danced.

Nangala, the one from Jinalku, put the minyirra head-dress on the boy, to show that she wanted him for her husband. They decorated his arms, his head, his neck. Then he lay down in the sun. They placed him there. The child lay there.

They took hold of him then. They stood holding his hand ready to go. All the men stood up together. They took him away.

"I am going to bring this, I am going to bring the nosepeg and the feathers." So Nangala said.

They all said good-bye. They all stood up together and said good-bye. Then those that were going on the journey started walking away. They buried it, the witi pole, in a cave lying in this direction.

On the way, they made flat ground out of crushed ant bed, and practised. There they stood all the witi poles together. Then they

nyanunguju, jakururlalu karrija. Wurna-yirrarnu cave-rlaju
kalkurnupurdalku. Ngulalpa milyingka-milyingka-yirrarninjinanu.
Ngulajangkalpa yangka pirrirljirla wala-parrurnu kulkurru,
pirlpanjirla. Ngulangka wangkarna-mardarlu manu,
kanmurrpajalalpa kangu nyanungurluju. Ngayilpanyanu
yurlpumiparlu maparnu wakujarra. Wanarrijarralpanyanu maparnu
nyanungurluju. Wupujupuju kangu kanmurrpa nyampujarrarla.
Yuwayi, yinyarlawiyijukujala wala-parrurnu.
Ngulajangkaju yirajakurla-pardija, yirrara-manu. Ngulajangkaju,
ngulajangkaju, kulkurrulku pirlpanjirla yarda wala-parrurnu.
Ngulangka yirrara-manu. Ngulalparla Wurrpardiki wara-
parnpinjinanu. Marnmarn-marn-yirrarnu ngulaju pirlpanjirlakula
kulkurru. Ngulangka wangkajarla ngangkarliji kankarlarra.
Ngayilpa wupujupuju kangu. Yarliny-kangulpa.
Ngulajangkaji, yalumpu kujaka pirdaparnta-karrimi nyanungu,
yapuntarlipa, ngulakurra rarra-kangu. Wari-yirrarnu
Kiriwarrangikirra. Ngulajangkaju, Kirriwarrangirla yarda yirrara-
manu. Ngulangka, yuwayi, yuwayi milyingka-milyingka-yirrarnulpa,
ngulangka, now.
Ngulangurluju, karlukarirli Parrjarrakurra pangkarl-kangu,
karlumparrawarnurlu pangkarl-kangu. Kakarrumparrawarnurlu
Wardilykakurra kangu, nyampukurra kankarlarrakurra. Kuja
ngawu. Wartardikirra wari-yirrarnuju –
kakarrumparrawarnujangkarluju, puralykangarrkarlu,
puralykangarrkarlu, kakarrumparrawarnurluju.
Ngulajangkaju, yangka rarrarni-manu warringiyipuraji
nyuntukupalangu, Marrawaji kuja karrija. Really ngajukupalangu,
my father karrija. Ngulangkaju, ngulangkalpa rarra-kangu.
Ngulangkalpa rarra-kangu. Ngulangkalpa rarra-kangu.
Ngulangkurla, ngulakurralparla yukaja. Ngulakurralpa taarn-
karrija. Ngulangkalpa jarnakurrarni-jarrija, turkey-ilkilpa
jarnakurrarni-jarrija.
Nganayijangkaju Kurlurrngalinypajangkarlulpa nguurl-nguurl-
kangu. Ngulajangkaju, yalumpu ngulayijala wurruru ngari ka jinta
nguna karlarni. Jinta-jinta-jarrijalparla nyanungu Marrawajiki
jintaku. Yuwayi, wurruru side-i. Ngulajangkaju, nganayiwana
nyanungujangkaju Marrawajijangka, wurra kajirna purda-nyanyi,

carried them along, one pole in each hand. They rubbed red ochre alone on their arms. They also rubbed red ochre on their thighs. They travelled in a long straight line carrying the poles in each hand. They had first practised the ceremony during a break in their journey. They all stood up. They made the boy stand up.

Then later, on another ground they had made from ant bed, they practised again, at another place. They stood the boy up. There they came across the path of the Wurrpardi dreaming, and pointed it out. Then they put the poles down one by one. On a ground made out of ant bed, during the journey, at that place, they made the ngangkarli [clouds of leaves] talk by shaking them at the top of the poles. Then they carried them away again, on their shoulders, walking in a long line. They dragged them to a place where people had been buried, the fathers we have lost, and then, later, they climbed up towards Kiriwarrangi.

Then at Kiriwarrangi, again they made the boy stand up. There some poles were buried, at that place. From there, westwards to Pajarra, one group separated off from the others. One group travelled along the west side. The other group went along the east side to Wardilyka, to a place on high ground. They threw away the poles that had been damaged.

Coming back from the east, the men with long legs, the long-legged men, climbed up towards a sacred place, in the east. There they came upon the Marrawaji dreaming, where your grandfather, your relative, actually my father, the Marrawaji, stands.

They travelled along, still dragging the poles with them. Then they came into that place where there were a great many people standing about, like an army. Other people were coming behind them, the people from Wardilyka were arriving there from behind. However, those who had come from Kurlurrngalinypa jostled and shoved them and sent them away.

In that place, a dreaming belonging to the people who are in-laws to me comes from the west. It meets the Marrawaji dreaming and joins up with it at that place. That belongs to those who are in-laws to me.

Then, along that way, from Marrawaji, as I understand it, at Warluwangu, they were left without the means of making a fire, at Warluwangu. They travelled on, huddled together at night, past Lung-

Warluwangurla, Warluwangurla jarrurnu-karrija nganayirla
Kulpurlunurla, Lungkardajarrarla kakarrarapurda. Warluwangu.

Kujajarra ngayilpa jarri-jarri-parnkanjinanu, kujajarra ngayilpa
parnkaja kuyungarranypajarra nyanunguju. Ngulangkalpa
purljanparla-jarrinjinanu. Ngulangkalpa purljanparla-jarrinjinanu
ngalipanyangu, ngalinyangu.

Ngulajangkaju, nganayikiji yanu karlumparrawarnujuku yalumpu
ngapakurlanguku watiki. Watikirla, ngapakurlanguku yanu
karlumparrawarnu nganayikirra Purrparlarlakurra. Wali ngapa
nyangu wirrinjirl-pakarninjakurra kakarrumparra kaninjarra.
Ngulajangkaju, "Aw, ngapangkulku ka waraly-kanyi nyampuju."
Wirrinjirl-pakarnu ngapangkulku. Yunparnulu yalumpuju ngapa
nyanungu. Ngulajangkaju Purrparlarlakurraju.

Purrparlarlarlaju, kurdiji yirrarnulku, now. Wirntijalkulpa
ngulangkaju – kurdiji yirrarnulkulu. Ngarru-ngarruju parnkaja kuja
yangka yarda-yardarlujuku yatijarni. Yakiji-manulu
kirrirdikirrawarnuju, yuntalurla yirrarnu really-nyayirni ka karrimi.
Nyampujarra ka pankijijarra yangka wanarli. Kujalpa ngulangka
wirntija, jarri-manulpa, jarri-manulpa, jarri-manulpa, jarri-manulpa,
wirntijalu. Ngulangka yilpalu wirntija.

Nangalajulpa palkaju kangu. Wurra. Ngulajangkaju, wirlinyirli
kujalpa wiri-manurra kujapurda. Ngulalpa wakalarrangiji pakarnu
karlarrapurda. Pakarnulpalunyanurla, warurnulpalunyanurla.
Ngakalpa kanmurrpa-kanmurrpalpa kangu nyampujarrarlu.
Ngakalpanyanu yurlpangku maparnu yangka mingkirrirla.
Ngayilpanyanu yurlpamiparlu jawirri-maparnu and
kuruwarrimipalpanyanu jawirri-kujurnu. Ngulajangkaju,
ngakalpanyanu kujajarrarlu pakarnu, kuly-kuly-kuly-kuly-kuly-
kuly-kuly-kuly-kuly-kuly-kuly-kuly-kuly-kuly-
marrayangkarra-manulkulpa.

Ngulalpa wirntijalku. Wati-manulkulpa. Watikilpa wirntija
wakarlarrangurlalku.

Ngulajangkaju, wirntinjarla kalalpa karntangku warlungku kardu-
yungu nganayirla Jalayanpirrirla. Nyanunguju really swamp ka karri,
wirijarlunyayirni.

Lukurl-pungulpanyanurla, lukurl-pungulpanyanurla, alright,
jamalya. Ngulajangkaju, wirntinjarla, rdirri-jarrijalkulpalu yangka

kardajarra towards the east, towards Kurlpurlurnu, always without any fires.

They rushed over there, they divided into two ceremonial groups and ran over there. They, our people, noticed in that place that their feet were wet, they noticed that their feet were wet.

From there they travelled along the west side, into the country belonging to the man who owns the rain dreaming. They went along the west side in the country of the rain dreaming towards Purrparlarla. They looked back and saw rain and thick black clouds along the eastern horizon, low down. Then, "Oh, those little clouds are moving rapidly this way. Later the rain will be coming." The rain had gathered into a thick black cloud. They sang as the rain fell, towards Purrparlarla.

At Purrparlarla they prepared everything for the kurdiji [initiation] ceremony. They danced. They prepared everything there for the kurdiji. There they made a path for the witi poles to a sacred place nearby just to the north. They cleared the path by removing all the spinifex ready for the tall poles. They built a wind-break. They heaped up the wood for the two fires. Later they danced between them. They made the young boys dance more and more. They danced. It was at this place they danced.

They had brought Nangala with them. She was there. While hunting, they made a road leading away from there. Then they cut the witi poles, out towards the west. They cut them down and tied up the leaves. Then they carried them along, one in each hand. Then, at the dancing ground they had made out of ant bed, they rubbed red ochre on themselves.

They sat down and rubbed red ochre on themselves, and they painted themselves with the designs belonging to the dreamings. They clapped their hands against their thighs, making the witi poles attached to their legs shake and all the leaves on top swish about.

Then they danced. Then all the men, including the men who make the boy into a man, danced, after the women had danced. After they had danced, the women cooked vegetable food on the fires at Jalayanpirri, which is actually a big swamp, a very big one.

They had pulled up ngalyipi vines for themselves, they had pulled up vines. After dancing they got themselves ready for another journey

wurnakurralku yinyakarikirli kurdukarikirli. Well-i, nyampu ka
nyina warluwariji ngalipa-side-ji. Wirntinjarla yampinja-yanu
yalumpurlajuku, Jungarrayili wirntinjarla yampinja-yanu,
Jungarrayiyijala.

Ngulajangkaju, pardijarra kurlirrapurdalku. Purlajarra, purlajarra.
Jijarralkulu manu nyanunguju kurdu. Ngulayijalalunyanurla jakarra-
mardarnu. Yanu. Pirliji kujajarra yarriki-side-ji Wapurtarlijipalangu
ngujuly-pungulu kuja wali, watingkiji. Ngujulyparralu pungu.

Well, jintilykakulparla yujuku yalumpujuku karrija.
Ngulajangkaji, nyangulu jintilykakurlangu yujuku. Ngulajurlurla
ngayirra rdilypirr-rdilypirr-luwarnu. Ngayi raalurla rdilypirr-
rdilypirr-luwarnu.

Ngulajangkaju rarra-kangu nganayikirrarlulku. Yarda kayi purlaja
Yanjilypirikirralku. Yantarliwarralunyanu pungu,
purturluparntapaturlu. Yantarliwarralunyanu-pungu
Yanjilypirirlarluju. Ngulajangka, yuurlparnili kangu nyanungu
kurdu. Kurdulu yuurlparni-kangu. Marrararlulpanyanurla
ngurrarntijarlu warurnu. Yangka yilpanyanurla waralji
pajurnunjunurra. Wakarlarrangulpalunyanurla ngayirla yangka
kakarrarninginti warurnu. Yuwayi. Nyangurluju
yurlpamiparlulpanyanu maparnu Yanjilypirirlalkuju.
Maparnulpanyanu, yatijarni wapirrirli yinyarlakula, yinyarlakula.

Pamarrpa kajikanpa jajipuraji nyanungujuku nyanyi.

Maparnunyanu yurlpamiparlu and kuruwarrimipa yangka kuju-
kujurnulpalu. Wakarlarrangu kamparnulpa rarra-kangu. Yangka
wakarlarrangulu marrara kamparnulpa yanu. Ngulalpa wirntija,
wirntija, wirntija, wirntija, wirntija, wirntija. Ngulalpa riwirrparra-
parnkaja. Ngulapurulpa riwirrparra-parnkaja.

"Nyanungulku nyarrparakurlurlu ka yanjan-kanyi waja?
Nyarrparakurlurlu warrajakurlurlu nyanungurlulkulpa yanjan-
kangu?" Yuwayi, yatijarni wapirrilki. Yanjan-kangulpa.

Ngulajangkaju, ngakalpanyanu kujarlu pakarnunyanu, manu
pakarnunyanu, manu pakarnunyanu. Marrayangkarra-manuju,
manuyijala kuly-kuly-kuly-kuly-kuly-kuly-kuly-kuly-kuly. Yali kula
nganta nyiyarlulku manu, marrayangkarra-manunya. Wirntija,
wirntija, wirntija, wirntija, wirntija, wirntija, wirntija, wirntija,
wirntijalu, wirntijalu, wirntijalu, wirntijalu, wirntijalu. Marra-

with a different child. This child is sitting covered in red ochre on the side belonging to our people. After the ceremony they left Jungarrayi still there at that place. After dancing for him they departed and left that Jungarrayi there.

After their departure, they travelled south. As they went, they called out, they called out. They carried the child on their shoulders. They carried him along singing. At Wapurtarli they went through the middle of a hill, dividing it into two. The hill belongs to the people who are cousins to me.

Later they got to a place where there stood a humpy [hut] belonging to a grasshopper. Then they flattened the humpy, driving it right into the ground, they drove it right into the ground. They pushed it so far into the ground that nothing remained.

From there they travelled on, always dragging the poles and calling out, towards Yanjilypiri. There they all lay down quietly close together, they all lay down close together at Yanjilypiri. There they put the child down, they put the child down. The people who belonged to that place sat face to face and tied themselves to the witi poles. They had gone and cut down the poles and brought them back to tie on to their legs. They tied the poles to themselves sitting on the east side. They rubbed themselves with red ochre at Yanjilypiri. Those who had come from the north rubbed themselves with red ochre at that place.

You can see the hill that belongs to your father, still the same.

They rubbed themselves with red ochre only, and painted themselves with ceremonial designs. They dragged the witi poles down to the first dancer, the one on the outside. Then the first man went to dance, facing the others. Then they danced and danced. Then they stopped. At that point they stopped.

"Which one is ready now with the witi poles? Where is the one who is standing ready lined up with the witi poles so that we can see him?"

So the men from the north lined up with the witi poles ready to dance. Then they danced, slapping themselves on the legs, slapping themselves on the legs, making the leaves at the top of the poles shake, shake, shake, shake. The large clumps of leaves on top of the poles made a loud swishing noise as they were shaken. They danced and danced. They had reached the end of their journey.

The young man from Yanjilypiri cast his eyes around the scene,

pardija wurnajangu.

Ngulajangkaju, yungurla milpa-milpa rirringki-parnkaja
Yanjilypiriwardingki jimarrinyanu – ngalipa-side. Nyangu, milpa-
milpa-nyangu. Nyurrujalalu pungu. Pinjarlalu pajurnu, yuwayi,
jarakurlumanji, warri-warri yangka kujaka nyiyapiya yurdingka
yajarr-kirda-kirdarra-pinyi. Waraly-waralyparra-karrijalku.
Milpaju, yuwa, milpaju rirringki-parnkaja Yanjilypiri-wardingkiji
Jungarrayiji, rirringki-parnkaja. Well, kujalku,"Wayi waja
yarlpurru?"

"Nyurru waja lawa!"

Wirntinjarla, wirntinjarla, tarnngajukupala marrkarirlangu
kurlirrapurda-jarrija. Yinyapala nganayikirra, Parrayilpilpakurra
jaarr-karrija. Wurra.

Nyampu karna Yanjilypiriwiyi ngarrirni. Ngulajangkaju,
nyanungulku thought-jarrija. Yangka yarlpurrunyanungurlu
murrunyuntu-nyuntu-jarrija. Wamumpu-manu-uu. Kaninjarralpa
yarrardu-rrardu-karrijalpa, yarrardu-rrardu-karrijalpa, yarrardurlu
kujurnulpa, yarrardurlu kujurnulpa, yarrardurlu kujurnulpa.

"Ngajuju yarlpurruwangurlalku waja. Kulakarna ngajulurlu
yarlpurru mardarni ngajunyangu, lawa. Walyka yirrarnurnurnaju
waja. Yuwayi, ngajulurlujuku jalpingki yukanjarla kaninjarralpa
yarrarda-rrarda-ngarnu!" Nyampujuku yukaja.

Nyampu, yarda karna yitaki-mani yinyakurralku. Ngula, now,
nyampukurla ngayi nungku-nungku-jarrija now, ngayi, nungku-
nungku-jarrijarla kurduku. Nyampunyarla wali kartirdikirlilki
Ngiiny-ngiinytari karrija jarrmirntiji. Wali, yukajalu kanunjumparra.

Nyampurlaju karntangku jintangkujala manu. Kurdu manu jinta
Japaljarri Nakamarrarlu. Purrparlarlawardingkinyanu manu
Yumurrpawardingkirli Nakamarrarlu. Ngulakurlu, yukajalu.
Kanunjumparralu yanu rawungka. Yinyalu pina wilypi-pardija
yatijarra, yatijarralku. Ngalyakarijilpa, yuwayi, ngalyakarijilpa
jaljalku yukaja. Nyampu now Kartirdirla karlipa Ngiiny-ngiinytarirla
yirrpirni nyanunguju kanunjumparra. Yuwayi. Ngulajuku.

Yuwayi, nyampuju kapurna kurdukarikirli pina yitaki-mani. Kuku
witikirli yanu. Kuku witikirli yirrara-maninjinanulpa, nganayirla
wangkanamarrarlu manu Wangkinarlu. Ngulangka, wangkajarla.
Jalyirrpa lirlirl-manu. Yirrarniyijala kalu panungkuju. Ngulangka

searching for his twin brother, the one from our people's side. He looked all around, examining the people minutely. Before this, this young man had killed someone. Having attacked the man, his father, he had cut him into pieces in order to get the fat from the body, and hung the pieces up as we do animals so the fat can drain out. There he was, hanging up in pieces!

So the young man from Yanjilypiri, Jungarrayi, gazed around, searching for his twin brother, peering here and there. Then he said, "Where is my twin brother?"

"Already dead!"

After the dancing was finished, after the dancing, the married couple, Nangala and Jungarrayi, the one who had been initiated before, set off towards the south, towards Parayilpilpa. There they remained.

Now I will tell you the important story about Yanjilypiri. The man from Yanjilypiri considered the matter. Then because of what had happened to his twin brother, he turned around and came back. He made an empty space in the ground. All the men went down into the ground. He moved them all in under the ground.

"I have lost my brother. No longer do I have a brother. I will keep myself calm and peaceful. For this reason I have placed myself underground."

He went in. I can recount the story of where he went, to that place over there. When he got to this place he suddenly came face to face with the boy. At this place, there was a circle of people standing, with their mouths open and their teeth showing, all very undershot. Then they went underground. One woman took the child with her underground, one Nakamarra took that boy Japaljarri, the woman from Yumurrpa, Nakamarra, took that boy Japaljarri from Purrparlarla underground. She went with that one and they went underground. From there they re-emerged in the north. The other group stayed underground.

Now we shall leave these people with the undershot teeth there underground. I shall tell the story of the other boy. He had been taken along with the witi poles. They collected and placed many witi poles together. When they looked back they saw the crows standing around that place, heard their harsh cries. The leaves were rattling. Many

yirrarra-manu. Wirntija, wirntija, wirntija, jarri-manu, jarri-manu
kankarlurlu. Yanulpa karlarrapurdalku-uu. Ngulajangkarla muurr-
katurnu kulkurru. Yuwayi, jakutakutalu muurr-katurnu. Yirrarnulu-
uu. Yawirrilpirrili jamulurra-katurnu. Yirrarnulu. Ngula, ngulalpa
yangka pungkayi-pungkayi-jarrija. Manulpa nyampu witawangu.
Ngulajangkaju, ngulangka yangka pirlarlany-kujurnulpa.
Wantakurra kujurnulku now-lpa, wantakurralkulpa yirrarnu.
Pirlarlany-kujurnu nyanungunyangu witi.

Ngulajangkalpa yarda warangka-manu. No nyampu jurrkulku
nyanungu yaku nyanunguku. Ngula ka nguna kamparru. Yarliny-
kangulku ngulalpa, yarliny-manulku-uu. Kuku palka, kuku palka,
kuku palka, kuku palka, kuku palka, kuku palka. Ngulajangkaju,
kulkurru-kulkurrujuku muku-parntarr-parntarr-ngunaja. Putaly-
putaly-ngunajalkulpa. Well, wardijirla kanunju yurrpurnu.

"Pala-palarlulkurnangku waja, pala-palarlulku karnangku
yirrpirni wajarnangku. Yurrpurnurnangku waja, pala-palarlulku
wardijirla kanunju waja."

Yuwayi, wakarlarrangu.

Ngulajangkaju, maralpalkunyanu ngarrurnu yinyakariji.

"Ngarrjangarrjalku japa karna yani. Witi maralpalku waja karna
marlajarralku yani."

Ngulajangkaju, Yurrulyariparntarlalpa kulkurru marlurluju lurru-
lurru-wantija, lurru-lurru-wantijalpa. Ngulajangkaju, kilyi-nyangu
Ngulajangkarluju well purlkapardurlulpa nyampuju jawuru-
panturnu. Panturnulpa mangarri. Ngarnulpa, jalpingki, waparlkurlu.
Kujajarrarlarlu yirrki-yirrki-yirrarnu, kujajarrarlurlalu yirrki-yirrki-
yirrarnu, murralyparni warrurnu.

Well, panturnulpalu, panturnulpalu. Marlurlu palkangku tarda-
nyangu, kulkurru. Tarda-kujurnu. Wantija yangkajarralku. Marijirla
papardinyanurlu palkangku jirri-manu. Ngulajangkaju,
ngulajangkaju yardarralu manu kutulkujala Parayilpilpakurraju.
Yardarralu manu-uu. Ngulajangkaju yirrarnulurla.
Waluwarnuyijalalurla yirrarnu. Yirrarnulpalurla, yirrarnulpalurla.

Palkangkulpa ngardin-kangu Nakamarrarlu yatijarrawardingkirli.
Kujanyanurlulpa ngapujunyanurlu warlalja Japaljarri warlakurnu
witajangka. Follow him-maninjinanu Yumurrpawardingkirli.
Ngulajangkaju, yirrarnulurla. Nyangulpa, lipirriki-nyangu,

people had put witi poles in that place.

In that place they had collected many poles. They had danced and danced. They had sung, loudly. From there they went towards the west. After that, the women performed a ceremony. They performed the ceremony of the Takurtakurta. They put down the boy who was to be initiated. They danced around him one after another in a line. There were many people. They took up the witi poles, big ones. Then they threw them down in all directions, they threw them down in the sun, they threw the poles down in all directions. Then they picked the poles up again and put them on their shoulders. For this ceremony they had different designs painted on their bodies.

One of them set out before the others. He carried the poles on his shoulders, he carried them on his shoulders. Then he could not carry them any longer. He could no longer carry them. He left them lying halfway, all broken. They were lying halfway, all broken up. He left them there under the mulga trees.

"I am leaving you here because I am exhausted. I have left you here under the mulga trees because I am exhausted." Yes, the witi poles.

Then he went on, empty-handed. "Here I get closer and closer to the place where they are holding the ceremony and I have no witi poles."

Then at Yururlyariparnta, in the middle of the journey, the boy had taken cover, he was hiding. He looked around. One old man there was cleaning bush tomatoes. He was cutting them up and eating them all by himself, without noticing anything. He sat in the middle and the others went quietly around the outside, avoiding him. Then they all came together.

They speared him, they speared him. One of them threw the boy down in the middle, he threw him down. He fell. Then his older brother who was there took hold of him. Then they took him back again to Parayilpilpa, nearby. They carried him away again. There they decorated him. They put the Waluwarnu head-dress on him there, they put it on him.

Nakamarra, the woman from the north, had been following the boy's travels around. She was following the Japaljarri she wanted for her own husband, while he was still very young. The woman from Yumurrpa was following him. She saw him with the head-dress they had put on him. She winked at him. "That is my husband whom they

"Ngajunyangu ngarrka kalalu yirrarnu waja jalangurluju. Ngarijili kangkarra."

Kangu-uu, kangulu nganayikirra, Purayilpilpakurra-aa. Well, yangka, kuja wali pirri-manu wurnajangkaju. Kuja. Nyanunguju kuja kartirdikirli ngiiny-ngiinytari pirri-manu wali. Ngiiny-karrijalpalu. Well, jirramalupalangu, two marlanypalupalangu wiri papardinyanu, witalpapalangu ngayi yilyajarra. Yijardupala parnkajarra. Lurru-lurrulpa wantinja-yanu. Well-i karliparla yalikiji kurduku. Marlurlurna lurru-lurru wanti-yirrarniyijala. Karliparla jaka-mardarni, yuwayi, ngapilyilyi lurru-lurru, lurru-lurru-parnkayijala.

Ngulajangkaju, well, malyarrparalujana parnkaja. Nyanungujana kurdu kartirdikirli watiki. Ngulajangkaju yulajalpalurla ngiiny-ngiinytari wati kurdukuju nyanunguku. Yulajalpalurla, yulajalpalurla, yulajalpalurla. Yuwa, jamirdi, kirda, ngamirnipirdi, yangka kujapirdi. Kujarla cave-rla.

Nyampuju, jintakari nyampu marlurlukarilpa wardu-karrija nyampurla. Walirlalpa marlurlukari wardu-karrija yukayangi. And-i Japaljarrilpa kuja wardu-karrija, nganayi, Purrparlarlawardingki. Nyampuju yangka jurrkuwarnurla kujakarlipa ngurujinta ngarri-jarri, nyangka, Napurru, yangka jurrkuwarnurla, nyampu kujakalu yangka Mulyarri, julyurlparntaju. Yuwayi. Yilyayapiwarnurla warru. Ngulaju lawalkujala uncle-wanguju. Yuwayi.

Ngulajangkaju nyanunguju Nakamarrarlu nyangu. Nyampu yakurni-jarrija, yakurni-jarrija Nakamarraju, Yumurrpawardingkijala, yatijarniwapirri warlalja, yakurnu-jarrija, yakurni-jarrija. Nyanjarninjinanulparla, kujakurlurlulparla nyangu, kujarlulparla nyangu.

"Well-rli ngajunyangu kapurna ngarrka mani waja warlalja yatijarniwapirrikariyinyanu, ngajunyangu!"

Ngulajangkalparla yangka kuja manulpa, manulpa yijardujuku. Ngulajangkalparla marnparnulparla, marnparnu, kaa-kaa-mardarnu. Warrurnu. Kuja-jarrija, jarntarrurlulkulparla marnparnu.

Ngulajangkaju karrinja-pardijalku, kujapururlujala, ngirrmirriripururlu jarrmirntipururlu. Manulku!

"Ngajunyangu karna wati warlalja yatijarniwapirrikariyinyanu waja. Nganayi Purrparlarlawardingki karna kanyi Yumurrpawardingkirli Nakamarrarlu. Ngajunyangu karnaju

have dressed and decorated today. You can all take him around for me."

They took him away to Parayilpilpa. They sat down after the journey. The people with the undershot teeth sat down. Their teeth were visible. The tooth people sent the two brothers, one older, one younger, away. They ran off. Running behind, the younger one kept himself hidden.

We sing about that boy, the one who was hiding. He ran along, hiding behind the bloodwood trees. Then they ran through the rocks. The boy was the child of the people who bared their teeth. Then the people with the bared teeth all cried out for the child. They called and called, the grandfather, the father, the uncle, all of them. They were all in a cave.

Now this one, another one, another initiate was lying down on the ground. That other initiate, grandson to me, was lying down. And at the same time Japaljarri, the one from Purrparlarla, was also lying down. It is because of this that we have all become one family and one country, all from the same dreaming, because of those who were all brothers and sisters, our relatives. They were all there sitting around the boy ready for the ceremony. However, he was without an uncle.

Then Nakamarra saw him. Then Nakamarra from Yumurrpa painted herself with the ceremonial designs. The relative from the north got herself ready. Without appearing to, Nakamarra looked around, trying to see the boy.

"Well, I will get my man indeed, my relative, the one from the north, mine!"

She tried to get the boy by feeling around for him in the dark. She searched around for him, feeling around, moving around on her knees. Then everybody stood up and stood around in a circle. She got him!

"I have this man, my relative from the north, and I shall keep him for my own. I, the woman from Yumurrpa, Nakamarra, am taking this man from Purrparlarla. I am taking him because he is my relative."

She took him. They went underground together. He went in underground from that place. He entered there. From that point on he was no longer seen in that place. After he had travelled underground, and after he had emerged, he sat in an open space. As he sat there, his hair was still covered with the fluff from the ceremony.

warlalja mani."

Kangu. Jirrnganjarla kanunjumparra-jarrijaju. Nyampungurluju
kanunjumparrayijala yukajalpa. Yukajalpa nyampungurluju
yinyalku. Wurru kulalpanyanu ngaka nyangu. Ngulalpa rduul-rduul-
pardinjarla wilypi-wilypi-pardinjarla yakijirlalku nyinaja.
Maningirrirla ngarilpa nyinaja.

Yuwayi, nyampuju, nyampuju, nyampu nyanungu wali kartirdi
nyanungu nyampu, walypalirlilki muku pakarnu, nyampuju ngiiny-
ngiinytari pinjakurra, jukurrpa nyanunguju. Nyampujukurna
yurrpurnu. Yangka nyanungu nyampu kujaka kujapurda rurrpa
karrijalpa, walipurda cave-i, ngulangurlulpalu yukaja. Ngayi
nungku-nungkulunyanu pina-yirrarnu. Nyanunguyijala karliparla
jaka-mardarni. Ngayi nungku-nungkulunyanu pina-yirrarnu,
yukajalpa, yukajalpa, yukajalpa.

Yinyalkuyijala wilypi-pardija, wilypi-pardija yatijarra ngurungka
ngalipanyangurla, ngula, nyarrparawana mayi? Karija.
Kurlurrngalinyparla marda. Kurlurrngalinyparla marda,
Kurlurrngalinypakurra now-lpalu cave-kirra-jarrija pina. Yukaja.

Recorded at Yuendumu, 23 May, 1990

Now at that place belonging to the people with the jutting out teeth, well, the rocks which are their teeth have all been broken up by the white man, the teeth that in the dreaming were exposed.

Now I will leave this story. All the people who were in the cave sat down in a circle. The ones who had gone in placed themselves again in a circle. We sing about them as well. They placed themselves back in a circle. Then they went in.

They did also come out, in the north, in our country. I do not know exactly where, perhaps Kurlurrngalinypa, or in that direction. Then they returned to the cave, and there they went in.

TRANSLATORS' NOTE

The tale of the travels of the witi poles is a central Warlpiri myth. The witi poles are long sticks with bunches of leaves at the top. In initiation ceremonies, at the point just before the women leave and the boy is circumcised, a number of men dance with a pole bound to each leg with the ngalyipi vine. In the dance, the feet are stamped to make the leaves at the top of the poles swish and rattle, described in the story as making "the ngangkarli talk by shaking them at the top of the poles".

The story of the travels of the poles involves a complete description of all the procedures relating to a boy's initiation, both the ceremonies, and the travels that precede and follow the ceremonies. Thus, the story is both an account of how this mythic initiation was done and a description of how later initiations should be done.

The initiation ceremony (kurdiji) is the major ceremony of Warlpiri life, and one of its functions is to reinforce the structures which bind Warlpiri society together. So, in this story, several initiations take place and the narrative follows a number of journeys to a number of different places. The purpose of this is explained in this passage:

> It is because of this that we have all become one family and one country, all from the same dreaming, because of those who were all brothers and sisters, our relatives. They were all there, sitting around the boy ready for the ceremony.

This narrative has two features of great interest. One is the style of the narration, a stately, high, formal Warlpiri with a distinctive and elegant diction. The other is the profundity of the myth itself, including as it does a visit by one of the initiates to what seems to be the land of the dead, where he finds his brother:

> When he got to this place he suddenly came face to face with the boy. At this

place, there was a circle of people standing with their mouths open and their teeth showing, all very undershot. Then they went underground.

During the initiation, a ceremony parallel to mourning takes place, in that the child is said to die in order to be reborn as a man. After the dance with the witi poles, the women leave the ceremonial ground, wailing as if for the dead.

The other function of the initiation is the boy's marriage, although he may not meet the girl for some years. Prospective wives appear in the narrative, both at the beginning and at the end. In both cases links are celebrated between major sections of Warlpiri society and landholdings, between Kurlurrngalinypa (Jungarrayi-Japaljarri) and Jinalku (Nangala-Nampijinpa), and between Purrparlarla (Japaljarri-Jungarrayi) and Yumurrpa (Nakamarra-Napurrurla). The description of the emergence of the second boy in the company of his new wife is very beautiful:

After he had travelled underground, and after he had emerged, he sat in an open space. As he sat there, his hair was still covered with fluff from the ceremony.

PATILIRRIKIRLI

About Patilirri

TOLD BY

Jimmy Jungarrayi

Ngayirnangku ngarrirni kuruwarri nyampu. Yali karnangku wangka – yali Ngatijirripurda ngulangurlu ngula yanurnu. Kuja puwaly-ngunaja. Well wiri yaliji ka ngunami, wiri ka nguna nyanayiji Patirlirriji ngalipanyanguju. Wiri ka nguna Patirlirri. Yalumpungurlunyapala yanu yangkaji yalikirra. Kuja yimpijirri wirrinykuru yalirlilki purda-nyanyi, yalirralu yingajili.

Yalingirlipala yanu. Karipardujarrapala yalingirli yanu, watijarra we call them, watijarra karlipajana ngarrirni ngayi.

Yalingirlipala yanu watijarraju. Yanupala kankarlu. Yalirlapala walyangka-jarrija. Ngulajangkapala yanu kujalku. Kurlarralkupala yanu Yurlpawarnuwana, Yurlpawarnuwanapala yanu. No more yalumpujuku karnangku wari-yirri-pura.

Ngulapalarla yali pajurnu yatijarra jatipijirla. Yangkaju jungarni ngajulu yingajulu purda-nyanyi. Jatipijirlapalarla pajurnu. Kujapala yanu, Yurlpawarnuwanapala yanu. Yangkalkupala nyangu, nyanungulkupala nyangu.

Kala, karlarra ngulajulpa pakurnu yalumpurlaju jalpiyijala karlarraji, separate-yijala yaliji karlarrakungarnti. Ngulapala yanu, travel-jarrija young-fellow-jarrinjarla Owl-jangkalku. Ngulaju ngulajukupala nyangulku. Nyanungujarrapala yanurnu yalumpukurrajuku. Ngulajangka yalumpurlajukupala nyiya manngi-nyangu. Nyampurlulkupalangu ngurungku pina-manu? Yalumpurlu Jarra-jarrarlupalangu ngurungkuju pina-manu?

Kankarlulkupala yanurnu Jarra-jarrakurraju. Yalumpurlajukupala rdakurl-pungu Jarra-jarrarla. Jarra-jarrangurlupala yanu, Jarra-jarrangurlupala yanu, Patirlirrikirrapala yanu.

Well, nyarrpara-jarrija? Ngayi kujajuku karnangku ngarrirni Patirlirri nyarrpara-jarrija.

Ngayilkipala yanurnu Patirlirringirliji. Ngayi karnangku, kujajuku jaljakurra karnangkupala yirri-pura kuruwarri. Kala ngulapurujukupala thought-jarrijalku, manngi-nyangulkupala, manngi-nyangupala. Nyarrparapala yalumpungurluju manngi-nyangu yinya? Jinta yaliji ngulapiya yanu karlarra.

Yangkajukupalangu nyampu Jangalarlu, Jangalarlupalangu kangu karlarra Warlangarrakurra. Jutu-pinyi karna yaliji. Parnkajalu Warlangarrakurraju. Yalumpupala yanu kuja kurntaju. Ngulakarna yampimirrayijala yalumpu Ngarnkakurra. And nyampujarrapala

Well, I will now describe this section of our Law. I have the right to tell this story, and I can tell it truthfully. The budgerigars belonging to the dreaming came from that place. There were so many they covered the area bright green. Well, Patilirri, our place, is a very, very important place. Patilirri is a very important place.

Two men came towards that place, from some distance away. Please try to follow what I say closely so that when you tell the story later others can learn from you. The two men set out from over there, the two men in the dreaming. We call them "the two men".

The two men set out from that place there. They went up into the sky. They returned to the ground. Then they came this way. They went towards the south, past Yurlpawarnu. Past Yurlpawarnu they travelled. I am not going to follow their story any further in that direction.

While they were in the north they had collected food, jatpiji, a kind of yam. This is the story as it has been demonstrated to me. At the place where there are many jatpiji, they collected them. In this way they travelled, past Yurlpawarnu. They had seen the place, that was one of the places they had seen.

One of them went by himself to hunt in the west. He prepared himself to go alone into the west. This is how those two young men travelled, the two young men from Wawarlja. Later they saw each other again. The two of them travelled together this way to a place just over there. Then they arrived.

What were they thinking about? Were they missing their own country? They were becoming homesick for Jarra-jarra, for their own country. They flew up into the sky and went to Jarra-jarra. They came down right at Jarra-jarra. Then, later, they left Jarra-jarra, they left Jarra-jarra and came to Patilirri.

What happened then?

Now I will tell you what happened after Patilirri. From Patilirri they came towards here. I know this story well. They went to a very sacred place. I am going to continue revealing this law to you. All this time they had been thinking, thinking.

Where did they go after that?

One person had been considering where the two young men should go and what they should see next. He went east, this older person. This

ngulapuru yanurnu, nganayijarra, you know, ngarrkajarra.
Yankirripala yalumpurla panturnu. Nyampukurrapala purajarni.
Nyampurlanyalujana jajarnu. Ngayilkijanarla lawa-karrija. Now,
ngulapuru, ngatijirriji kuja-jarrijalku. Nyanungulu Ngatijirripur-
dangurlu yalingirli kurlirra Ngarnaja karluwarnunya kuja Ngarnaja,
kujakankulu yangka parnkamirni, Pulupujuwana karlipa. Ramp gate
there karriyarlarni, gate ramp ngayi ka karri. Nyanungurlaju kuja
karlarrapurda Patirlirrikirra karlarrapurda ka nguna.

Kuja-jarrijalku ngatijirriji yalumpungurlujuku – Jurntikirra,
Yinapakakurra, Warlangarrakurra and Karntawarranyungukurra,
Murinjayikirra. Murinjayingirli ngarnu. Wangu Ngayirrirntingirli
ngarnu. Nyangu. Ngayirrirntingirli jingi-jingi kuja-jarrijalku
Kumpurlawurrukurraji.

Kampurlawurru yangka karnalu ngarrirni Karntawaljanyungu,
Pussycat Bore-rla kakarrara. Yalikirra karna wurrangku yirri-pura
kuruwarriji. Aa, nyampuju, nyampu ngula karnalu nyina ngatijirrirla.
Kankarlarni karnalu nyina. Wapu-pungu kujapurdarlu ngatijirrirli,
ngatijirrirli.

Kakarrara-purda yanu. Nyampuwarnu Yamuruwukurra
kakarrarapurda yanu ngatijirriji. Nyampu kurlarninyarrarnu yanu
Pujupakurra yarturlukungarnti ngatijirriji. Yakuranji kala yanu. All
over-lku kala yanu, ngatijirri jintangurlujuku yalumpungurlujuku.
Nyampu karnalu nyina ngatijirrirla wirliyarla.

Ngatijirrirla karnalu nyina nyampu. Ngulajangka, nyangulku.
Nyanungu rdirri-jarrijarni warrkirri yangka kujaka wilypirirla nyina.
Purluwanti we call him. Warrkirri, wiringarri, yirdipatuju,
yirdijarraju, yanurni-ii.

Nyampurlanya nyangulku. Yalumpu wantija kuruwarri-ii.
Nyampurlanya luwurl-manu wijingkilki. Yalumpurlajukulpa manyu-
pungu, manyu-pungu, manyu-pungu, manyu-pungu.
Yalumpungurlujuku kangu wijingkilki. Kala Yinapakarlalkulpa
warru-nyangu, Yinapakarlalkulpa warru-nyangu-uu. Warrulpa
nyangu Yinapakarla kujakurlurlulku. Nyampungurlu ngula kangu.

Tarrukuju kuja yangka ngarranparla pirrarnijala purda-
nyangkarla kajinpa yantarlarni. Warrulpa nyangu. Tumpa,
tumpakurlu Yinapakaju nyanungu pangkarla rduyu-karrija ngatijirri
karlarrapurda.

Jangala took the two men to Warlangarra. I cannot say any more about this. They ran to Warlangarra. The two men went there. However, because it is a matter of shame, I cannot tell you about the journey to Ngarnka.

Later the two men, the two initiated men, came back in this direction. Over there they speared an emu. They had been following it as it came towards here. All the other people ate the emu. They ate the lot. They left nothing. Then, at this point, the two men came across a whole flock of budgerigars. The budgerigars, the budgerigars of the dreaming, had come south from Ngarnaja in the west. You can also travel that way yourself. We go by Pulupu, where there is a ramp gate. This all lies on the way to Patilirri, in the west.

From Patilirri, the budgerigars flew away spreading out towards Jurntu, towards Yinapaka and Warlangarra and Karntawarranyungu and Murlinjarri. Coming from Murlinjarri they ate, but coming from Ngayirrirnti they did not eat. From Ngayirrirnti they went straight to Kumpurlawurru. Kumpurlawurru is the place we also call Karntawaljanyungu, beside Pussy Cat Bore, in the east. I will tell you this dreaming as it goes over there. All this story lies in the country belonging to us, the people of the budgerigars, and we the owners always live in the country that belongs to us.

Then the budgerigars went across, towards the east, to Yamuruwu. The budgerigars went toward the east. Then they went along the south side toward Pujupa, expecting to see the hill. They went to Yakurranji. From one single place, that one just over there, they had spread out everywhere. They went everywhere, and we follow in their tracks.

Then the white cockatoo saw them. The cockatoo, the one who lives in hollow trees, got ready. We call this cockatoo warlkirri, purluwanti or wiringarri. It has many names. He approached. He saw them.

At this point another dreaming, a yam, came rolling along. The cockatoo grabbed the yam in his claws, like a thief. Then he began to dance with the yam, playing with it, playing with it. At that place, he stole the yam and kept it. At Yinapaka, the cockatoo looked around, to see if there was anything else. While he looked around, he sang. Then he took the yam from there. If you had been here yesterday, you would have heard that ceremony. This next part at Yinapaka is very sacred.

Kujakurlurlulku warru-nyangu. Awu, tarda-yanulku. Kurdu pilya-
pilya-manu yalumpujuku. Ngulangurlu yarda yanu Ngarnajaku.
Ngarnajajangka yanu right Murinjayiki. Ngayirrirntirla nyangu,
Ngayirrirntijangka yanu Murinjariki, ngurra kurlarninyarralku
jintangkakurralku. Nyampu karnanyarra kuruwarri pura, karna
jungarnijiki jintakurralku. Well, jintalku ka ngunamirni kujarni yarda
pina ngunamirni.

Murinjayijangka, Karntawarranyungujangka ngarnurnu right
back Ngarnajaku. Ngarnajajangka ngatijirri yarda yanurnu
Yinapakaku. Yinapakajangka yanurnu Patirlirriki. Nyampurla jingi-
jingi puwaly-ngunaja ngatijirri ngaka Patirlirri. Patirlirrijangka yanu
yangka pirli kujakalu Yarnmarnpatu parntarri, yangka yali
Yurntumurla yangka kujaka parntarrimi. Ngula ngarnu.

Ngulajangka yanu right up-ji Jurntulku. Ngulapuruyijala karlarra
yalingirli nyangulpa. Warlangarrangurlu kujakurralku kuja puwaly-
ngunaja. Yinyay Docker River-purdalku mata-jarrija. Docker River-
rla mata-jarrija. Yinya, wurnturunyayirni.

Yalilki, yali now karna ngajulurlu level-mani. Ngula karna muku
wapa. Yuwayi, ngatijirri nyanungu karna wirliyarla muku wapa.
Kakarrarapurda karna yani wirliyarlayijala. All over karna
wirliyarlaju muku wapa ngajuju. Nyampuju karna ngarrirni
nyampuju kuruwarri ngulaju ngajunyanguyijala yanurnu yalumpuju.
Ngulapala purajarni nyampu kuyu, emu. Aa, nyampujuku, ngulaju,
ngulaju.

Nyampunya karnangku ngarrirni kuruwarriji, nyampu karna
ngarrirni kuruwarri, kajilpa yalirlimalku, waji-purda-nyangkarla
ngawu-ngawukarirliji glass-parntakarirliji ngulakarna nyina –
ngawu-ngawulku kuja. Well, nyampunya karnarla kuruwarriji yirri-
pura. Walya karna kuruwarri ngari yirri-pura. And too much karna,
you know. Yilpa nguna yalumpuju kurlarni ngalipanyangu ngatijirri.
Yuwu, Patirlirri nyanungu yirdi.

Ngulapala ngulangurlu warru-karrija yali yangka nyanungu
Granite-wana, yalumpungurluju. Kujakarnangkupala ngarrirni.
Jintangurluju ngatijirriji all over wapaja, all over panu-jarrija, all over
jintangurlujuku. Nyampu ngula karnalu jungu yapa nyina, yali
karlarra, kurlarninyarra, yatujumparra, jintangurlujuku.

Jintanyalpa wijiji warru-wapa nyampurlajuku yangka

In the west, the budgerigars were standing in the smoke.

While he was singing the cockatoo was looking around. He sat down. In that place he created many children. Then he came back from there to Ngarnaja. From Ngarnaja he went to Murlinjarri, to the place in the south where the dreamings met together.

I am telling you the truth about these events when all these dreamings met up together. They met together, they went their separate ways, they met again.

From Murlinjarri and from Karntawarranyungu, they ate on their way back to Ngarnaja. From Ngarnaja, the budgerigars went back again to Yinapaka. From Yinapaka, they came directly to Patilirri. There were so many, they covered Patilirri, turning the whole area bright green. From Patilirri, they travelled to the hills that stand along Yarnmarnpatu, near Yuendumu. There they stand.

There they ate. Then they travelled all the way to Jurntu. From Warlangarra, other budgerigars looked toward the west, watching them land at Jurntu, turning the whole area bright green. They went all the way to Docker River where they stopped because they were tired, over there, a long, long way.

I know the whole of this dreaming, the songs, and also I have walked around the whole of this country. I have followed the tracks of the budgerigars. I have followed their travels to the east. I have followed them everywhere they went. I can relate this law.

Then the one which is mine came back this way. At that place, the two men came, following the emu.

Since I am telling you about this dreaming, perhaps my brother might like to listen to it, the other one who is not well, and who wears glasses, the other one who is no longer very well.

I can tell you about this law, and also the country that belongs to it.

Well, the budgerigars that belong to us lay down and slept there just in the south, at the place whose name is Patilirri. From that place, from Patilirri, the two young men walked around visiting different places near the Granites. The budgerigars spread everywhere and multiplied, all coming from the one place. Because of this, we people who live in the west, in the south, along the north side, are all from one family.

The other one, the thief, the one who lives in a hollow tree, the one also called purluwanti, still walks around in this country as well. He

wilypiringawurrpa purluwanti, warrkirri. Ngulanyalpa wapaja wijiji.
Wijingki too much-lpa manu. Ngula kurlarninyarralku
yalumpungurluju yarnkajarni Pawungurlu yarnkajarni,
nyampungurlulpa warru-wapanja-yanu, warru-wapanja-yanu,
nyampuju, warru-wapanja-yanu. Nyangu. "Kari nyampu ka tari-tari-
parnkamirni, waja! Yalumpu ka tari-tari-parnkamirni-ii."

Warrurla maaly-pungu. Kururr-wapajayi-ii. Nyangulku. Kutu
lanturru-manulku. Luurl-manu wijingkiji. Manyu-pungulkulpa
kujarlulku. Yalumpuju kakarrarapurda plain – manyu-pungulkulpa.
Jawirrijana ngunanja-yirrarnu jukurrpanya warrkirri, cockatoo-jana
ngunanja-yirrarnu. Nyanungu wiringarri wijiparnta. Yanulku,
Kuwangkarnikirralku yanu, Kuwangkarnikirralku.

"Kuwangkarnikirralku karna yani." Yanulku. "Nyurrulajulu
nyinaka. Ngayi karna yani Kuwangkarnikirra." Yanulku. Yangkaju
yanu Murinjayikirra. Yanulku nyanunguju wijiwarnu.

Too much wiri jantalypa, you know. Nyampunya karna kuruwarri
right way-ji karna ngarrirni. Ngulajuku kanpa mardarni. Nyampuju
karnalu nyina ngurra yatujumparrawarnurlajuku, nyampunya Payiji
– Watiyajirrijangkaju yukajarni. Nyampuju ngula ka kuruwarri
nyampu karri, yalumpu ka karri, Payiji. Ngurra kurlarninyarrawarnu
Watiyajirrijangka nyampuju yukajarni. Yali yukajampa
yatujumparrarnu, yinya Wangkapurluwarnujangka. Yuwayi.
Nyampuju kajinpala pirrarni yantarlarni, yinganpala little bit marda
purda-nyangkarla jawurrukari nyampuju. You know, nganayi,
Warumungkukurlangu Warnmanpakurlangu ngayirla kankarlu.

Warumungu-side, Warnmanpa-side jawurru yuka karnalu
kujapurda kankarlu winarrpawangungurlu. Not Jardiwanpapiya
nyampu. Kankarlu karnalu pura ngarakurra, nyampu Warnmanpa-
side, Warumungku-side karnalu pura wirliyaku yatuju kujarni –
kuruwarriji. Nyampunyarna ngarrurnu. Ngurra nyampuju karnalu
nyina ngurunyanurla. Everyway nyampu kajikankulu yaninjayani
ngurunyanukurra nyampukurra, ngari, no worries. Yali ngakalu
wirliyarlaju nyinayayi.

Kunangunjungunju yirdi yaliji yuwarli ngulakula,
Kunangunjungunju. Yalirlapala purajarni. Nyangunkulujana
yalumpungurlu nyampukurraju?

Recorded at Willowra, 19 October, 1990

goes around stealing things. He has stolen many things. For example, when that other dreaming came into the south, the one who came from Pawu, well, while the thief was walking about he saw it: "I say, look at this thing bouncing along! That one over there seems to get along by bouncing."

Having flown around it and examined it, he picked it up, after he had circled it a few times. He looked at it. He picked it up and held it in front of his eyes. He picked it up and stole it. Then he played with it. Out on the flat country to the east, he played with it. Then he came across other people sleeping. From them he stole a sacred object and flew away, leaving them still asleep.

He went. He went to Kuwangkarni, to Kuwangkarni. "You can all stay here. I am off to Kuwangkarni!" He went. From there, he went to Murlinjarri. He travelled about stealing things.

There are many sacred stories here. I am telling you all this correctly, so that you will be able to pass this on. We also belong to the country just along the north side, which is the wind dreaming, which came this way from Watiyajirri. The dreaming which we find here, the wind dreaming, has its home just in the south and it came here from Watiyajirri. It blew across in here along the north side from Wangkapurlawarnu. Yes. If you had been here yesterday you would have heard some of this one. It really belongs to the Warrumungu and Warnmanpa people.

The songs that belong to the Warrumungu and Warnmanpa side are ones that we sing loudly and quickly, not like the jardiwarnpa songs. As owners we also follow the tracks of these Warrumungu and Warnmanpa dreamings to the north and back again. We are sitting here in a place which is also one of their places. Later we will be able to go to all the places that belong to them. That one has come along to this place which is one of the places which belongs to it.

Kunangunjungunju, that is the name of the dwelling, Kunangunjungunju. The two young men followed the emu there.

Do you see them as they come towards here?

TRANSLATORS' NOTE

This story was told by Jimmy Jungarrayi, the senior traditional owner of the budgerigar dreaming at Patilirri, to Peggy Rockman Napaljarri, who is a

younger owner of the same dreaming, which belongs to the Jungarrayi-Japaljarri men and Nungarrayi-Napaljarri women. The main purpose of the narrative is therefore to instruct, but this does not detract from the sonorous and stately poetry of the way it is told.

However, the selection of items to include is influenced by the presence of Peggy, whose dreamings include that of the Jungarrayi from Wawarlja (for her account of this, see pp. 149–159). The two sons of this Jungarrayi in Peggy's narrative are the two men who appear in this one. Jungarrayi's central concern in telling the story is to place all the associated jukurrpa – the two men and the emu, the thieving cockatoo and the yam, the budgerigars, and the wind – in their correct relation to the place, Willowra (or Wirliyajarrayi) where he is, to Patilirri which he owns, and to Peggy, the interlocutor, and her associated jukurrpa. This follows the pattern of Warlpiri modes of address in which two people are addressed according to their relationship both to each other and to the speaker.

The most important part of the story is the point where the multitudes of budgerigars gather at Patilirri. There are so many they turn the whole area a luminous green, the colour of the Tanami budgerigar (ngatijirri). From Patilirri, the centre of the jukurrpa, they are described as spreading out and multiplying. It is important to remember that the birds of the jukurrpa are also people, the ngatijirri people of whom two are Jimmy Jungarrayi and Peggy Napaljarri. For the Warlpiri people these ancestral beings are always present. That is why Jungarrayi ends the story with the question, "Do you see them as they come towards here?"

WAPURTARLIKIRLI

The Battle at Yumurrpa

TOLD BY

Liddy Nelson Nakamarra

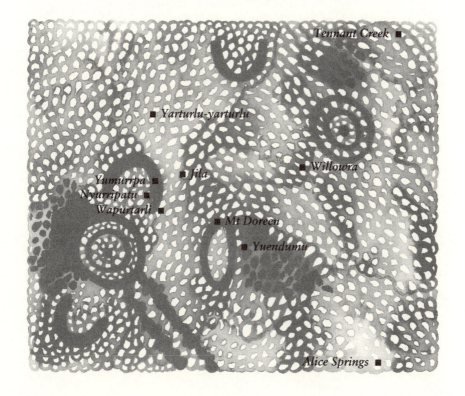

Nyampu ngaju Liddy Nakamarra karna wangkami yangkajarrakurlujuku papardirllanguparduкurlu Yumurrpakurlu manu Wapurtarlikirli. Ngulapalanyanu kuli, kulu ngulalu jangkardu yanu, yuwurlarri-manu, yuwurlarri-manu, yuwurlarri-manu. Jangkardu parnkajarla, jangkardu yaninja-yanurla.

Wurrawiyilpa Wapurtarliji ngunaja. Karlarrangurlu yanurni, Nyurdipatungurluwiyi ngajukupalangurlajangarra yirdingkaju. Yangka kuliparnta nganayi watiya kujaka muku ngarni, laju yangka purrjulyulyu, kulinypa yangka, kulinypa kajika yaparlangu warruwani muku, warruwani muku, warruwani muku. Kulinypanyayirnirli kujaka watiya parla muku ngarni. Ngayi karna nganayirlangujangarra wangka, my father-rla you know, my father-rlajala, ngajukupalangurlajala nyampu. Yalkarrkarla kujajana tarda-nyangu kujarla. Milya-pinyijala kalujana walypalirli, Land Council-rlangurluju yirdiji, not yirdi, ngayi kuruwarrirlajala.

Ngulawiyi yanurnu Nyurdipatungurlu. Ngulawiyili ngulakurralurla kulu-jarrija kamparruju. Ngulalu luwarnu. Ngulawiyili luwarnu nganayirli Yumurrpawardingkipaturluju yapangkuju – yapayijalajangarra. Luwarnulu nganayijala jajutuma. Kuja. Ngajunyangu kirdarnakurlangu. Last one-lki yangka lawarra-jarrija. Ngula lawarra-jarrija yangka purdangirlikirralku. Yangkarnalu tarda-kujurnu. Ngulawiyilirla luwarnu jukurrpaju. Luwarnulu, luwarnulu, luwarnulu, luwarnulu.

Yarnkajarnirla kukurnunyanulku kurlarrangurlu, Wapurtarlilki. Yapajana manurni. Nyanungulku, nyanungurlulkujana luwarnurralujana whole lot, panulkujukujala. Luwarnurralujana, luwarnurralujana, luwarnurralujana, nyanungujurlu Ngardilpirli. Ngardilpili karrijarni. Ngardilpirlijukulunyanu luwarnu luwarnu ngulangkaju, Ngardilpirli. Ngardilpijuku ka karri ngulaju. Ngurrayi ngula Ngardilpijuku ka karri. Ngardilpirlinyanu luwarnu, Ngaliyarlunyanu luwarnu, Ngardilpirli, Ngaliyarlu. Ngurra ngula kujaka karri Yumurrpa, ngurraju Ngaliyarlunyanu luwarnu, Ngardilpirlinyanu luwarnu kulungku waja.

Ngardilpikirlangu, Ngardilpikirlangu, Ngardilpikirlangujuku ngulaju Yumurrpa ka karri, Yumurrparlu kujanyanu Ngardilpikirlangurlujuku luwarnu. Lirra jintajuku,

This tale I, Liddy Nakamarra, tell always about those two, about the two brothers, Yumurrpa and Wapurtarli. Now they became angry with each other, and in the quarrel many went to fight each other. They took up weapons, they took up weapons, they took up weapons. Threatening, they ran there, threatening they went along.

Before that time the one who slept at Wapurtarli had come from the west, from Nyurripatu, the one who bore the name of my father, that one, the one that stings and eats all the leaves of the tree, the caterpillar that is purrjuyulyu, the stinging one, the stinging one that makes people too itchy, itchy all over, the very dangerous one that eats all the leaves of the tree. Indeed I can speak of the caterpillar person, the one belonging to my father's place, you know, at my father's, here.

Yalkarra's people are those who saw the dead in this place. Some white people and also the Land Council people know the story, no, not the story, the Law.

Thus, first they came from Nyurripatu, thus first to this place. They were the first to become very angry. So they killed them, the people who lived at Yumurrpa killed those who were people like themselves. They killed them, the caterpillar people, my father's people, right down to the last man. We saw them die. There they became nothing. Thus at first they killed them there, in the jukurrpa, they killed, they killed, they killed, they killed.

The younger brother set out from the south, from Wapurtarli. He gathered his people. That one, that one then killed them, the whole lot, many, many of them indeed. They murdered them, they murdered them, they murdered them. Those ones, the Ngardilpi speakers. The Ngardilpi faced this way. The Ngardilpi went on killing each other at that place, the Ngardilpi. That place is still the place of the Ngardilpi. The home of the Ngardilpi speakers is at that place. The Ngardilpi killed each other, the Ngarliya killed each other, Ngardilpi, Ngarliya. That place is Yumurrpa, the place where the Ngarliya speakers killed each other, the Ngardilpi speakers killed each other, in the great battle.

Belonging to the Ngardilpi, belonging to the Ngardilpi, to this day belonging to the Ngardilpi, thus stands Yumurrpa, Yumurrpa where the Ngardilpi murdered each other, the people of one tongue. It belongs to the Ngardilpi still. That place is Yumurrpa where the

Ngardilpikirlangujuku. Ngurraju ngulaju Yumurrpaju.
Ngardilpikirlangu ngulanyanu luwarnu Ngardilpikirlangurla
ngurrangka, Ngardilpikirlangurlanyanu luwarnu. Luwarnunyanu
yinyakujurla, yinyakula.

Wapurtarli kunkarni pardija. Yangkaju karlarningirli kujalu
yanurnuwiyi. Marnkurrparlujukujalalunyanu luwarnu.
Nyurdipaturlu, Nyurdipatuwiyi kamparruju luwarnu. Jalpi
ngurrapuka yalumpujukulpanyanu luwarnu ngurrapukarlu,
yalumpuwardingkirlijuku, one family-rli jintangkarlu
ngurrapukarlulpanyanu luwarnu. Nyurdipatuwiyili luwarnu.

Ngulajangkajulu luwarnu Wapurtarlilki. Wapurtarliji ngari
kunkalkujala yarnkajarni kankarlarra yangka Yilkirdingirli.
Ngulangkarlujurlayi tarda-kujurnurnurla papardinyanuku,
tardarnirla-kujurnu,

"Kari nyurru-manu wajalu Ngardilpirli. Nyurru-manu waja
ngajukupurdangkaju."

Nyanungulkurla parnkajarni. Yangkalku kujakapala
palkanyayirni karri jungalku. Luwarnu nyanungurlulkulpajana,
luwarnurraju. Kirdanyanulkulpalanyanu nyanungujarra
pariwarnpajarra jangkardu tarda-yanu, wirijarlijarralku, Ngardilpi
manu Wapurtarli, yarla manu Wapurtarli. Jangkardupalanyanu
tarda-yanu. Ngarilkilpapalanyanu ngarnu, ngayilkilpapalanyanu
ngarnu. Ngulangkajukulpalunyanu luwarnu, ngayilpalunyanu
panungkujuku luwa-luwarnu, panungkujukulpalunyanu. Kujarlu-
kujarlulpalunyanu luwarnu. Panukarijukulpalujana ngarlkinpa-
karrija, ngarlkinpalpalujana karrija.

Ehh, kutulkulpalanyanu yangka yungulpalanyanu walyka-
yirrarnulku. Yangkalku kujakapala karri karluwarnu manu
yatujuwarnu. Yangka jungu kujakapala karri. Kulaka yani
yalumpukurraju, wu, yapa mardukujarlangu, kurdurlangu, walku.
Ngayi karnalurla ngarrirni yika pinkajuku kapala karrimi.
Karnalupalangu Jinkalyarraju yangka nyanyi pinkakurrajuku.
Walkujala. Ngulaju ka tarrukujala karri. Ngulaju ngayi yika karri
secret-waja, walku. No-lpa yantarla kurdurlangu nyanungukurra.
Ngaka kalu yani yangka yakurimipajuku, kurdungurlu kalu yani,
watimipa, no mardukuja.

Kujankulupalangu kapatinjakarra yani nganta watiyajarraku

Ngardilpi murdered each other, in the home of the Ngardilpi, in the home of the Ngardilpi they killed each other. They killed each other over there.

The man from Wapurtarli set out for revenge. They came at first from the country in the south. The people from three places killed each other. The people from Nyurripatu were killed first. All the people who killed each other were from one place, all from one family, all one, all belonging to the same place they killed each other. They killed the Nyurripatu people first.

Then the people from Wapurtarli were killed, the people from Wapurtarli who had come there for revenge up from Yirlkirdi. At that place he saw his older brother lying dead, he saw him lying dead.

"I see the Ngardilpi have already taken him, they have already taken my brother." He ran to the place. Indeed, they both still stand there, still truly present.

Then they all slaughtered each other, they killed each other off. Then the two fathers of their people, those two, the two elders sat down to fight each other, the two most important men, Ngardilpi and Wapurtarli, big yam and little yam. Threateningly they sat down. Savagely they wounded each other, savagely they wounded each other.

At the same time many of the others killed each other, many, many of the other people killed each other in this way, in this way at that time. Many others continued to defend themselves by warding off the blows, they warded off the blows.

The two drew close to each other in order to make peace. They are the two who still stand there, one to the south, one to the north. They truly still stand there. Women and children do not go to that place, no. We can tell the story while those two stand a safe distance away. We can look at those two at Jinkalyarra, but only from a safe distance. We cannot go there. That is a very sacred place. In fact, it is a secret place. No children may go there. Later my brothers will go there, and the kurdungurlu, men only, without women.

Lest you go to the two trees without understanding, blasphemously, men or women, lest strangers like you go close to there, lest you approach there ignorantly or blasphemously, lest the Land Council people should take you about, lest perhaps you go south by that place

ngulajarraku mardukuja watirlangu, yapakarirlangu kajikankulu
kutu yani yapakari, kapatinjakarra yangka kajikankulu karrka,
kajilpanyarra yangka Land Council-rlangurlu warru kangkarla,
kajikankulu marda yani yinyawana kurlirra. (Ngayi karnalu
yatujumparrawarnujuku nyina nganimpaju warlaljaju yangka
ngurrapukaju, yanirra karnalu, yangkarnalu malurnparlaju
yuwarlirlajuku nyina.) Kajinkili kurdu-kurdurlangu yangka
kajilpankulu yangka ngurrpa-ngurrparlu, walku, kajikankulu
nyiyarlu nyanyi, watiyakurra alright kanparla watiyajarraku
kanparla kapati, kajikalunyarra yunparni ngayi kuukurlu kapankurlu
mirlalparlu, mirlalparlu kajikalunyarra pakarni manu
yunparnirlangu. Palka kalu karrimi mirlalpaju.

And nganimpa ngularnalu yanurra jalangu. Well-rnalu
wangkajarnalujana jitinjarla. Yanurnalu and ngunajalparnalu.
Ngunanjarlarnalu Napaljarrikirliji jukurra-pardinjarla pirnpiji
ngarninjarla yanu Yurntumukurra. Kuja.

Kala nyampu, ngulapalanyanu luwarnu. Junga ngulajupalanyanu.
Ngula kaju warrarda wangka nyampu Napurrurla. Ngulangka ngayi
karnarla yimi ngarrirni yangkajarraku waja jimarrikarra. Ngari
karnangku. Ngaka wajangkulu yimi ngarrirni yinyarrarlu yapangku.
Walkujuku karna puta-puta wangka. Wingkingkijuku kaju japirni
yikaji nyampurluju. Wurrangkujuku ka jilypi-yirrarni. Karna nyina
wangkanja-wangu. Ngula, ngulakuju, ngula ka warrarda wangka.
Ngula kapala karri, ngurrpangkupalangu nyangu nyampurluju
Napurrurlarlu watiyajarra yangka. Ngulajuku karnarla yimi-
ngarrirni. Jungu kapala karrimi ngulaju. Yungupalangu purdayi-
nyanyi nyampurluju . Kulungkupalanyanu luwarnu. Yawuruju
yangka nganayi-manulkulpalanyanu. Marrara kapala karri.

Kulanganta kajikarnalu warlkakula wangkami, nyampuju karnalu
nyinami one family-nyayirni, junga.

Kuturla yinyangurlu Wapurtarlingirli jangkardarnu-yanu. Kujaka
karrimi, kapu pungulpalunyanu, luwarnulpalunyanu.
Luwarnulpalunyanu. Junganyayirni karnalu nyina. Karlarrangurlu
yanurni. Ngayirla kunka-pardija yinyaju papardinyanu
kukurnunyanuku kurlarrajangkaju yinyaju. Kujarla
karlarrajangkaku, karlarni kujajangkalkuyijala, Nyurdipatujangka.
Yangkakujukunya watiya ngula ka muku ngarni. Yapawiyi

(although we stay on the north side, we the one family belonging to the one place, we go over to the shade where the houses now are), lest you bring children to that place when you approach for the first time, lest you see something, lest you ignorantly or wrongly approach the two trees, powerful and vengeful spirits will immediately sing to you and curse you. The spirits will strike you and curse you as well. There the powerful spirits stand.

Well, we left today. Having got down from the truck, we spoke to the others. We went there and slept there. Having slept there with Napaljarri [Peggy Rockman Napaljarri], the next day, having eaten the first meal, we came to Yuendumu. So.

Here those two had killed each other, true, those two. This is what has always been told to me, Napurrurla [Lee Cataldi], and thus I tell the story in this way. I tell you the story about the two brothers, the two men initiated together. Later you will tell the story to other people. Perhaps I should talk no further of this lest someone should accuse me of breaking the Law. I still have this [microphone] attached. I will remain without talking. No, it is for this reason, to avoid this, that we talk about those two standing there, lest out of ignorance Napurrurla look too closely at them. That is why I tell her the story. True, those two stand there. Enough. So that this person may understand about those two.

In anger they killed each other. Then they made peace with each other. They are now both spirits.

If anyone supposes wrongly that I tell lies about this, we are all the one true family. Furiously they came close from there, from Wapurtarli. Where that place is, there they fought and killed each other, killed each other. We are the right people for here. He came up from the west, he came to revenge his older brother, the younger brother came up from the south, and then from the west, from the place in the west, from Nyurripatu. It is still marked by the tree that is always eaten. They used to be people. This is where they used to kill.

Here the people belonging to Yumurrpa killed them. Consequently, the ones from over there came for vengeance. Two groups of people set out from the south for vengeance, the water people as well, two groups of people set out to perform the revenge, our wurrurru relatives from Karlingkaturu, and the people from Wapurtarli, both peoples came

ngarilpa nyinaja.

Ngulawiyili luwarnu – nyampurluju Yumurrpawardingkipaturlu. Luwarnulu. Ngulajangka yinyalkurla kunka-yanu. Kunkaju yarnkajarni kurlarrangurlupalarla ngaparlangu. Kunka-pardijapalarla, jirrama – wurrurru, Karlingkaturu, Wapurtarlipalarla kunka-pardija nyampukuju. Nyampu, yinya kuja yangka watiya muku ngarnu, watiya kujaka parla muku ngarni yapaku. Yapangkuwiyiyijala. Jirramapalarla kunka-pardija. Luwarnupala nyampuju jintajuku nganayi Ngardilpi nyampuju. Yumurrpapala luwarnu yarla jirramarlu, ngapangku. Nyampurlapala luwarnu kunkangkuju. Luwarnupala. Luwarnupala. Luwarnupala.

Walyka-yirrarnu yangka kujakanyanu yapangku ngula kapala watiyajarralku karri. Walyka-yirrarnulkulpalanyanu. Ngulajukulunyanu luwarnu kuja yawarra wirijarra waja. Kujalkupalanyanu wangkaja:

"Ngulajuku. Luwarnurlunyanu yarlpurru, yarlpurru."

"Yawarra wirijarra waja? Ngayi karnalu nyurnuwatilki waja karrimi nyampukula kulpa waja."

"Nyampu karlinyanu ngalijarra waja walyka-yirrarni wirijarrarlu, pariwanpajarrarlu ngalujarrarlu. Walyka-yirrarni karlinyanu."

"Ngulajuku yarlpurru?"

"Luwarnurlunyanu. Kulpalku karna Wapurtarlikirralku."

"Yuwayi. Nyina karna ngajuju nyampurlajuku Yumurrparlajuku."

"Yuwaw!"

Yanulpalu. Kurlarralpalu yanu. Kurlarralpalu yanu. Kurlarralpalu yanu. Yanu kulpalu. Yangkalpanyanu yunparninja-yanu. Palkajalarnalu yunparninjakurlangurlawarnu. Kujalpanyanu yunparninja-yanu kurlarrapurda. Kulpari-yunparninja-yanu ngulalpanyanu. Yunparninja-yanulpanyanu kulpari.

"Yungkurnurlu panturnu, nyirawurlu ngurrju-manu, yungkurnurlu panturnu."

Yalumpurlu wiripirdinyparlu kujalpalanyanu jakuru-pungu. Ngulangkulpanyanu yunparnu. Yungkurnurlulpa panturnu yirlara. Well, manulpanyanu nyirawurlu. Ngurrju-manulpanyanu. Minti nganayi-manulpanyanu, mijurnulpanyanu, mijurnulpanyanu, mijurnulpanyanu. Turnu-manulpanyanu yungkurnu, mijurnulpanyanu, mijurnulpanyanu, pulykulpanyanu mijurnu.

here for revenge. Here, there where that tree stands all eaten, the tree all of whose leaves the people eat. Two armies set out for revenge. Here they killed each other all together, the Ngardilpi people, at Yumurrpa they killed each other, the yam people and the water people. At this place they fought out the vengeance. They killed each other, they killed each other, they killed each other, they killed each other, they killed each other, they killed each other.

Then the two men made peace.

And now they stand at that place, the two trees. At the end they made peace. After they had struck each other with deep and open wounds, thus they spoke to each other.

"This is enough of killing each other, brother."

"Brother, enough of these big wounds. You see me standing here with all the dead. Let it stop."

"Here let us make peace with each other, the two important ones, the two elders. We two, let us make peace."

"Enough, brother?"

"They have all died. I am going back to Wapurtarli."

"Yes. I will stay here at Yumurrpa."

"Yes."

They went. They went south, they went south, they went south. They went back. That one went along singing, that one we know to be there from the place belonging to the song who sang himself back to the south. He went back singing. Thus he went along, singing himself back.

There, the two foremost men bade each other farewell. There one of them sang himself. The bone of his leg had pierced the flesh. He got the nyirawu vine. With it he healed himself. He bound up his leg, he joined the muscle again, he joined the muscle again, he joined the muscle again, he reunited the bones, he joined the muscle again, he joined the muscle again, he joined the muscle again, the tendon he joined together.

Then singing he went along. He did not die, because he had joined the muscle, because he had reunited it, because he had sung himself. He felt better. He could stand up.

"Because of my leg, my head waves about . . ."

You might wrongly think we are not singing the truth, you might

*"Yungkurnurlu panturnu, nyirawurlu ngurrju-manu,
yungkurnurlu panturnu."*

Kujalpanyanu yunparninja-yanu. Nyampu walkujala.
Ngarilpanyanu yangka mijurnu, mijurnu. Turnu-manulpanyanu,
yunparnulpanyanu. Ngurrjulkulpanyanu purda-nyangu. Karrinja-
pardijalku.

"Ngarnajintarna parlpirri parlpirri."

Kulanganta kajikarnalunyarra warlkangku, kulanganta yunparni,
kulanganta kajikankulu nyurrularlujuku yijardujuku yunparni. Kala
nganimpaju kulanganta karnalunyarra kulanganta warlkakula
wangka!

"Ngarnajintarna parlpirri parlpirri."

Jarntiny-jarntinypalkulpa yanu, pinkalkulpa jarntiny-jarntiny-
karrkaja Wapurtarlikirralku jintapurdanjilpa jarntinja-yanu.
Yangkangkalpanyanu wiripirdinyparlu yunparninja-yanu nyampuju
pariwanparlu kirdangku Jakamarrarlu.

"Ngarnajintarna parlpirri parlpirri."

"Jintapurdanji waja ngayi karnaju jarntiny-jarntiny-karrka!
Kujakula waja."

"Ngarnajintarna parlpirri parlpirri."

Yangka pulyku taarlpalkunyanu purda-nyangupalanyanu,
yilpapala yirdija jirrama yanu, panu ngayi, panu yanu.

"Taarlpalku kujarnaju purda-nyanyi yaninja-yaninjakulku
yinyarlakulku."

"Kurnpalurnparlurla wangkanya. . . ."

"Mayalkurna kuja yaninja-yanu. Mayalkurna nyampuju yaninja-
yanu. Kiljilkirnaju pulykuju rarrarlpapardulku yani. Taarl-manurna
kuja, pulykujarraju. Yuwa, ngajurlangu kuja.

Yilpalunyanu panuju ngayi Luwarninjawarnu yangkaju
kankarlarra. Kutukurralkujangarra. Warrkarnurralpalu ngayi.
Walyakurrawiyijala ngulaju pirlilkijala jardu-karri."

Kala jukurrpa yilpalu yanu yangka walyakurrawiyi.

"Ngurrjupardu karna pulykulypaju, ngayi karnaju purda-nyanyi."
Yaninja-yanu kala waja Wapurtarlikirraju.

"Yukamirralku karli ngurrakurralku, ngulakurrakula."

Yukajarrapala ngurrakurralku. Yukajarrapala ngurrakurralku,
ngulakurra.   *Recorded at Yuendumu, November 9, 1990*

wrongly think that you can sing this more truthfully, but it is wrong to think we are telling you lies.

Limping, he travelled along. He travelled slowly, limping, towards Wapurtarli, lame in one leg. So he went along singing, the great one, the elder, that one, my father Jakamarra.

"Thus I go, lame in one leg, in just this manner."

He heard the muscles in his wounded leg grating. Two people or more people went along.

"I can hear the grating as I go along.

I continue to travel further, always toward that place there.

My wounded tendon is rapidly getting stronger.

My two wounded tendons were grating together.

Yes, I am also stronger.

They have placed there the ones who were slain nearby at that other time and are now stones having first returned to the ground."

For thus in the Jukurrpa they returned first to the ground.

"Now I can feel my tendons have got much better."

So he went along towards Wapurtarli.

"Now we enter our homes, we enter there."

The two of them went into their homes. The two of them went into their homes, into there.

TRANSLATORS' NOTE

This narrative is an account of a major battle, the battle between the small yam (ngarlajiyi) people from Wapurtarli and the large yam (yarla) people from Yumurrpa. The climax of the narrative, its turning-point, is when the leaders of the two groups decide the slaughter is so great that they should settle the matter by engaging in single combat, sitting cross-legged on the ground, a gruesome method which allows neither to escape. When the hero from Wapurtarli convinces the other that continuing to fight is useless, he does this without loss of face, which may well be the cultural achievement the jukurrpa celebrates. As the severely wounded hero limps back towards Wapurtarli, mourning as he passes the ranks of the dead now turned into stones, he heals himself by singing. This capacity to heal may be another gift to the culture.

In both the matter and style of this narrative, we can see the classical face of Warlpiri culture, a culture which has much more in common with the open and clearly understood laws of society and the universe of the Achaeans of the

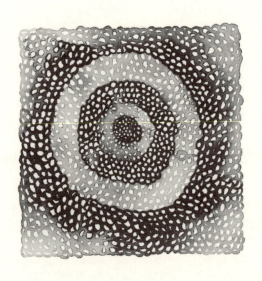

Iliad than it has with the haunted gloom of romantic ninteenth- and twentieth-century versions of the "primitive" – the Warlpiri hero is much more like Hermes than he is like Prester John. Liddy Nakamarra's account of the battle at Yumurrpa is a great narrative, a living example of the heroic style – elevated, uncluttered, sustained.

JARNTUJARRAKURLU

The Two Dogs

TOLD BY
Popeye Jangala

Yarrajalpa
Wirninginpa
Karljawarnu
Jinarli
Warlarla
Yurlpuwarnu

Tennant Creek

Yarturlu-yarturlu

Willowra

Yuendumu

Alice Springs

Nyampu karna start-i-mani. Start-i-mani karna ngajuku-palanguku father-ku kujalurlajinta pungu marntiwa. Marntiwalurlajinta pungu ngajunyangu, my father-ku yangka muljungka nganayirla Yarrjarlparla, Yarrjalparla muljungka. All right, finish-yi-manulu yi yuwa nyanungurla muljungka.

Ngunajapala ngurrangka. Pardijarrapala kakarrara nyanungu jarntujarra, yananyarrapala-aa Wirnirnnginpaku. Yatujumparrakirlipala yanu Wirnirnnginparlajupala yatujumparra. Kakarrarapala rdakurl-pungu warnirri-kirra, yangka kujarna nyanja-yanu. Pardarnu yilpankujulu, pardarnurnu kuja karlarra – Wirnirnnginparla kulkurru. Mukirrirlalpankulu nyinaja. Ngajurna, rockhole-wiyirna ngapa ngarnu.

Nyanungu jarntujarra kujapala warrku-pungu, mawupala ngajarnu. Ngulajangka yanurrapala jarntujarraju kakarrara nganayikiji, Jinarlikiji. Jinarlirlapala ngurrangkaju ngunaja country-rla, Jinarlirla ngajunyangurla. Yalikariji karlumparra, ngulaju kajana karrimirni purdangirlilki. Ngunajapala. Jukurrapala yarnkajarra kakarrara yangkakula. Yarnkajarrapala-aa. Kakarrarapala parrawariny-yanu nganayikirra Karljawarnurla.

Yangkapala ngunaja rockhole-rla Karljawarnurla ngurrangkaju, ngunajapala. Warlu, warlulpa purajampa kurlarnimpala, warlu ngarilpa jingi-jingikirla purajarra. Ngunanjarlapala. Pardijarra kakarrara. Yanupala-aa kakarrara-aa. No-more-pala Jiliwirrpakurra yanu kurlarnirra. Yatujumparrawarnujukupala yanu, yanupala-aa. Yinyapala warrku-pungu nganayi Waanjurna, ngulakurrapala yanurra, ngurrakurra Waanjurnakurra. Waanjurnarlapala ngurrangka ngunaja.

Ngulajangkajupala mayi yanu kakarrara-aa. Wulyu-wulyupala pungu muljungka, warnirrirla mayi Tapungka, Tapungka. Tapungka wulyu-wulyupala pungu, ngarnupala. Ngulajangkapala yarnkajarra kakarrumpayi.

Wangkajarla jinta, "Ngaju karna yani kujanya kurlarnimpalawarnu." Ngamaju isn't it?

Ngamaju yanu kurlarnimpala yinya Ngamarnawarnukurra – Ngamarnawarnukurra. Yatujumparrawarnu wirriyapardu yanurni. Yangkakula yananyarra Pawuruwana maraju karrupardu.

Jalangu kujarna karrija pirlingka Mukurrirla.

I begin this story at this place with my father, whose initiation finished at that soak, his soak, at Yarrajalpa, at the waterhole Yarrajalpa. They finished the ceremony there at that waterhole.

The two dogs slept in their camp. Then those two dogs left to go away towards the east. There they were going away to Wirninginpa. They went, in fact, along the north side, north from Wirninginpa. Then they crossed over to the east to those rockholes – you know, the ones I went and found while you all waited for me over to the west. From Wirninginpa it is halfway. You stayed by the little rocks, while I drank first from that waterhole.

There, the two dogs had dug out a waterhole. They also urinated. Then the two dogs went east to Jinarli. They slept one night at Jinarli, at Jinarli in the country that belongs to me. Along the west side that country at the back belongs to other people. They slept. The next day they continued east from there. In the east they went around to Karljawarnu. Then at Karljawarnu they slept at the rockhole. At Karljawarnu they spent one night.

The fire, the fire burnt its way past along to the south of where they were. In fact, the fire went straight past them and away.

After they had slept, they set off towards the east again. They did not go to Jilwirrpa in the south. They kept on going along the north side. They went on. They scratched out a little rockhole at Waanjurna. They went away to Waanjurna. At Waanjurna they camped. Then they probably continued east. At the soak, they hunted little mice, or maybe that happened at the rockhole at Tapu, at Tapu. They hunted little mice. They ate them. They they set out to go a long way to the east.

One of them said, "I will travel this way along the south side." It was the female dog.

The female went along the south side that way towards Ngamarnawarnu, towards Ngamarnawarnu. The male dog went along the north side. In this way they travelled separately. Along past Paruwu, he walked slowly, at the little creek where I stopped at the hill at Mukirri. They both travelled on. He walked slowly along that northern route. He had already stayed at Ngarnka, on this side, at a soak near paperbark trees. There he hunted little mice. He sniffed the air.

Yanurnipala-aa maraju. Yanurra-aa yatijarra, yangka ruutu kala nyinaja nyurru Ngarnkangka kujarninginti pakarlikurlu mulju. Ngulangka pungu, wulyu-wulyu. Pungu. Parnti-nyangu, "Kari yapa ka nguna kankarlarni – Ngarnkangkaju."

Pawururla kankarlarra jarda-jarrija, yungu jarda-jarrija. Jardalkulpa ngunaja. Nyanunguju kurtaji – ngulawardingki – jamirdipurajikariyinyanu. Warurra yanu pinkajuku yangkakula karlarninginti nganta. Warurra-yanu kankarlarra. Parnti-nyangu. "Kari ka . . ." Yanu-uu. Nyangu. "Kari ka nyampu jarda ngunanya!"

Juurr-yarnkajarla. Pungu-uu, pungu, pungu, pungu, pungu, pungu, pungu, pungu, pungu! Nyurnu yirrarnu. All right. Lawapulkulpa nyinaja – wirriyaju.

All right, yinyarla ngamapardukulkurla wapalpa yulaja yangkaju yilpinji. Yulajarla wapalpa-aa. Junga jangku-manu kurlirra Ngamarnawarnuwana. Yangkakula parnkanjarni-yananya yulanjakarrayijala. Yaninjarla-aa yapa-aa, "Nyampu kuyupardu kala!"

Yulajarla yilpinji kuja karlipa yunparni, jinta-jarrijapala. "Kari nyampu ka ngunanya yapa!"

Ngarnupala, ngarnupala, ngarnupala. Kankarlarniji Pawururlaju, ngarnupala, ngarnupala, ngarnupala. Kari parljakurlulku – two-pala bin tuckered out, full up-i, pirda. All right. Wangkajarla, "Yanirli!"

Yanupala mayi kanjayi nganayikirra, yuwa, Yinirntikirlikirra, yangka muljukurra – nganayikirra, Ngarnkakurra. All right, ngulangkakula warri-warriji nyangulpa yangka kuja kalu jarntu nyinanya, kuja now, nyinajarnilpa kujarni. Ngula wirriyarluju nyangu, "Kari rduju karnaju jurnta kanja-yanu, rduju, kuja – warri-warriji."

Ngulapala yarnkajarra kaninjarra.

Wangkajarla, "Nyinayalku. Yani karna wirlinyi." Yanu kakarrara-aa kaninjarra nganayikirra yangka. Nyiya yangkaju muljupardu, muljuwangu nganayi ayi? Yirnintipatu, Yirnintipatu? No. Nyiyarna yali kawarli-manu jalangurlu? Mulju yangka, muljuwangu, Larrka – muljukurlukulajala. Warlangkarla wurduju-manu, waapuru-manu, wurduju-manurla-aa everything-i, nyampu, nyampu waluwarnu, minyira, yangka, wurduju-manunyanu, nyanungukulkunyanu thought-jarrija-aa, "Finish-i!"

"There is someone lying up there at Ngarnka, on top at Pawuru."

He was asleep, he was asleep there. While he was sleeping – that kadaija [man sent to enact a sorcerer's pay-back], the one who lived there, your grandfather, was sleeping – the dog crept around very slowly, he crept around by the west, up on the top. He sniffed the air again. "Maybe . . . ." He went closer and looked. "I say, here is someone asleep!" He sprang on the sleeper, and bit him. He fought and fought and finally left him dead.

The male dog was becoming very lonely. The female dog was still over in the other direction. The male dog howled. He sang a love-song to try to find her, he called out to try to find her. Well, he heard a reply from the south, from Ngamarnawarnu. She came straight to him, running all the time, and calling out as she ran.

When she got there she saw the dead body. "Why, this is meat!" The dogs had been crying out their love-songs like those we sing. They met. "I say, there is someone's body lying here."

They ate it, they ate it, there up on top at Pawuru. They ate until they were completely full. Those two ate until they could eat no more. Then one said to the other, "Let's go!"

They went as far as, maybe, yes, Yinirntikirli, that is to the soak, to Ngarnka. There he realized that the dog lying next to him was female. As she was sitting facing him he looked at her closely. "I say, it is a female dog I have brought with me. Oh, please excuse me, lady."

They went into the place. Then one said to the other, "You stay here while I go hunting."

He went toward the east, into that country where there is a soak, no, not a soak. What is it I have forgotten? Larrka, it is a soak. That is the place. At that place in the soft sand he made head-dresses, he made everything there. He made the man's and woman's marriage head-dresses for himself and his bride. Then he looked at them and decided, "Yes, these are finished. Good."

He went back westwards to the camp. He put the man's head-dress on and took the woman's one back to give to her. Then he looked back towards the east.

"Yes, look, my husband!" She ran towards him. He tried to cover the paintings on his body, done with white clay, that is, with the white clay. The woman took his head-dress off. They went towards the west,

All right-i. Pardijarrarla pina karlarra. Waapuru nyampu yirrarnu. Minyirajulparla kanja-yanukirli. Nyangu kakarrara.

"Yuwa, ngumparnalu nyangka kakarrara!" Wapirdirla parnkaja. Palupaturlajinta nyampurla kujarlu. All right-i. Yuwa, karlji yangka, white one, all right, nyampurla. Rurruny-pungu waapuru. Yanurrapala ngurrakurra ngamirljikirlilki. Karlarrapala yanurra, ngamirljikirlilki. All right, ngurralkupala yirrarnu yunta ngurra. Ngurrangkalkupala yirrarnu ngapuju warri-warri, ngapujurlangurlu now. Ngapujunyanulkulpapala ngunaja jungulku tarnnga. Ngunajapala, ngunajapala, ngunajapala warri-warri-ii. Rangkarr-ngarnupalangu. Yarnkajarrapala kakarrara.

"Nyampu mayirli?" Lawa-nyangulu warra wiyarrpa, wiyarrpa nyampu now. Ngurrangkapala ngunanjarla jukurra-pardija. Yarnkajarra-pala. Maraju yangkakulapala yananyarra kakarrumpayi maraju, marajupala, marajupala. Yananyarrapala kakarrarninginti Kurduwijawijarla kurlarnimpala. Yanupala. Kakarrarapala warrurra yanu-uu. Kakarrara ka Ngarnka nganayikirra Yurlpuwarnukurra, isn't it, rockhole-patu, yangka wiri-wiri kujakalu nyina ruuturlajuku kuja-purda kaninjarra. No-more-rnanyarra show-manu yet, Ngarnkangka kankarlarrapurda-aa, nganayirla.

Nyiya yalumpu karru yirna kawarli-manu? Warlarla, Warlarlarla. Parnpijapalanyanu ngulangka purlapa now little bit. Ngurrangkapala ngunaja ngulangkakirli. Early-palapala pardijarra. Yangka cross-ju manu maraju. Yananyarra-pala kakarrara. Nyangurrapalanyanu jaarlparra-kujurnu Rabbit Flat-wana yilpinjiji.

Yananyarrapala kakarrumpayi. Parnkajarrapala. Kankarlarrapala. Kaninjarra yangka jintapardu-jangarrapala pila-parnkaja kakarrara Yurlpuwarnukurra, Yurlpuwarnukurra. Ngulangka Yurlpuwarnurlapala ngurrangkaju ngunaja. Yaa, rockhole-rla kujapurdajangarra ka ngunanya wirijarlu – karlarrapurda Yurlpuwarnukurra. Ngurrangkapala ngunaja – ngulangkakula.

Ngulajangkajupala pardjarra. Pardijarrapala jukurralku yinya kakarrumpayi. That far, ngajunyangujurna puraja. That's all, Napaljarri. Yangkakari kujarna nyurrukari yapakarikirlangu. Yuwa nyampunya karna jalangurlu pura, ngajuju.

Recorded at Lajamanu, May 30, 1990

their arms around each other. They made a camp with a wind-break. The man and the wife, the married couple, put everything they needed in the camp. Then they lay down together, for always. They slept together, they slept together, the man and the beautiful young lady. Dawn came.

They set off toward the east. "This way perhaps?" They only had eyes for each other. How sweet. They camped again for one night. The next day dawned. They set off again, walking slowly. There they were, travelling toward the east, walking slowly, walking slowly, the two of them walking slowly. There they went on into the east, to Kurduwijawija on the south side. They went. They turned around to the east, at a place near Ngarnka, on the way to Yurlpuwarnu, a place with several rockholes, very big ones which lie beside the road in this direction, at Warlarla, at Warlarla.

There they performed a ceremonial dance, a little one. Then they made camp there, right there. Early the next day they set off to go across, walking slowly. From there they went toward the east. They kept on looking across at each other. Near Rabbit Flat, while singing love-songs, he scattered little rocks behind them.

From there they went a long way into the east. There they ran along. They ran up hills, they came down. Together the two people from the dreaming ran eastwards towards Yurlpuwarnu, Yurlpuwarnu. At Yurlpuwarnu, then, they slept one night. There is a very large rockhole at that place, lying in the direction of the high ground towards Yurlpuwarnu. They slept at that place one night. Then they left that place the next day, that place which lies a long way over to the east.

That is as far as I can follow it. That is all. Napaljarri, the rest which I now leave belongs to other people. This is what I can relate now, this is what belongs to me.

TRANSLATORS' NOTE

The Warlpiri jukurrpa of the two dogs (jarntujarra or malikijarra) concerns the travels of two black dogs all the way from Yarrajalpa in the extreme west of Warlpiri country to Alekarenge on the eastern edge where they settle. Alekarenge means "belonging to the dogs". Popeye Jangala, who lives at Yaruman in West Australia, follows the adventures of the dogs as far as Yurlpawarnu. The later part of the story is told by Joe Jangala from

Alekarenge in the east (see pp.129–137).

The dogs which are black are clearly also people, since the Australian dingo is usually a reddish brown. In Popeye Jangala's account, the protagonists beautifully combine characteristics which clearly belong to dogs with those which clearly belong to people, particularly when they fall in love. In this story, the dogs create important features of the landscape as they travel, especially soaks that they dig out. The performance of the marriage ceremony provides a description of how marriage ceremonies should be performed. Ideally both partners are willing and very happy. The telling of this tale is distinguished by the sharpness of the observation and the delicacy of the characterization, the dogs acting convincingly as both dogs and people.

MALIKIJARRAKURLU

The Two Dogs

TOLD BY

Joe Jangala

Warlarlangurlu ngari parnkajarni nganayingirli, Ngarnkangurlu, Ngarnkangurlu now, Ngarnkangurlu parnkajarni. Warlarla, Warlarlakurrapinanguju parnkanja-yanu wurnturu wurrajuku. Kulkurruwangu lawa, kulkurrujarrajuku parnkanjarni-yanu, parnkanjarni-yanu, maliki – nganimpanyanguwiyi – nganimpapatukurlangu nganimpangurluwiyi, Jangalaku, Jampijinpakuwiyi.

Parnkajarni-ii, parnkajarni-ii, parnkajarni-ii. Kujajuku parnkanjini ka – nganimpa side-wiyi. Like kirda nganimpaku, nganimpanyanguwiyi –Jangalaku, Jampinjinpakuwiyi parnkanyarni karlumpayingirli Ngarnkangurlu. Parnkanyarni Warlarlakurrapala. Yungkaparri-yungkaparrilkipala Warlarlakurralku parnkaja. Ngakarra-ngakarralkuju. Yungkaparri-yungkaparrilki. Warlarlakurralkupala yanurnu. Warlarlawanapala parnkajarni jingi-jingi ngula kujaka yangka yuwarlilki karri, pub. Parnkanyarni kulkurru-kulkurru yangka yali Lajamanukuju parnkaja kurlarninyarra, kurlarninyarra parnkaja Lajamanukuju. Parnkanyarni yalumpu manangkarra kulkurru-kulkurru.

Yuwayi, Yurlpuwarnu, Yurlpuwarnukurra parnkajarni. Yuwayi, paarrpari-yanupalarla ngulakuju – Yurlpuwarnurla. Yaliji wara-parnpija. Well-i, yunparnu yalumpurlarluju. Yangka tururru witangkulpa pirlirl-pirlirl-yungu.

Ngulangka, Yurlpuwarnungurlupala yarnkajarni. Parnkanyarnipala, parnkanyarnipala. Tarnngajukupala yaninjini kulkurru-kulkurru, kulkurru, kulkurrulku. Jimanypakulkulpa warlulkulpala rduul-yungu. Yilpapala warlu yurrparnu kujarlu, light-manu yangka nganayi warlu, jimanypa. Luwarnupala, luwarnupala.

Ngulalpa yangka jintakarirliji jinyijinyi-manu, "Warlujurla manta! Janjinjanjinngi (nganjin-nganjinngi). Ngalyin-ngalyinngijirla warlu manta!"

Watiyakari-watiyakarilpa pajurnulparla. Kangurnulparla. Well-lpa paka-yirrarnu. "Yaliji maninjintarra, yali nganjin-nganjin-ngalyin-ngalyin!"

Lawa. Warlulpa manunjunurra. Parnkajarralpa. Manunjunurralparla, kangurnulparla. "Nyampunya?"

"Nyampuwangu! Ngaljin-ngaljinngi maninjintarra, ngaljin-ngaljinngi! Yangkajala ngaljinngi."

He ran this way from Warlarla, that is from Ngarnka, from Ngarnka now, from Ngarnka he ran this way. At Warlarla he went along running, right to Warlarlarla. He was still a long way from here. He ran right through the centre. The dog was still running along, running along, coming straight through this way. The dog belongs to us first, to all of us first, to Jangala and Jampijinpa.

He ran this way, this way. There he is, still running this way. He belongs to our side. We are the owners, and it was ours first, belonging first to Jangala and Jampijinpa. He is running this way from a place a long way to the west, from Ngarnka.

There they both are, running to Warlarla. They were running to Warlarla, getting closer and closer, for just a little longer. Closer and closer they came running to Warlarla. They ran this way straight past Warlarla, right past the place where the building stands today, the pub.

Then they ran on through the country to the south, to that place owned by Lajamanu people, on the south side. They ran then to the place owned by Lajamanu people.

They ran to Yurlpuwarnu. They went out that way to Yurlpuwarnu to avoid coming across a ceremony. He had noticed that people were singing there. At that place they were singing to the accompaniment of clapsticks.

From there they ran this way, from Yurlpuwarnu. There they are, both running this way, both running this way. They ran for a long time towards here through the country in the centre, through the middle.

They started a fire using a stick and a spear-thrower. They made a fire and lit it using the stick, the jimanypa. To light the fire, they pushed the stick backwards and forwards on the spear-thrower.

Then one of them gave orders to the other, "Get me some firewood. Get me some ngaljingi-jangilgni wood, get me ngaljingi-ngaljingi wood."

She cut wood off this tree and that. She brought it back but he refused it. "No, go and get that other type, that one, ngaljingi-ngaljingi."

Still nothing. She went and collected more firewood. She ran off. She went around and collected more. She brought it back.

"This sort?"

Ngakarra-ngakarralku, ngakarra-ngakarralkurla pajurnujunu.
Ngakakarilki. Jungarnilkirla pajurnunjunurra. Kangurnurla.
Yungurla.

"Yawu, nyampunya kuja wali ngaljin-ngaljingiji!"
Parnkanyarni. Kulkurru yalumpu, kulkurru-kulkurru. Parnkaja,
parnkanyarni kulkurru-kulkurru, kurlarninyarrajuku.
Kulpurlunukuju kuja parnkaja, kuja parnkaja Kulpurlunuku
ngapaku nganimpanyanguku japiyaku. Parnkaja.
Ngumurlungukurrajana rdipija. Ngumurlungukurrajana,
rdipijajana. Running-jarrija kamparruwarnupatu jarntuku again.

Yalumpujulpa wartarirla nyinaja. Nyinajalpa. Nyangulu wapirdi.
Wapirdili nyangu.

"Awu, awu jujukurranpa running-jarrija, nyampu jujukurra,
jujukurranpa. Nyampuju karalya-karrija, yanurnunpanganpa,
rdipija."

Nyanungulku, nyanungu yarnkajarra pina. Yalumpurlanya,
yalumpukurranyajana rdipija kamparruwarnukuju wurnajangu –
jarntuju. Nganimpanyanguwiyi yanurnu yalumpukurraju.
Ngulajangkaju, yalumpu kamparruwarnulu, yilpalu nyinaja
business-rla – nyampurla jarntungka – jarntupatuyijala. Jukurrpa.
Jukurrparla nyanungurla.

Ngulajangkaju, jintaku, jintakujuku ngari nyinajarni. Yarnkajarni
wurnajuku. Parnkanyarni-ii, parnkanyarni-ii. Yananyarnipala
jirrama. Parnkanyarnipala-aa wurnturu Ngumurlungujangkalku.
Parnkanyarnipala. Kalkurnu-kalkurnu-jarrijapala, wurra
wurnturujukulpala wapanjarni-yanu. Ngaja-ngaja-jarrijalpala-aa
yalumpulku kulkurru-kulkurru. Kalapala wurra parnkanjinani
kulkurru-kulkurru yangka, nyampulku yangka kulkurru-kulkurru
parnkanyarni, yangka yalumpu Jarramardawana. Parnkanyarni
Yankirrikirlanguwana.

Parnkanyarnipala kurlarninyarra, parnkanyarnipala, nyampupala,
nganayipala paarl-mardarnu Yalikarangi. Malikilpalu nyinaja
nyampurlaju. Yanurnupala-aa Yalikarangikirra nyampukurralku.
Yatijarra yalumpukurra parnkajarnipala-aa. Nyangupalajana panu
jarntupatuyijala nyampuwardingkipatuyijala. Nyampu walya
ngulalpa nyinaja. Nyangulujana. Panulpalu nyinaja, lirri-nyinaja
maliki wita-witakurlu, kurdu-kurdukurlu, kirdanyanu-kirdanyanu,

"No, not that sort. Ngaljin-ngaljingi, go and get it, ngaljin-ngaljingi, you know, ngaljingi!"

A little later on, a little later on, having gone to cut some more, she returned. She had cut the right sort this time. She brought it back and gave it to him.

"Yes, this sort. This is the real ngaljin-ngaljingi wood."

There they go, running always in this direction, but still in the country in between. They ran. There they are in the middle, running still, still towards the south. They ran to Kulpurlunu, to the water, to our place, to that very important place. On they ran.

They met the others at Ngumurlungu. They met up together at Ngumurlungu. They were the ones he had caught sight of earlier, the dogs. He ran to meet them with the high-stepping run used in ceremonies. Then they all sat down together to perform the ceremony. They sat down. They looked closely at each other.

"Oh, oh, you who came running up to this sacred ceremony using the high-stepping run, this is not for you. It belongs to us alone, but you have come here and joined us."

So he went away. It was in that place that he had met up with the other dogs that he had seen before on his travels. The one who is ours had gone towards that place where those ones, the ones he had seen before, stayed and performed the ceremony. It was at that place which in the dreaming also belongs to dogs.

During this, the other dog had been waiting alone. The two dogs set off again on their journey. There they are, running this way. There they are, both coming towards this place, the two of them. They are still a long way off, running from Ngumurlungu. They are both running this way, getting nearer and nearer. Now, walking this way, they are still a long way off. But there in the middle they are approaching. They go on running this way, across all the country in the middle, there, running this way along past Jarramarda. They run past Yankirrikirlangu.

Now on the south side they run along, the two of them. The two dogs arrive at Alekarenge. Many dogs were living here. The two dogs came to Alekarenge, to this place. At first they went just to the north. They had run this way. They had seen the others, the many, many other dogs like them, living in this place.

ngamardinyanu-ngamardinyanu. Ngari, panulpalu nyinaja.

Ngulajangkajulpalu wirlinyilki wapaja. Maliki, malikimipa, malikimipalpalu nyinaja nyampurlaju. Ngulalpalu nyinaja. Nyampurralpalu parnkaja yalumpungurlu kakarrumparra, nyampurla kaninjarra nyampu wali. Parnkajarrapala nyampurlaju. Nyampuju kakarrumparra mirnilpalu parnkajarra.

Nyampuju Kayitijikirlangukurralpalu parnkajarni – karlarrangurlu Warlpiri, Warlpiripatu, Warlpiri again. Nyampukurra yanurnupala, Warlpirrikirra again. Nyampukurraju yanurnupala, Warlpirikirra. Kayitiji, Warlpiri, yuwayi, jurrku yangka ńgula karnalu nganimpa wangka jungarni, jurrku.

Well-i ngula nyampujukupala parnkaja – malikijarra karlarni wurnajangu, wurnturuwardingki, West Australia-wardingki, yanurnupala. Wurnturu-wardingki, nganimpanyangu, Jangala Jampijinpakuwiyi. Ngunamirni kujaka yaliji kuruwarri. Ngulawarnulu, ngula kulkurru-kulkurrjukulpalu parnkajarni Jangala Jampijinpakurlanguwiyijiki.

All the way. Yanurnu. Catch him up-manu Ngumurlungu, yalumpuju Jakamarrakurlangu, Jupurrurlakurlangulku. Kujarnijipala yarnkajarni nyampukurraju. Nyampukurrapala yanurnu Yalikarangikirra, mm, Warlaku, we call him Warlaku. Maliki.

Ngari, yalumpujukupala karlarra yinirnti kujalu pakarnulku, ngulangkanyapala, karrijalpapala. Yalumpuju no-rnajana payurnu yalumpurlajuku.

Yalumpukurrajukupala parnkajarni. Ngula yalumpurlajukupala panungkalku mixed up-jarrija. Maliki kamparruwarnurla. Yuwayi, jintawangurla panungka. Mapirri-jarrija kujalu.

Ngulajuku.

Recorded at Alekarenge, December 3, 1990

They stopped here, in this country. They looked at the other dogs. There were many of them sitting down. They were sitting in circles, at a meeting, with their little ones, their children, fathers and mothers and uncles. There were many there sitting down. Then they all went hunting.

There were only dogs, only dogs living here. It was here where they were living. Well, they all went from there to the east side, to here, to this place right here. The two dogs ran from here to a place a short distance away in the north. Then the two dogs ran towards Kaytij country from the west. Then they came back here into Warlpiri country. Here it is both Kaytij and Warlpiri country. This same country we can both really say is ours.

Well, then, the two dogs from the west lived and hunted around here, the two travellers, the two whose home was a long way away, in West Australia, our people, Jangala and Jampijinpa. And that law stays right here. From over there it came this way right through the country in the middle, and it belongs from the first to Jangala and Jampijinpa.

It came all the way. It met up at Ngumurlungu with the one that belongs to Jakamarra and Jupurrurla. From there the two dogs left and came here, here, to Alekarenge, to the place we call Warlaku, belonging to the dogs. In the west they went and cut yinirnti wood. There they stood, the two dogs. I did not ask to know any more.

From over there they came back this way. Then they settled down and lived with all the others living here. In the beginning they were all dogs, not just one but many. As this story has shown, this is how they became all one family, one people.

That is all.

TRANSLATORS' NOTE

This account by Joe Jangala of the later, eastern part of the story of the two dogs follows the progress of the couple from Warlarla, in the centre of Warlpiri country, to Yurlpawarnu and from there to where they finally settle, at Alekarenge (whose Warlpiri name is Warlaku). Whereas Popeye Jangala's narrative (see pp.119–127) deals with the dogs as a couple and provides a model for marriage, this section of the tale concerns the customs and protocol of living in the world, particularly in relating socially to other, different

groups of people.

The slightly irritated exchange between the husband and wife over the wood used for kindling is also a description for future generations of how to make a fire. However, the central concern of this jukurrpa relates to how people of different groups and different tribes behave in order to maintain peaceful relations with each other, particularly if they settle in the same place.

Alekarenge has always been on the border of Warlpiri, Kayeteje and Warrumungu country, and it has always been important for the different groups to be able to live together, something which the development of the modern settlement intensified but did not basically alter. In this jukurrpa the different tribes have in common that they are all dogs. The arrival and acceptance of the Warlpiri dogs from the west explains how the Warlpiri people came to live and settle there: "In the beginning they were all dogs, not just one group but many. As this story has shown, this is how they became all one family, one people."

WARNAJARRAKURLU

The Two Snakes

TOLD BY

Tiger Japaljarri

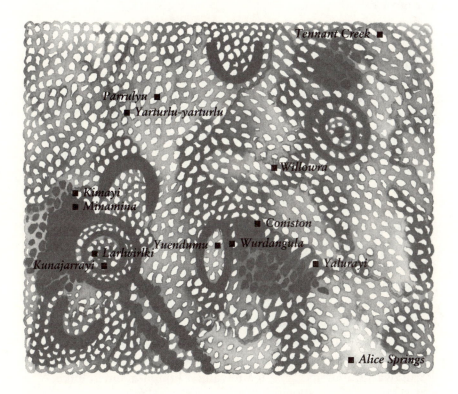

Yangka jarlupardu yanu. Yangkajurlupa yanu, round kuja. Kujarlupa yirrarnu Warnukurdupaturla, Toyota nyampu. Yirrarnurlupa. Ngulajangka, kangurnanyarra, kankarlarrarnanyarra kangu pirlikirra. Ngarrurnurnanyarra karntakurlangungarna yirdiyiwana. Yanurlupa, wari-yanu kankarlarra pirlikirra. Ngulajangkaju, show-manurnangku ngulaku warnangku warirninja-yanu, kujarlu kankarlarra.

Nyangunkulu. Kaninjarrarlalpa jitija muljukurra. Pirnkingkarlipa ngapa nyangu. Show-manurnanyarra pirnki, ngapa. Kankarlujuku ka nguna ngapaju. Wita ka karli kaninjarra – pirnki – wurnturu. Well ka kankarlujuku nyina ngapa yaliji – mulju.

Ngulajangkaju, turnu-jarrijalu yapa. Yamakarili turnu-jarrija. Nyangulupalangu kulukurralku warnajarra. Ngulapalanyanu, warurnulpalanyanu, you know, warirninja-yanulpalanyanu. Warurnulpalanyanu. Kuja jinta, kuja jintalpa kakardaju karrija. Warna, nganayi warna, nyanungu warna, warnayarra wirijarlu, warnayarra.

Ngulangka kuja yaninja-yanulku Ngardilypakaju yirdi nyangurra yatijarra. Well, nguruyu Kunajarrayiwardingki wina-jarrija, wina-jarrija. Well, he's the big winner.

All right. Yali ngajarri, yali ngajarri jingi-jingi yanu. Pinjarla yilyaja. Jingi-jingi yanu, nganayikirra Yarturlu-yarturlukurra yanu. Ngulangka early-pala warlu yungkurnu kulukungarntirli. Karrijalpa warlungka. You know, well, here kujakarlipa daylight here, early, early-lki. Ngulapiya yarrpurnu warlu, kulungku that one, kulungku.

Kuja wangkajalu, "Kuluku yakarra-pardija, kulukujaku yakarra-pardija! Kulungkangku nyanyi, ngulangku kurlarningirli kapungku pinyi."

Well-lpalurla lutu panturnu. Panturnulpalurlaja purlkapardu yaliwardingkikiji, Lajamanuwardingkikiji. Not Lajamanu, nganayi Yarturlu-yarturlujangka. Ngulangkalpalu nyinaja.

"Kutu kangku jangkardu karri wara-wararla ngula kurlarni. Yakarra nyinaya! Kapunparla nyanyi, yarnka, kulu."

Ngulajangkajulu jangkardu yakarra pardija. Ngulawarnujulunyanu maparnu, mawunturlunyanu maparnu, ngalya and karntawarrarlu. Nyampurla nyampungurlu karntawarralu-jarrija. Well-lpalunyanu, "Jujupa-manu kululku."

At this time, all the people met together. They were all sitting together in the shade. They saw the two snakes in the middle. The two snakes at this stage in the fight were engaged in tying themselves up. They thrashed about tying themselves up. They tied themselves up in knots. One of them managed to get on the back of the other snake's neck. That one was a very big snake, a rainbow serpent, a very large rainbow serpent.

After this, that snake went to a place called Ngardilypaka. From there he looked north. The snake belonging to Kunajarrayi won the fight. He is the big winner.

Now, the snake who was a stranger, the stranger, left immediately. Having beaten him, the other sent him packing. He left at once and went straight to Yarturlu-yarturlu. At the place of the fight, he had lit a fire very early, ready for battle. He stood there beside the fire. You know how it is when we get up very early and it is just light. It was at this time that he built the fire, in great anger.

Thus they spoke, "He has woken up in order to fight, he has woken up ready to fight. He is looking at you in rage, and he is about to attack you from just there to the south."

Then they took the lice out of their hair, they took the lice out of the hair of the old men, the people from Lajamanu, no, not Lajamanu, from Yarturlu-yarturlu. They remained where they were.

"He is coming toward you. Look how terrifying he is. He is coming from just over there, from the south. Sit up, wake up! When he sees you he will come over here to fight."

Then they woke up and made themselves ready for battle. They rubbed themselves with white clay, including their foreheads, and also with yellow ochre. Because of the circumstances they painted themselves all yellow. They said to themselves, "The fight is beginning!"

They fought.

Then they spoke among themselves and said, "Sit down! Sit down, you two old men, for your own sakes, you two sit down. Sit down without fighting, sit down without fighting! Fathers of many sons, old men whose children are many, sit down, sit down, sit down!"

Now, many others went on fighting.

One of them began to give way. The other attacked him directly and pushed him down. Having been attacked again, the one from

Kululkulpalunyanu pungu.

Now-lpalunyanu, well-lpalu wangkaja, "Aaa, nyinayapala,
nyinayapala purlkajarra, wiyarrpajarrapala nyinaya! Kuluwangupala
nyinaya, kuluwangupala nyinaya. Kajakungarduyu panu, purlka
nyampuku kurduku lirri-nyina panu waja! Nyinayapala!
Nyinayapala! Nyinayapala!"

No. Pungulpalunyanu wurrangkuju panukari.

Ngulajangkaju, yukaja jintaju. Jingi-jingikari pinjarla yirrarnurra.
Pardija yaliwardingki, Yarturlu-yarturluwardingki, yardarra pungu.
Wina-jarrija yardaju wurrajuku jintajuku Kunajarrayiwardingki.

Ngulajangkaji yanu Parrulyukurra. Parrulyukurra yanu yatijarra,
Parrulyukurra yanu. Yali, jintakarijala. Parrulyukurra yanu.
Nyinajarra. Parntirri-nyangu, ngapa parntirri-nyangu ngurra, ngulya.

Yanu-uu, Mount Theo-kurra yanu Purturlukurra – kakarrara –
jingi-jingi. Ngulajangkaju, yukaja kaninjarra, ngulyangkaju yukaja.
Yanurnu kanunjumparra. Still, yalumpu ka nyina. Pina wilypi-pardija
yangka yalumpuyijala. Still there ka nyina.

Ngulakurra pinarni yanu, ngulakurra warlaljawarnu
nyanungunyangukurra. Kanunjumparralku yukaja ngulyangka.
Yanurnu. Wilypi-pardija.

Ngulajangkaju, yingalpalu wirntija. Wirntijalpalu kurdijirla, the
young men's time. Well-lijana pakarnu. Wati-manulpalujana.
Pakarnulu. Wirntija. Wirntija. Wirntija. Wirntija. Wirntijalu,
wirntijalu.

Kujalu jukurrpanyanu karntaju yanu nyampu kakarrara.
Kakarraralu yanu nganayikirra Yarlarnkirri-kirra wurnturu.
Nganayiwardingkipatulu yanu: Kimayi, Kimayiwardingki and Mina-
minawardingki. Mina-minawardingkili yanu, karnta. Every place-
ngirlili yanu ngayi, panungurlulu ngari – yuwayi, ngayi kirrikaringirli,
kirrikaringirli – yanulu.

Ngulajangkalu yanu kakarrara. Yanulu, yanulu kakarrara. Yanulu
yatuju, kurlarninyarra kulkurrujarra. Kulkurrujarrajukulu yanu.
Nyampulu yanu Yurntumurla jingi-jingi and Kakutuwana.
Kakutujangkaju, Coniston-kirralu yanu – kakarrara.

Ngulajangkajulu come out-jarrija Yalurayirla. Yalurayirla
panukari kamparruju. Jintakariji nganayiwanalu come out-jarrija.
Every way-li yanu, kuja, line up – maturnu. Nganayikirra

Yarturlu-yarturlu left. Again, the one from Kunajarrayi was the winner.

From there he went to Parrulyu, straight to the east. Then he went down underground, into a hole. He came back this way under the ground. He is still there. He came back out there, and he is still there. Then he went back to where his family is, to his own country. He had gone down into a hole. He came this way. He came out.

Later they danced. They danced for the kurdiji [initiation ceremony], in the young men's time. Then they initiated them. They made them into men. They initiated them. They danced and danced.

At this point, the women went to the east, following their own dreaming. They went east to Yarlarnkirri, some distance away. The women who travelled were from Kimayi, from Kimayi and Mina-mina. The people from Mina-mina travelled, women. They came from everywhere, and many, many women travelled with them. They journeyed from many different places. They went east. They journeyed on, always to the east. Then they travelled into the north, and then into the south, on this long journey. After that they passed through the places in the centre. They went straight to Yuendumu, and on past Kakatu. From Kakatu they went on to Coniston, in the east.

Then they appeared at Yalurayi. Many others had gone to Yalurayi before them. They also appeared at other places. They travelled in every direction, moving along in a long line, one behind the other. They went to Yarluyampu. From Yarluyampu they went to where? Where have I forgotten? They went to Yamakungku. At Yamakungku they sat down. They stopped there. Then they went to Yakurranji. At Yakurranji they climbed straight down into the river bed, into the bed of a very large river.

They journeyed on. They climbed up to Waranpi. They came to Waranpi. They came to this important place and stayed there. They walked, in a long line, one behind the other. Many women in this way walked along together. They journeyed long distances. They travelled this way to Waranpi, and from Waranpi they returned home. For a long time at Yarlarnkirri they went underground. There they went in. They travelled, they rested. They stayed in some places for a long time.

Then they all went down into a hole. They went in. There they became monsters, and evil spirits, down there, under the ground. The

Yarluyumpukurra, Yarluyumpukurralu yanu. Ngulajangkajulu yanu
Yarluyumpujangkaju nganayikirra, nyiyakurralu mayirna waja-
waja-manu? Yamakungkukurra. Yamakungkukurralu yanu.
Yamakungkurlalu nyinajarra. Karrijarralu. Yanulu Yakuranjirla.
Jingi-jingili jitijarra Yakuranjirla, karrungka, wulpayi wirijarlu,
wirijarlurla karrungka. Jitijalu.

Yanulu. Yanurralu, warrkarnulu Waranpiyirla. Waranpiyikirralu
yanu. Really japiyakurra, really japiyarlalu nyinaja. Ngarili wapaja,
line up – maturnu. Ngarilpalu wapaja yuurrku-yuurrku. Ngarilpalu
wapaja wurnturu. Ngulajulu yanu, yanulu nganayirla,
Waranpiyijangkajulu yanu nganayikirra, ngurrakurrajulu yanu.
Tarnngalkujulu yukaja Yarlarnkirrirlalku. Ngulakurralu yukaja.
Yanulu, nyinajalpalu. Tarnngalkulu nyinaja. Nyinaja.

Ngulangkajulu muku yukaja ngulyangka kaninjarra. Mukulu
yukaja. Nganayi pangkarlangu-jarrijalkulu, kinki-jarrijalkulu muku
kaninjarra. Mardukuja kaninjarra, yukajalu, yukajalu. Ngulajuku.

Yalumpuju jintakariji, jintakariji yanu jaljakurra. Milya-pinyi
kanpa Wakurlpu? Ngula. Yanu Wurdanykurla, yirdi Wurdanykurla.
Yuwa, Jungarrayipardu, Jungarrayi. Yanu, yalumpungurlujuku yanu
Kunajarrayingirli. Yanu. Come out-jarrija-aa nganayiwana,
Yarrungkanyiwana yanu kulkurrujarra. Mount Doreen-wana,
Mount Doreen-wana yanu kanunjumparra. Yanu, ngunaja.

Well, purda-nyangujana karntapatu.

"Karnta panu kalu lirri-nyinaja!"

Manyungkalpalu wirntija, manyungka you know,
manyungkalpalu wirntija. Well-ilpalu wirntija. Well-i, purda-
nyangujana nyanungurluju purlkapardurlu, purda-nyangujana.
Yura-kangujana. Yanu. Yura-kangujana. Yanu. Yuwurrkuwanalpa
yaninja-yanu, watiya nyampupiyarlalpa yatijarra, karnardi. Kujalpa
yanurra. Yalipiya kanjayirlalpa wilypi-pardija. Watiyakarirlalpa
wilypi-pardija. Watiyakarikirralpa yanu. Nyangulku. Well, well,
juta-yungu karlangurlu, kurupapiyarlu, yangka karlangurlu kujarlu.
Ngarntu.

"Ayi!" karntangku jintangku pupu-jurrurnu, "Nyiya mirnimpiji,
ayi?"

"Ngarntu ka pupu-wangka. Kankarlu. Pingkangku!"

"Yii!"

women went in, under the ground. And that was the end of that.

Then another one, the snake, travelled into the centre. Do you know Wakurlpu? There. He went there, to Wurdangula, to a place called Wurdangula. Jungarrayi, little Jungarrayi. He had travelled from just over there, from Kunajarrayi. He went. He appeared near, where was that, near Yarrungkanyi. He travelled through the middle past Mount Doreen, underground. After arriving there, he lay down.

He heard women. "I say, there are lots of women here together!"

They were dancing, just for fun, for their own enjoyment. They were dancing. He heard them, that old man heard them. He began trying to creep up on them. He went along in thick bush, in trees like those around here, trees standing in straight lines. He travelled along in this peculiar way. He came out eventually about as far away as that tree over there. He emerged among the other trees. He sneaked from one tree to another. He watched them. They were dancing, with digging sticks, like kurupa, that is with digging sticks, they were following the cracks above the yams.

"Hey!" One woman felt something underneath the ground. "What's that just here?"

"Something is down there in the crack. It is coming up. Slowly."

"Yii!"

"Yes, it is soft, really soft!"

"I say, this one is just like a prick, just exactly the same!"

Larlwirlki, at that place, at Larlwirlki, that is what I call that place, Larlwirlki, Larlwirlki, well, there he had raped that woman, against her will at Larlwirlki, at the cave you have seen. That is the name of the place, Larlwirlki. There is water there, a rockhole and a soak.

Well, he inserted himself down along under the ground, he pushed himself down under the ground. He inserted his big prick, as big as that of a horse, or like that tree over there. He went under the ground, where the yam cracks were, as far away as that tree standing over there. Then it came up, wriggling.

Well, the women were now digging under the cracks for yams, like they had been doing in the dancing. They were pushing their digging sticks down into the cracks to see if they could find anything. But now, they were using their real digging sticks, ones they had made really sharp. They had these sharp digging sticks.

"Yuwa, yuwa, kapu runyu-mani, runyu-mani waja nyampuju!"
"Kala ngirntingkiji nyampupiyayijala, same one, yalumpu kuja!"
Larlwirlki nganayirla, Larlwirlki yangkaju karnarla warrirni,
Larlwirlki, Larlwirlki. Ngula larlwirl-mularnu yalumpu now
Larlwirlki, that one, pirnki you been look. Yuwayi. That's the name,
yirdiji, Larlwirlki. Ngapa there kuja, warnirri, mulju. All right.

Ngulapiya, walili yangkaju yurrpurnu kanunjumparra walyawana,
kanunjumparra yurrpurnu. Yuwayi, nantuwupiyarlu. Ngirnti
wirijarlurlu yurrpurnu. Nyampu, not nyampurrapiya, nyampupiya,
nyampu kuja karrinya watiya.

Well, yukaja kanunjumparra-aa. Kuja yalipiya-kanjayi – ngarntu-
yirrarnu. Yinya watiya karrinyampa, pupu-yirrarnu. Kankarlu julyal-
yirrarnu. Well ngarilpalu wirntinjangurluju yangka kujalpalu
wirntija, ngarilpalu ngarntu-jurrurnu. Pupu-pupu-jurrurnulpalu,
well. All right. Nganayilkili manu, karlangulu jampalypa-pungu, yiri.
Manulu karlangu.

Well, jungajukulu yangkaju panturnu kujarlu.
"Ngayirlipa pantirni, waja! Nyampurla marda ka pupu-wangka.
Nyampurla marda ka nguna waja nyampu yiwirri kuja pungu."

Well-li panturnu purturlu. Finish. Tarnngalkulu panturnu. Yuwayi.
Nganayirlaju yangka nganayi, Larlwirlkirla, yatijarnipirdinypa.
Ngulangka, now. Well, yaliji, yalijana jijaja nyampungurluju
tarnngalku. Yuw, ngulajangka, now, yalumpujangka. Yuwa, yuwaw,
tarnngangkulu panturnu. Yuwaw. Ngayiji, Jungarrayimanjili yangka
jamirdimirda. Yuwayi.

Ngulajuku. Ngulajuku witajukurna finish-manu.

Recorded at Kurntarnu, 19 September, 1990

146

Well, in fact, they stabbed him with those digging sticks.

"We are stabbing something. There is something that I can feel down here. There is something that has been killed down here under this crack." They had stabbed him in the back. He was dead. They had stabbed him to death. It happened at a place some distance north of Larlwirlki. That was the last time that he travelled away from here, the last time. They stabbed him to death, Jungarrayi, that one, your grandfather.

That is the end. I have told you a little story. Finish.

TRANSLATORS' NOTE

Tiger Japaljarri's account of the dreaming of the two snakes is also an account of another very important Warlpiri jukurrpa, that of the women. The two narratives are inseparable. Since the snakes clearly symbolize the masculine, the fact that these two jukurrpa cannot be separated, while at the same time they are two distinct jukurrpa with different owners and different key locations, may reflect the fact that the lives of men and women in Warlpiri society, although inseparable, often continue with quite different activities in different locations.

This pattern of connection and opposition underpins the narrative. The men's battle is followed by the initiation ceremony, which, although it seems to be another very masculine affair, has women as some of the crucial functionaries. The narrator's attention then switches to the women, the most numerous and impressive group in perhaps any Warlpiri story.

It is unusual to find an encounter between men and women in Warlpiri narratives which ends to the advantage of women, as happens here. However, the field of activity is sexual, rather than territorial or ceremonial; the time-honoured practice around the world of using comedy to confront male fear of female sexuality and power finds its place in Japaljarri's gallant and witty salute to the women's dominion.

The jukurrpa of the women is, of course, a very popular subject in painting and dance for those women to whom it belongs.

WAWARLJAKURLU

The Man From Wawarlja

TOLD BY

Peggy Rockman Napaljarri

Jungarrayi kala nyinaja panujarlukurlu karntakurlu – yirdingkaju
Wawarljarlaju. Kala nyinaja. Panujarlu karntaju kalajana
mardarnu warrura, nyiyakantikanti, Napangardi, Napaljarri,
Nangala, Nungarrayi, Napanangka, Nampijinpa,
nyanunguparntawati. Warrurarlu Jungarrayirli.

Kalalurla kurdu yimi-ngarrurnu Jungarrayiki, "Nyampuju karnta
kurduju palka-jarrija karlarra jilimirla."

Wangkaja kala Jungarrayiji, "Walyalujana tirnngi-yirraka!" Kala
wangkaja Jungarrayi, "Mardakalujana yarnarntiki ngurrju.
Mardakalujana yarnarntiki jinyjinypaku."

"Yuwa!" Kalalu mardarnu karntaju.

Ngulajangkaju, kala palka-jarrija jintakarilki kurduju – wirriyalku.
Kalalu yanurni. Yimi ngarrurnu kalalurla. Mungangka kala palka-
jarrija. Kalalurla yimi ngarrurnu ngurrakurra nyanungunyangukurra.
"Jungarrayi, kurduju ka ngunami wita, wirriya waja kuyujardungu."

Kala Jungarrayiji wangkaja, "Walyalujala tirnngi-yirrakarra!
Ngampurrpawangu karna nyina wirriyakuju." Kalalu junga-pakarnu
kurduju. Kalalu milyingka-yirrarnu kurduju witaju pirltirrka.

Kala yanu wirlinyi, kala pungu warru kuyu nyanungurluju.
Kangurni kala panujarlu. Kalajana yungu. Kala ngampurrpa nyinaja
karntamipaku nyanunguku kurdukuju.

Ngulajangkaju kalalu wangkaja karntapatuju, "Yuu, wiyarrpa
karlipajana pakarni wirriya-wirriyaju.
Mardakarlarlangulparlipajana kurduju."

Ngurdin-purda-nyangulpalu nyanungurluju karntapaturluju.

Jirramalkurla kurdujarrapala palka-jarrija wirriyajarra. Kulalurla
yimi-ngarrurnu Jungarrayiki, walku. Mardarnulpalupalangu.

"Kanyirlipapalangu wurnturu. Mardarnirlipapalangu."

Mardarnulupalangu. Kujarningintirlilkilipalangu kangu, jilja
kujarningintikirra. Kalalupalangu ngapurlu yungu. Kalalupalangu
ngurrangka mardarnu yalirlajuku. Kalapala nyinajayi witajarrawiyi-
ii. Wirijarlu-jarrijalkupala. Kalapala manyu-karrija,
nyanungukarijarralku yirakarilki. Kalalupalangu ngatinyanurlu kuyu
manu mangarri yungu manu ngapa. Kalapala nyinaja Wawarljarla
nyanungu yamangkaju ngurrangkaju.

Ngulajangkaju, nyanungujarrarlupala purda-nyangu
kurdujarrarlu wirijarlujarrarlulku, "Yanirli!"

At a place called Wawarlja, there lived a Jungarrayi man with many women. Many women lived with him at that place. He had wives of all the wrong skins, all sorts, Napangardi, Napaljarri, Nangala, Nungarrayi, Napanangka, Nampijinpa. He was married to them all. That Jungarrayi took the wrong women as wives.

When a child was born, they would go to Jungarrayi and tell him, "This woman has given birth to a child in the women's camp in the west."

Jungarrayi said, "Bury them!" He used to say, "Keep the girls, look after them. Work hard and look after the little girls."

"Yes." They kept the girls.

Then another boy was born. They came to him, and told him about the baby boy. He had been born at night. They came to him in his camp and told him, "Jungarrayi, there is a new-born child, a little boy, a future man."

And Jungarrayi said, "You all go and bury him in the ground. I don't want any boys." So they hit the child and killed it. Then they buried the tiny body in the ground.

The man used to go hunting, and catch animals to eat in the country all around. He brought plenty of meat back with him. He gave it to the women. But he only wanted girl children. Then all his wives said to him, "We find that having to kill these boy children is making us very upset. Let us keep all the children."

His wives thought the matter over at length. Two boys were born. They said nothing to Jungarrayi about this. They looked after the two of them. They kept them both. "Let us take these two a long way away. We will look after them there."

They kept them and carried them off to the other side of a big sand-hill, out of sight. There they gave them milk. They looked after them in that camp over on the other side. While they were small those two children lived there.

They grew very big. They used to play with each other. Their mothers gave them meat, vegetable food and water. The two boys lived there, with their own bough shelter in their own camp near Wawarlja.

Eventually, the two boys discussed their situation and that of their father. They came to an understanding.

"Yanta kakarrara wapirrakurla yanta jintakariki Munkupalpaku –
Jungarrayiki jintakariki."

Yanurla kakarrara. Yimi-ngarrurnurla, "Wapirra, kapu nganta
puntarni nganta ngapujunyanuwatiji. Nyampurluju karlarrarlu
pinjarla kapungku luwarni waja."

Kulanganta junga, kala walku. Ngayipala nyanungurlu ngurrju-
manu yimi. Kujalpa nyanungu nyinaja ngampurrpawangu wirriyaku
mardarninjaku, ngula-panurlapalarla jangkardu purda-nyangu
kurdujarrarlu.

Jungajuku parnkanjarla yanu maninjarla karliwatikirli
panujarlukurlu karlikirli, kurlardakurlu. Yaninja-yanupala.
Kirdarlangupala yaninja-yanu. Pirri-manu.

Jungarrayi jintakari yanu wirlinyi kuyuku, pupulpa nganta.
Luwarnu warru. Kunalkulparla manu watiyarla yarunparla.

Nyanungu kurdu parnkaja jingi-jingi ngurrakurra
yarlpurrunyanukurra.

Nyanunguju, kunalkulparla manu, kuyu watikiji malaku.
Manulparla. Yanurni. Wurru-kangurla that Jungarrayi jintakariji.
Wurru-kangulparla. Nyangu. Ngulajangkaju kutulkulpa karrija.
Waku-karrija. Wakurlingki-karrijalkulpa karlikirliji.

Yalirli jintakarirliji nyangulpanyanu malurnpa, nyangunyanu
yama, shadow. Yamanyanu nyangu. Wangkaja Jungarrayiji," Yii-ii,
nyampu karna nyina ngajuju." Yurirrijalpa. "Nyampu karna nyinami
ngajuju. Kala nganangku kaju nyampuju wurru-mardarni?"

Ngayi, puljantarrarlu luwarnu boomerang, karlingki
jintangkujuku. Muku wantija yirlaraju wurnturu-wurnturu,
jurrupinki, nyiyakantikanti, warri-warripinki! Karrijalpa wurrajuku
jintakari Jungarrayi luwarninjarla.

Nyanunguju, nyuyu-nyuyu-manunyanu. Yangkapiyalkujala
kulpari nyinaja. Karli manu nyanungurluju. Tarnnga luwarnu
nganayiji Munkurrpalpa. Wantija wurnturu-wurnturu yirlara manu
palka yapa. And purturlu wantija kakarrara nganayikirra,
Jarrardajarrayikirra, Yinapalkukurra. Wantija purturluju.

Ngulaju kapu nganimpanyangu karriyarla, ngulaju
nganimpanyangu. Jungarrayijarrarlupalanyanu luwarnu. Well
walku. Japanangkaku manu Japangardiki kajana karrimi wurruru-
side yaliji – Yurntumurla yatijarrapurda – wurnturunyayirni.

"Let's go!"

"You go east, to see our other father, our father's brother, go and see that other Jungarrayi, the one called Munkupalpa."

One of them went east to see him. He told him a story about something that was about to happen: "Father, I believe that other one is about to try to take all your wives away from you. That one who lives in the east is about to attack you and try to kill you."

He believed him, but it was not true. The two boys had made the story up. While their father had been living there, killing all his sons, the two boys had thought things over for a long time, planning their revenge.

So then the other Jungarrayi, Munkupalpa, having run and collected all his weapons, many boomerangs and spears, set out. The two departed together, Jungarrayi and Japaljarri, they went along together. Together they sat and rested.

The other Jungarrayi, the man from Wawarlja, was out hunting for meat. This was in the dry season. He speared various things. Near a big tree, a yarunpa tree, he sat and cleaned the carcasses.

Meanwhile the boy had run straight back to where his brother was at their camp.

The man continued to gut the animals. The meat was that of the hare wallaby. He was sitting cleaning the meat. The other man approached. He came very quietly creeping up to where the man with the meat was sitting, the other Jungarrayi. He watched him. He came closer. He raised his hand with the boomerang, ready to throw. He stood with the boomerang ready to throw.

The man sitting near the tree saw a shadow. He was also able to see his own shadow. He said, "But I am sitting here!" He moved. "I am sitting here. But who is standing behind me?"

Then the man with the boomerang threw it, with terrible force, smashing it to pieces over the other man's head. Bits of his body flew all over the place, pieces of his head, of his genitals, of his arms and legs. Having thrown the boomerang, the other Jungarrayi, Munkupalpa, still stood there, behind where he had been sitting.

But the man who had been sitting near the tree put himself back together again. He restored himself to his original shape. He got his own boomerang. He killed the man from Munkupalpa. Now, pieces of the body and limbs of that man fell some distance away. His back

Ngulajangkaju yarnkaja that Jungarrayi, yarnkaja pina.
Warlarnuwiyi walkulkulpa kiripa-kanja-yanulku, matalku. Yukaja
yaninjarla. Nyangulpalu Nangalapaturlu nyiyakanti-kantirli ngayi
panujarlurlu yapangku. Yarnkajarni. Yanu wurnalku. Yarnkaja.
Kulkurru ngunajarni ngurrangka.

Wangkajajana Nangala yapakuju karntapatuku
nyanungukupurdangkawatiki warrurawatirlanguku, "Ngapalu
maninjingkaw!"

Ngulakarla karrimirni wala marnikijiji Wawarljakuju. Kulpari
yanulpalu, kulpari yanulpalu. Manunjunulpalurla ngapa.

Ngulajukulpa yaninja-yanu-uu. Nyanja-yanulpa maarr-
maninjakurra wurnturu kulkurru-kulkurru. Yanurni. Ngunaja.
Puyungkalku ngunajarni. Ngulangurlujana karntapatu yilyaja,
"Yantalu. Ngapalu kardirninjingka!"

Yilyajarralujana yalikarilki. Yaninja-yanulpa. Ngulajangkaju yanu
mungalyurru. Yilyajajana, "Ngapa kardirninjingka!"

"Yanirlipa! Ngapalu kardirninjingka nyurrularlulku!"
Walkujangkalu wangkajalparla karntapatukariji.
Kulungkulkulunyanu pakarnu. Ngulaju nganayirla ngapangkaju
yirdingkajunyanu pakarnu Jirda-jirdalparla. Pakarnulunyanu.
Ngulajangkaju yanurnili. Kurrangkalku Mata-jarrijalku. Jungarrayiji
ngunajalpa tarnnga. Ngunaja, ngunaja, ngunaja.

Pardijarlajinta Kurralku, ngayilpa wilaly-pungu Kurraju –
punkunyayirni. Yirrilji-kanja-yanulku. Karrinja-pardija.
Yarnkajarni. Yanurni. Kulkurru ngunajarni yapurnurla yirdingkaju
Kuturdawurnurla.

Ngulajangkaju pardijarni. Warlurla wantija yirnti ngijijangka.
Papijarralku warluju karlumpayi Warlukurlangukungarnti.
Nyanungu yarnkajarni. Yanu. Nyinajarni marrangki – yamangka
kankarlarni. Jururrku jintapardu pardijarni. Ngulajangka
Nganyanyirla. Nganyanyijangka yanurnu. Ngunaja. Yanurnu.
Kulkurru ngunaja Warranparla, ngunaja marlurirla. Kutulkulpa
nyangu maarr-maninjakurraju ngapaju.

Kujakarlipa yangka yapangku nyanja-yani ngapa maarr-
maninjakurra. Ngulaju kutulku. Kulanganta yarlungka maarr-manu.
Kala kanunju nyampuju pirnkingka. Ngulajangkaju,
karntapaturlulpanyanu narri-pungu. Ngapa jirrajalu.

landed a very long way away, at Jarrardajarrayi and Yinapalku. For this reason, these two places ought to belong to us as well. Those two Jungarrayi men struck each other terrible blows. But no, it belongs to Japanangka and Napangardi, the people who are in-laws to us. The place is over there to the north of Yuendumu, a long distance away.

The Jungarrayi from Wawarlja returned to his own home. At first he was walking, but then he became so tired he could only crawl along the ground. He managed to get to his camp, and went inside. All the Nangala women and the other women looked at him. He went away again, he went away and stayed away. He slept in another place.

One Nangala took charge, saying to the women, to her own sisters and to all the other women of the wrong skins, "Go and get water!"

Now there is a big marnikiji bush growing right near the Wawarlja waterhole. The women returned to the waterhole. Again, they had to go back to the waterhole.

The man continued his journey. He saw lightning in the distance, over near the centre. He came this way. He slept. He slept at Puyu.

Then the woman sent the other women out again.

"Go and get water!"

"No, we are going somewhere else. It is your turn to get water." These women told the other women they would not do it, and it was their turn. They grew angry and began to fight. They began to hit each other. This fight happened near the waterhole called Jirda-jirda. They beat each other. Then they went to Kurra, where Jungarrayi was lying, exhausted and ill.

He lay there at Kurra, and had been there for a long time. He slept and slept. There his boils had burst. The pus was seeping from all his unhealed wounds. He was covered in disgusting boils. He had been so ill he could only crawl. Later he was able to stand up again.

Jungarrayi and the women set off. They travelled this way. On the way they stayed by a pond called Kuturdawurnu. Then they left there. Flames and sparks flew from their firesticks. This started a fire which burnt a long way towards the south, where it stayed and met up with the fire dreaming.

They travelled on, they went on. They sat down in the shade of a desert walnut tree up on a sand-hill. There was just one growing there. Then they went on to Nganyanyi. They came this way from there,

Nyangujana. Pukurdilkinyanu warurnu. Pukurdinyanu rurruny-
pungu Jungarrayirliji.

Yarnkajarni. Rdipijajana ngatijirriki panujarluku. Waja-
wajakurrajana rdipija. Ngulajangkaju, yanurni. Yanu. Nyinaja
kulkurru. Ngurrangka ngunajarni. Kutulkulpa nyangu maarr-
maninjakurra. Ngulajangkaju pardijarni. Karrija watiya walakarri.
Palkajuku marnikijiwati. Parnkajarni-uu.

Wangkajalpalu yapakariwati Ngardikirliwati, "Malingka,
malingka, malingka!"

"Kujawiyi ngulaju malirdinyanu mardawangu. Ngajupirdinypa
yanirra. Purraku-jirraja."

Kankarlarra warrkarnu. Rarrja-rarrja-pangurnu. Kaninjarralku
pangurnurra. Tarnngajukulparla yaralyu-ngarnu. Pangurnu manu
yapa Jungarrayi. And karntapatulurla yarralparni-yukaja.
Ngulajuku.

Ngulajukurna Jungarrayi yirri-puraja nyampuju. Jarnamirla
yukaja pangirninjarla. Kulpari ngunamirra ka kujapurdayijala
Wawarljakurra.

Ngulajukurna wangkaja.

Recorded at Lajamanu, 5 March, 1990

from Nganyanyi. They slept, they travelled. On the way they slept at Warranpa, they stayed there beside the swamp. They saw lightning and rain close by. This is the way we Warlpiri people watch out for rain falling while lightning strikes when we are travelling, in order to follow it and find water.

They were under the impression the lightning was striking in the open air, but really it was striking down inside a cave. Then the women, his wives, put earth on themselves to make themselves cool. They did this because they were very thirsty.

He saw the rain. He tied up his hair. Then he pulled all his hair down again, to celebrate the rain. They set off towards it. On the way they met large numbers of budgerigars. They came upon them as they were performing the Waja-waja ceremony. Then they travelled towards here. They went on. They sat down and rested during the journey. They slept one night. They saw the lightning coming closer. Then they set off. There was a tree standing there, a supple jack. There were also ripe marnikiji. They ran towards them.

Then the other people spoke, the Ngardi speakers, "Keep away! Mothers-in-law, mothers-in-law, mothers-in-law! Here, here, here!"

"I am sure there are no mothers-in-law here. Certainly I am going over there to the water. I am very thirsty."

They climbed up the hill. They dug down under all the rocks. They dug right down inside. Then he slipped right underneath forever, the man Jungarrayi and the scoop he had been using to dig. All the women also went in there together. That was all.

So now I come to the end of the story about Jungarrayi. After digging there, he went in, at the Tanami rockhole. His body stretches under the ground from there to Wawarlja.

And that is all I have to say.

TRANSLATORS' NOTE

This jukurrpa story of the man Jungarrayi from a place called Wawarlja concerns a man who collected a large number of wives regardless of their kinship affiliations, a practice locally described in English as "marrying people of the wrong skin". For Warlpiri people, for whom the kinship or skin system is pivotal in both social arrangements and in the relationships of people to the land, such breaches of marriage law are particularly serious.

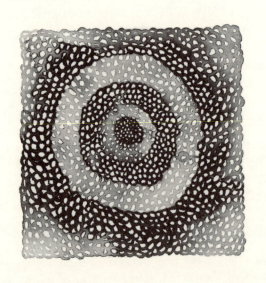

Moreover, when children are born to his wives, this Jungarrayi has the male children killed. And, as in other myths which concern the systematic killing of male children, some children escape; two mothers take their sons away and bring them up in secret. These two sons, who take revenge on their father in this story, become the culture heroes of a whole cycle of myths concerning the Two Men. They make their appearance in the east in Jimmy Jungarrayi's account of the ngatijirri (budgerigar) dreaming at Patilirri (see pp.93–103). There is also a major sequence concerning the Two Men centred around a place called Yakayaka, country belonging to the Ngardi people to the west of Warlpiri country, which includes such typical culture hero activities as teaching people to use fire and cook their food.

YURRKURUKURLU

The Events at Yurrkuru

TOLD BY

D. M. Jakamarra

Ngulapalangu warrkiki mardarnu, warrkilparla karrija — nganayiki kawartawaraku — yilpa maninja-parnkaja, well-i jintalpa yalumpu mardarnu Keeper marda-wu — nganayiji jawirrirli mardarnu ngulaju old man nganimpaku-palangu-again Panjiji Jampijinpa, ngula mardarnu Coniston-rlaju.

Well-i, nyampu, yalumpujulpa mardarnu keeper — yangka nyampurlu — pirilyiji. Yilparla maninja-parnkaja kawartawara, you know, wirlinyirli yangka, yilparla maninja-parnkaja. Ngunaja, ngunaja, ngunaja, ngunaja, yilpala ngunaja, nyanungu-jarraju. Yirdija nyampu-wardingki-jarra kala-pala wapaja old man-jarraju. Kalalu every way through-jarrija nyampuwana. Kala nyinajayi. Right. Nyangulkupala nyanungu. Kulanganta ngurrjulku. Yilparangulkupalanyanurla janyungukujala ngulaju — janyunguku, tobacco-ku.

Jungajuku. Yanupala. Kalapala keep going-yanu. Miyi, miyikila kalapalangu murntu, no flour, ngayi, murntu kalajana yungu — murntu. Wurrangkuwiyijiki kalajana look out-i-manu, ngayi, jintaku-jintaku. Right. Tarnngalku, tarnngarra manulkupalangu ngapujunyanujurlajinta. Old man, Walypali-pakarnukuju, Japanangkapardu. Tarnngarra manulkurla jurnta, tarnngalkulpa jawirdiki mardarnurra.

Well, yangka nyanguparla, nyangu, nyangu, nyangu, nyangu.

"Nyarrpara, nyarrpara-jarrija yangkaju, ayi? Nyarrpara? Tarnngalku nyarrpara?"

Ngaka yangka kalalupalangu, kalalu wanti-wantinjinanu yangka kulkurrukarirlalku. Kalapala wapirrija. Ngakalku yangka kalapala wanti-wantinjinanu. Ngaka-kula rangkarrkurlu-rangkarrkurlurlangulku. Well, jawirdikijala yangka kalapalangu mardarnu. Walypali yalirliji kalapalangu mardarnu jawirdikijala.

"Might be walypalirlangurlu or yaparlangurlu? Kala yalumpuju Jakamarrarlu majuyijalaja. Ngula marda kalalujana jarnku-mardarnu?"

Jungajuku — nyinajalu, might be month-i marda or might be three months-i marda, might be two months-ili nyinaja. Warri-warri yalirla little bit, rdangkarrku-rdangkarrku pinarra yanu. Jawirdikilkijala yangkajulpa yali walypalirlilkilpa-jana mardarnu.

Nganimpajukurnalurla marlaja pimirdinaku — ngula.

He kept them there at work. They were both working with the camels, which they used to go out to round up. Well, he also had another worker called Keeper. He also kept there for a little while our father's brother-in-law, Jampijinpa, whom he kept at Coniston.

Well, that white man had those two working here together with the charcoal sometimes, while the other one went out to round up the camels, you know, went out for the day to collect them. For quite a while he slept there. They all slept there, including those two, my relatives, the two who came from this place. They used to walk around here, those two old men, in the old days. They all used to travel right through here. They all used to live around here. They used to send each other to get tobacco, tobacco.

True. They went, they kept on going. He did not give them uncooked food or flour, only food already cooked. For a long time he really looked after them, day by day. Right. But he took and kept their wives for very long periods of time. He killed the old man, the white fellow. He took Japanangka's wife away and he kept her for a long time. He did not bring the woman back.

Well they realized this, after a while they realized what was going on.

"Where, where has she got to, ayi? Where, where has she been all this time?"

Later those two, the aunt and her niece, came back to the two men very late, in the middle of the night. Later on they used to return even later, very late indeed. Later on, they would even come back just at sunrise. Well, he was keeping them for himself, and not letting them return to their husbands.

"Might it be a white man or an Aboriginal man? It might be that Jakamarra doing the wrong thing as well. Maybe they are both keeping our wives for themselves."

So they all stayed there maybe for one month or two months or three months. That lady used to come back just in the morning. The white man was keeping the women for himself. She was our aunt. He won her for himself for a long time.

The husband waited. The women used to give them their supper in the late afternoon. They gave them their tea and meat and then went

Tarnngakurla jurnta winirr-manu. Karnuru wait-i-jarrija.

"Ngayi yangka kalarla miyimipa yinjarra-yanu wurajingirlirli."

Tiyi, kuyu kalalurla yinjanurra. Yangka plate-iki nganta kala yanu.
Kala plate-iwangu yalikila tarnngajuku yanurra, ngurrakurralku.
Waku-mardarnu, waku-mardarnu, waku-mardarni-ii. Jiringi
yirrarnulkupalangu makurntarlangurlu.

"Ayi, ngakakarilki? Month-ikarirlalku?"

"Ayi, nyarrpangalpa nyampuju ngapujupurajingki jurnta tarnnga
manu?"

"Nyarrpa?" kujarlupalanyanu makurntarlangurlu,
makurntarlangurlu ngarrurnu, "Ayi, nyarrpa?"

Nyanungujulpa kirringka nyinaja nyampu nganayirla – kakarru
–Yanyurdurla, Yanyurdurla, kalkurni yangka nyampu kulkurru.
Ngulangkalpa nyinaja. Yanyurduwana nyiyarla mayi? Yirrimirnjirla.
Yirriminjirla kalkurnu. Yapajulpa nyinaja kirringkaju. Nyampuju
marnkurrpanyalpalu nyinaja. Now, yangka panukarilpalu, nyampu
kurlarra nyinaja, nyampu wurnturuwangu. Nyampurralpalu
marnkurrpa nyinaja, few nganta.

Jungajuku mungalyurru-jarrijalku. Yanulku. Wangkajalparla,
"Ayi, nyampurlungku ngari karnta puntarnu tarnngalku waja."

"Nyarrpa-jarrirli wajamirnirlangu?"

"Aaa, jalangurlu karli pinyi. Pinyi karli jalangurlu waja."

"Jungajuku, pinyi wajarli jalangurlu."

Jungajuku, wangkajapala. Wurajingirlipala wangkaja
nyinanjakarra.

"Ngariji karntaju puntarnu, jurnta-manu."

Jungajuku yanu. Well-i kawartawarakurra yanu maninjaku warru,
early, yapaju. Yuwayi. Maninjaku warrkirniji yanu. Manurla.
Nyanungukulpa nyinaja tarnngajuku yalumpurlajuku. Married-ilpa
ngunaja.

Right. Yangkajupala payilirlipala yarri yiri-manu kamparruwarnu,
aa, wurajingirlijiki, yapajarrarlu nyanungujarra makurntarlangurlu,
ngunyarripurajirli kapu warringiyipurajirli. Warlkurrupala yiri-manu
– payilirli. Ngulajangka sharp fellow, pakarnipiya, yiri-manupala.

Jungajuku rangkarr-ngarninja-yanulkulpa, little bit, rangkarr-
ngarninja-yanulku. Aaa, nyurrupala ready-jarrinjarlalku,
ngayilkilpapala ready nyangu. Ngurulpapalarla nyangu nyanungu

away. They said they were going back to wash the dishes, but back at his camp he did not have any dishes. They used to go back to the other camp for the whole night. He kept them there. He had taken them for himself.

The two men thought this over carefully.

"Well, what next? And what happens next month?"

"Ayi, why has he taken our wives away from us?"

"Why?"

This is what the two cousins discussed with each other.

"Ayi, what indeed is going on?"

The white man was camping in the creek to the east at Yanyurdu, that is at this place in the middle. The others were camping over there, near Yanyurdu, at, now, where, at Yirriminji. At Yirriminji on this side, other Aboriginal people were camped together. There were three people camping at this place. Many others were camped to the south, not far from here. Here three people were staying, only a few.

The next day dawned. One of them, Keeper, left for work. The two men talked together.

"This one has taken my woman for good."

"What are we two cousins going to do about it?"

"Well, now we'll kill him. We'll kill him now."

"Right, we'll kill him now."

This is what they said. They discussed it in the late afternoon while they were sitting in their camp.

"He really has stolen my woman and kept her."

Now, the other one had gone, the other Aboriginal man, Keeper, had gone to the camels, to round them up and bring them back. The other man, the white man, was still camped in the same place. He was sleeping with the woman, like a married couple.

Right. The two of them sharpened it with a file, beforehand in the late afternoon, ready to kill. The two Aboriginal men, the two cousins, your father-in-law and your grandfather. They sharpened the axe with a file. They sharpened it ready to strike.

Then, very early in the morning, before first light, just in the very early morning, ahh, they both got ready. They saw that each one was ready. They saw the morning star in the night sky. It was setting.

In the hot weather, the man and the woman used to sleep outside, outside the tent. They actually lived in a tent, as you could see from the

nganayiki mungaku parraku yanjilypiriki. Jungajuku kanunju-
jarrinja-yanu.

Nyanungujulkulpala ngunaja pardayirlaju yangka outside, tent-
iwangu, outside. Ngulaju tent-ingkapala, tent-ingka, pipangka yali
nganayirla – tent, tent-ngkajulpa live-jarrija. Well, outside
ngantalpapala ngunaja – might be.

Junga, jungajuku-uu nyanungupala yanurnu.

"Yanirli kuja-side. Nyurru wajarli pinyi ngayi. Nyanyirli married-
japa!"

Jungajukupala yanurnu warru. Kuja-aa, kujarnipala yanurnu.
Yangka, you know, married is wurnturu. Yanurnu, yanurnu,
yanurnu, yanurnu, yanurnu. Now!

"Nyampu kapala nguna!"

Karlarninginti yangka little bit wurnturu-manu. Kuwiiij!
Warlkurrurlu yangkangkujuku walyalku jingi-jingi panturnu
kulkurru. Yuwayi, that walypali pakarnu, government man-ilki
nyinaja, isn't it, government man. Yuwayi, government, government-
lpa nyinaja, yuwa. Finish.

Ngula nyanungu karlarningintipala marda kurlardarlu panturnu.

Well, yalumpurla warrkarnirra tarnngajuku Japanangkaju –
nyampurla pirlingka. Nyampu jintakari Japaljarri parnkaja yalikirra,
Mawukurra. Nyampu Mawu, yangkajala kujarlipa nyangurnu,
ngulangka pirlingka yalumpu kankarlarra. Wijirrkirla warrkarnu.
Warrkarnu. Yukaja.

Well-i, yalumpurla kalalu panukari nyinaja kurlarni, nyampurla
kalkurnu. Yalilpalu kurlarnipirdinypa panukari nyinaja.

Right. Yangkaju yapa yanurnu, yali kawartawarakurlu,
kamurlukurlu. Well, nyanja-yanulpajana kajilpalu wangarlalku
turnu-jarrija. Too late.

And-i, "Now, might be, might be-ilkipala yangkajarrarlujuku
purlkajarrarlu pungu waja? Yawu, nyampuju nyampurrarlangu
warru pungu, ngularrarlangu, yuwayi."

Nyampu well-i nyanungurlukirli nyampuju yalumpujangka jurru
nyanungurlulku yarripalangu yilyaja. Jungajuku, yuwa, jungajuku
rdipijarnilkilpala. Ngulajangkaju, yuwayi, yanulku yangkaju.
Jintaparnta kawartawaraparnta yarnkanjunu. Nyampurlajukulpala
panukariji karrija.

story in the newspaper. However, they were probably sleeping outside.

The two men came near.

"Let's go this way. Ready! We'll kill him. We'll see if he's really married to her."

So they came from around the back of the camp. They came closer and closer. The couple were still some way off. They came closer and closer. Now!

"Here, they are sleeping together!"

He moved the woman away from the man. Whiisst! Just like that, with the axe he struck right through him into the ground. That white fellow was a government man, a government man. Yes, he worked for the government, for the government. Yes. He was dead.

Then they might have speared the woman, with a spear.

Well, then Japanangka climbed up into a cave, and stayed there for a long time. The other one, Japaljarri, ran further off to Mawu, you know, the place we have just seen, Mawu. At that place he climbed up the hill to the fig tree. He climbed up there and then took cover.

Well, many others were camped just to the south of the white man's camp, on this side. There in the south many others were camped.

Right. Someone approached the camp, the one who had rounded up the camels. As he came closer he saw the crows that were gathering. It was too late.

"Now, maybe, maybe those two old men have killed them. Ugh, look at his arm. Ugh, the other arm as well!"

Well, this man decided to send a radio message about the two men to warn the police. He met up with another man. Then he set off with one camel while all the other Aboriginal people stayed where they were. He went. Which way did he go? To Coniston. There he wrote a message, no he did not write a message, he told the people their names. The white man wrote down where it had happened, he wrote and wrote. That Jakamarra gave him the names and the story. He alone told the story to Randall, he told Randall everything.

"Get the police. The old man, our father, is running away!"

Then that same Aboriginal man, Keeper, went with one other and one camel to Capiss. There, at Yinjamurru, the white man gave the message to the man who lived there who took it to Alurayi, no, not to

Yanu-uu nganayikirra – yanurra Coniston-ikirra. Pipa nyanungurluju yirrarnujalanyanu? Ayi, yirrarninjawangurlu lawaju. Yalirlakirli read-manu. Yirrarnu, yirrarnu, yirrarnu, yirrarnu, nyarrpara, nyarrpara? Yimirlangu yangka yirrarnu yalirli Jakamarrarlu. Read-manu yangka yirrarnu.. Jintangka ngayi yangka yinyarla yimi-ngarrurnu Randall-ikilki, Randall-ikilki ngarrurnu, ngarrarnu, ngarrarnu, ngarrarnu-awu.

"Wardangkaji. Wirnmani, ngalipakupalangu ka yani."

Ngula yapa jintalparla yanu Keeper Kapiss-kirralku, Kapiss-kirralparla yanu jintakurlu kawartawarakurlu. Ngulangkapala, right, Yinjamurrapalarla. Walypalirli yaliwardingkilki kangurra Alurayikirra, not Alurayikirra yangka, kanunju Kanajurlakurra, proper town-ukurra, old station-kirra. Ngulakurra yanu. Tarnngalkurla yinja-yanu ngayi nyarrpakarrarlu. Nyanungu walypali kapankurnu rdipija Old Murray yirdi, policeman, Old Murray.

Yanurnu, you know, right up nyampukurra. Alright, nyampurlalu panukariji yanu. Ngayi yangka yalumpu kujarlipa water cross. Karrimirni ka ngapa yalumpujuku. Well, pirli yalumpujuku, water yalumpu, kirrirrparla nyinaja, water hole, really big water. Water hole. Ngulaju, lawajala. Ngulaju yangkakurrawarnulkujala, nyampupurujala lirrirl-pangurnu. Yuwa, larripala pangurnu nyampurlu nganayirla.

Right. Jungajuku yali wantijarra yalumpurla whole lot. Search-i-manujana. Manu yali kurlarnipirdinypa kujalpalu nyinaja muljungka, kalkurni. Yirdiminjikirla, kalkurnilpalu nyinaja. Ngulajangka yanu-uu. Nyampurrarlajulpalu every way wapaja. Yaninja-yanulpalu every way.

You know that, yanurra nganayi jingi-jingi yalumpuwiyi. Nyanungu yukaja. Nyanunguju yali purlka walyangkajalalpa nyinaja. I'll show you that, nyanungu yujuku. Walyangkalpa nyinaja pirnki. Jalangurlu karnangku show-mani, jalangurlu karnangku show-mani. Kutujala, isn't it? There, Yilpijaminirla, not far. It's half mile. Nyanunguwanaju pirnkirlangu karlipa nyanyi.

Ngulajangkaju, yuwayi pirnkingka yukaja, yukaja tarnngaju. Well, pirli, round one there witawangu nyina, well nyampujulpala jirrnganja shut up-jarrija, yunparnulpa, shut him up-manu, marnta. Yunparnulpa shut him up-manu, shut him up-manu yali pirli. Kala

Alurayi, to Kanajurla, right into town to the old station. Keeper had irrevocably given them the information and the white man very quickly went to find Old Murray, the policeman called Old Murray.

You know, he came right up this way. Many people came here, right to that place where we crossed the river, where that water lies over there. Well, one of them had been staying in a cave near a hill at a really big waterhole over there. That is, it used to be a waterhole once, but now they have graded it and put in a concrete causeway.

Well, a great many people came down to this place. They searched for them. They collected all the people who had been camped on the south side by the soak, towards here, at Yirdiminji. Then they all set out. They walked in every direction. They spread out moving in every direction.

Remember the one who at first had gone straight over there? He went right into the earth. That old man lived right underground. I will show you his humpy. He lived underground in a cave. I can show you today. It is not far. It is there, at Yilpijamini, not far, half a mile, just over there. We can see the cave as well.

He used to go into the cave. There has always been a big round stone there. Well, with the stone, he would shut up the cave, while singing to it, to make a closed-in space. He used to sing to close up the cave with the stone. Later he would look about carefully. If he saw nobody, in the afternoon, he would go out and spear game until it was late. He used to store the meat some distance away.

The other man, he went past this way, past that hill, past Minyiparntiparnti. He climbed up and went away, and he remained over there.

They shot many, many other Aboriginal people, a completely different group of people, who, poor things, had had nothing to do with the murder. Murray travelled about shooting them, all the while unable to find the old man who had killed the white man. He was the one who had killed the white man, old Japanangka, my uncle.

Murray went right up past Wakurlpu. Over there he caused Egan great sorrow as well, who now has no brother. He killed everybody. There was nobody left at Mission Creek, you know, to the west. No-one again was left of groups of people returning from ceremonies who Murray met up with, none of them survived either.

wirtirla nyangu kala. Wurajirlijiki kala kuyuju panturnu, until late-irli. Wurnturu kalanyanu yirrarnu.

Jungajuku, yuwa, nyampuwana yanu, pirliwana. Minyiparntiparntiwana-pinangu kankarlarra warrkarnurra. Nyampurla jintakari warrkarnu. Tarnngajukulpa yalumpurla nyinaja.

Panukaripukalpalujana muku-luwarnu, different mob-puka, karnuru, nothing to do. Luwarninja-yanujana-aa. Yangka nyanungurlu missing-manurra again, old man-i, Walypali-luwarnu. He was the walypali-pakarnu, old Japanangka, uncle again, old uncle.

Right up yanu, Wakurlpuwana yanu-uu. Yalirlajukujana wajampa-manu, Egan, Egan-i, like, nganjuluwarnuju, nyampu again, whole lot. Lawajala yangka yali nganayirla, Mission Creek-rla, yangka kuja karlarra. Lawa again. Yangka nganjirni-nganjirni, minijangka, warrmurlujangka. Lawayijala.

Well, first time-wiyi. Ngulajangkaju-uu, yuwayi, kujapurdarlulpa yalurra pinja-yanu, kujapurdarlu yali yalurra pinja-yanu.

Nyanungujarralpala tarnngajuku live-jarrija. Jungajukulpala live-jarrija. Yalumpujuku tarnngajukupala no come out-jarrija, lawa.

Kujapurdarlu tarnngalku pakarninja-yanurnu nganayi warru yatujumpayi Yalaninjikirra.

That far. Nyurru.

Recorded at Yurrkuru, 17 October, 1990

Well, that was the first expedition. Then he went away on the other side, still killing all the people. He went over there killing all the people.

The two old men lived for a long time. Truly, those two lived for a long time. They stayed over there for a long time without coming out.

From the east, Murray came back this way, always killing people, all around this whole area right up to the north, to Yalanjini.

That far. I have finished.

TRANSLATORS' NOTE

This story is an account of a major historical event which took place at Yurrkuru near Coniston in 1928 and later became known as the Coniston massacre, although the killings took place in different Aboriginal camps scattered over the whole area.

Although the narrator retained the use of traditional narrative techniques such as imitating the protagonists' probable speech patterns and feelings, and attributing his right to tell the story to his relationship to the protagonists and locations, the narrative is nevertheless a work of great originality. It can be described as the first Warlpiri text to enter the world of history, because the events are consciously realized in the field of the contingent rather than the timeless. An extra dimension of suspense arises from the knowledge that at any point the events could have taken a different turning. However, the historical necessity of this particular sequence of events is conveyed by the narrator's attention to certain details and matters which indicate the forces he knows to be at play; for instance, his elaboration of the period of the abuse of the women which drives the two men to the point where they have to act. Once they have acted in the only possible way, according to their law, the reaction of the local white community is well understood. In the dangerous tension which has been established in the narrative between white and black, given the disadvantage of the Aboriginal people in terms of weapons, and, most importantly, given the fact that white people do not recognize Aboriginal people or their relationships, the outcome – the indiscriminate slaughter of men, women and children who had nothing whatever to do with the original incident – is inevitable.

The final irony is not lost. The two men who killed the white man managed to hide from the police and the vigilantes and after a considerable period in hiding they returned to their families and lived peacefully until they were old.

MISS PINK-KIRLI

Taking Care of Miss Pink

TOLD BY

Ted Egan Jangala

Nyampu, nyampu karna yirri-pura, nyampu karna yirri-pura nganayi yilpalu mardarnu Miss Pink, yilpalu mardarnu Miss Pink nganayirla Pirdi-pirdirla. Pirdi-pirdirlalpalu mardarnu. Ngulajulpalu mardarnu kardiya, early day-lpalu mardarnu.

Pirdi-pirdirlalpalu mardarnu. Ngulalu kangurnu Puyurrukurra. Puyurrukurralu kangurnu. Nganayirlilpalu kanja-yanulpa bed-piyarlu. Watiyalurla, watiyalu wayurnu. Watiyalu pajurnu, watiyalu pajurnu, wayurnulu, wayurnulu, wayurnulu, wayurnulu, wayurnulu, wayurnulu, wayurnulu, nganayirlili wayurnu. Bed-piyalu ngurrju-manu. Nganayirlilu wayurnu kurrararlu, yangka nganayirli kujakarlipa, kuja karlipa nganayirlangu pajirni. Yangka nganayi kujakarlipa pajirni yutajiti, ngulapiyarlu.

Pajurnulu-uu. Nyampurlalu ngunanja-yirrarnu. Waa, kanja-yanulkulpalu, kanja-yanulkulpalu kujarlu jirramakari. Kujarlulpalu kangu-uu. Murru-murrulpalu kanja-yanu. Jijakurra nganta yungulu kangkarlarni . . . yii . . . nganayikirra, Nyuntukurra, Yarrunkanyikirra, Yarrunkanyikirra. Yungulu kankarlarni.

Kangurnulu, kangurnulu, kangurnulu, kangurnulu, kangurnulu, kangurnulu, kangurnulu. Yalilirla yirrkirnparni ngunaja nganayirla Mirlirlpa Bore-rla. Mirlirlpa Bore-jangkajulu pardija-aa. Kujalu yanu nganayikirra, Puyurrukurra. Puyurrurla ngayili mardarnu. Yirrkirnpalurla ngunaja Puyurrurlalku. Puyurrurlalu mulju pangurnu. Muljulu pangurnu ngapa. Watiyalurla yirrarnu, yirrarnu, yirrarnu.

Ngulalpalu mardarnu, ngulalpalu mardarnu.

"Karingantarlipa kanyi!"

"Ngapawiyili nganja yangka."

"Ngapalu ngula nganja yangka nganayi. Ngapakulu ngulaku yanta yalumpuku nganayiki, ngapa yangka yalumpu nganayi Jila Well-rla kujapurda."

"Yumurrpa. Yumurrpakulu parnkaya!"

Yumurrpakupala, parnkajapala jirrama. Nyanja-yanupala Yumurrpa.

"Karinganta ngapa palka."

"Oh, yalikirralku karlipa kanyi."

Yalikirralku kangu Yumurrpakurra. Yumurrparlalkulpalu mardarnu. Mardarnu, mardarnu, mardarnu, mardarnu, mardarnu,

These are the events I am going to recount – how they cared for Miss Pink, at, you know, at Pirdi-pirdi. They looked after her at Pirdi-pirdi. There they looked after the white woman, in the early days. They were looking after her at Pirdi-pirdi.

Then they took her to Puyurru. They carried her to Puyurru. They travelled carrying her in a thing like a bed. They had tied poles together, from trees. They cut the poles from the trees, then they bound them around, around and around. They made a thing like a bed. They bound it round with the kurrara vine. That, you know, is what we use, it is what we cut for that kind of purpose. It is what we cut like yutajiti, to be used for the same purpose.

They cut the vine. Then they placed her on it so that she was lying down. In this way they carried her along, in this way, two at a time. Thus they took her, they took the sick one along with them. They hoped to find a nurse, so they went up towards Nyuntu and then towards Yarrunkanyi. For this reason they went up.

They carried her and carried her. There they slept together, they slept at Mirlirlpa Bore. Then they left Mirlirlpa Bore. From there they went to, you know, to Puyurru. They looked after her at Puyurru. They slept all together at Puyurru. At Puyurru they dug out a soak. They dug out the soak for water. They made a bed for her there, there they made a bed.

And so they were looking after her.

"Maybe we should be taking her on somewhere else?"

"Let's all drink plenty of water first."

"You know, they should all drink plenty of water. Therefore, you others must go to find more water, perhaps, you know, in the direction of Jila Well."

"Yumurrpa. Run quickly to Yumurrpa!"

Two men ran off to Yumurrpa. As they approached, they examined the situation at Yumurrpa.

"There will certainly be water here."

"Oh, then we can carry her here, to this place."

They carried her to Yumurrpa. They looked after her at Yumurrpa. That is where they looked after the sick woman. Then they took her away from there. They carried her to Jila.

Ah, they went looking for water at Yumurrpa. Then they took her to

175

mardarnu. Ngulajangkajulu kangu. Ngulajangkajulu kangu
Jilakurralku.   Ah, ngapalu nyanja-yanu Yumurrpa. Yumurrpalu
nyanja-yanu. Yumurrpakurralu kangurnu. Ngulajangkajulu
ngunaja-ngunaja again. Kirringkalu mardarnu, mardarnu, mardarnu
ngurrjukarrikarrilki. Kalalurla yungu wardapi. Kalalu ngangkayirli,
kalalurla yapangku manu, witch doctor-rlu. Witch doctor-rlu kalalu,
kalalu yunparnu. Kalalurla kuyu yungu wardapi, marlu, yurapiti,
kararrpa. Kararrpa kala ngarnu. Nganayi kala ngarnu yarla, yarla
kala ngarnu, yumurnunju kala ngarnu, yumurnunju means that . . .
yeah yarla wita, ngarlajiyi, ngarlajiyi. Ngulajangkaju janmarda,
janmarda kalalurla karlaja. Kalalu yirrarnu parrajarla. Janmardaju
kalalu nyanungukurra kalalurla kangurnu.

Ngulajangkajulu pardija-aa nganayikirralku? Kujapurdalkulu
pardijarra Jila Well-kirra. Jila Well-rlalkulpalu mardarnu, mardarnu,
mardarnu, mardarnu, mardarnu.

"Kakarrararlipa kanyi? Nganayi, walypalikirrarlangu yilparlipa
nyangkarla. Nyampurlaku, Braitling?"

"Yuwa."

Ngulakurralu pardija. Ah, Pirrpirrpakarnulurla yirrkirnpa-ngunaja
– kutulku – Pirrpirrpakarnurla – yangka karru karluwarnurla.
Ngulajangkajulu pardijarni-ii. Kangurnulu, kangu wurrurnulu
Jinirrpakurra, karluwarnukurra windmill kujaka karri. Nyampukula
kakarrara Luurnpakurlanguju, nyampukula pirliji
Luurnpakurlanguju. Nyampukurralu kangurnu Jinirrpakurra.

Ah, ngurrangkalu mardarnu, mardarnu, mardarnu, mardarnu.
Kangurralurla walypalikilki.

"Karingantalparlipa kangkarla. Yilpankulu yilyayarla town-
kurralku. Ngulajukurnalu yupujurlaju mardarnu. Ngularnalu
yapangku waja kangurnu."

"Yuwa, ngurrju waja!"

Purlka-purlkalurla wangkaja.

"Yeah, ngurrju yalumpuju waja. Kapurnalu yilya Alice Springs-
kirralku."

Ngulajangkakulalu yilyaja Alice Springs-kirraju.

Ah, nyanungurnalu, show-manunganpa nyanungukulku yilparnalu
yanu nyanjaku. Nyanungurlunganpa ngarrurnu-again,

"Karinganta yapangkujulu mardarnu waja yalirla Warlpirirli –

Yumurrpa. There they stayed. They looked after her at the camp, they cared for her, until she was a little better. They gave her goanna meat. She was treated by ngangkayi, by Aboriginal people, by witch doctors. The witch doctors sang to heal her, they used to sing to her. They used to give her goanna meat, kangaroo, rabbit, karrarrpa. She used to eat karrarrpa. She also ate yams, she ate yams, in particular the little yam, ngarlajiyi. After that, they dug up wild onions for her, which they used to put in a coolimon [long wooden dish]. Then they took the wild onions to her.

From there, they set off to, you know, in that direction, towards Jila Well. Then they stopped there and cared for her at Jila Well, there they cared for her for a time.

"Shall we take her towards the east? Perhaps we should go towards the place of the white man to see if we can find him, to Braitling's place?"

"Yes."

So they set off in that direction. They slept overnight all together at Pirrpirrpakarnu, nearby, near Pirrpirrpakarnu, at the creek on the south side. Then they set off again. They carried her, they carried her quietly, towards Jinirrpa, towards the south side where there is a windmill standing. It is at that place east of here, at Luurnpakurlangu, at the hill Luurnpakurlangu. They carried her to this place, to Jinirrpa.

Ah, they continued always to care for her at the camp. Then they took her to the white man.

"We have brought her here so that you can send her into town. Up to now, we have cared for her in the bush. It was we Warlpiri people who brought her along and looked after her. We have done the right thing," the old men said to him.

"Yes, very good. We can send her to Alice Springs now."

So then they sent her to Alice Springs.

Later she showed us how grateful she was when we went to see her. She said to us again and again: "It was certainly the Warlpiri people who looked after me there, the Warlpiri people from Mount Doreen."

Ahh, yes. But after that, she no longer lived with us, the dear person. That is all.

Mount Doreen-wardingkirli."

Ah, yeah. Well ngakarranyi nganimpapuru lawa-nyinaja, karnuru.
Ngulajuku.

Recorded at Yuendumu, 17 October, 1990

TRANSLATORS' NOTE

This is an account of how Mrs Olive Pink (1884–1975), the distinguished anthropologist and botanist, was taken on a vine stretcher to Puyurru and then Yumurrpa, after she became seriously ill while living at Pirdi-pirdi (Thompson's Rockhole) with a group of Warlpiri people. It happened in 1944. Mrs Pink was the only white person there, indeed the only white person many of the people had seen. At Pirdi-pirdi, she learned to speak Warlpiri and made notes on the language. She also made extensive notes on local flora and taught the Warlpiri people who visited her how to cook with flour and other European ingredients.

When she became ill, she was treated according to traditional Warlpiri medicine. Thus, she was taken on a stretcher made out of two poles bound with kurrara vine to places where the Warlpiri people knew they could find water and the kind of food needed to build up a sick person's strength, namely the meat of game animals – particularly reptiles – the wild potato, and a very small brown wild onion.

Later, it was decided to take her to Braitling's mining camp at Mount Doreen. From there, she returned to Alice Springs. She never came back to Pirdi-pirdi. However, it says much for the effectiveness of Warlpiri medicine that she lived until she was ninety-one years old.

In telling the story, Ted Egan Jangala has used repetition to emphasize the sustained effort involved in travelling considerable distances with the sick woman, and also the way in which the sick are given constant support and personal attention.

Although this is not a jukurrpa story, it is now considered to belong to the Jangala-Jampijinpa men and women of one particular family.

YAPUNTAKURLU

The Orphan

TOLD BY

Mary O'Keefe Napurrurla

Tennant Creek ■

■ *Yarturlu-yarturlu*

Jarrajarra ■   ■ *Alekarenge*
Willowra ■ *Yarrkumardi* ■

■ *Yuendumu*

■ *Alice Springs*

Nyangulparna nganayi pilapanu. Ngulalparnarla janji-pungu. Ngarnulparna, ngarnulparna, janji-pinjarlalparna ngarnu-uu. Pardijalkurna. Yanulkurna, karlarrapurdalku yanurna – jiljakurra. Jiljakurrarna yanu. Yanurna-aa. Kujapurdalparna karlarrapurda yanu. Yanulparna. Yanurna-aa. Nganayilparna kanta ngarnu wirrkarliwarnu, wirrkarliwarnulkurna kanta ngarnu. Ngarnulparna pantirninjarla. Yamangkarlulparna ngarnu. Pakarnulparnarla watiyarlu. Karlarrapurda again pardija again, pardijarna. Karlarrapurdarna pardija.

Yanulparna-aa. Malikilparna kangu, jarntuju wungujuku. Kangulparna, kangulparna. Yanurna. Ngunajalparna Yirlangkurrunyurla – jinta. Yuwayi. Ngunajalparna, yuwayi, yuwayi. Ngunajalparna Yirlangkurrunyurla. Kankarlarrapurda. Ngunajalparna kankarlarrapurda-aa. Well-i, nganayilki kujurnu ngapalku. Milpirrilki kujurnu mangkurdurlu kankarlarrapurda, kujurnu.

Well-lparna ngunaja. Ngaka turlurl-purlaja ngajunyangurla. Yunguju, Wapirrarluju yungu. Mm, yuwayi, yuwa, no-lparna purda-nyangu Wapirra. Walku. Ngayilparna wapala, wapalalparna wapaja. Yuwayi. Junga nyampuju karna yirri-pura, junga. Not-i karna manyu yirri-pura. Yanulparna-aa. Wayi, yarlurnuju ngapangkuju. Kujapurdayijala ngapaju pardija. Maarr-maninja-yanu kujapurdayijala karlarrapurda. Well-rna yalirlayijala pardija. Yanurna-aa, karlarralparna yanu, yanu, yanu, yanu, yanu. Yalirlajuku wantaju nganayi pardija.

Wanta yati! Mangkurdu yati muku parnkaja. Yuwa, wantapurujurna yukajalku. Well-rna yarda pardija. Karlarrarna yanu, karlarra, karlarra, karlarra, karlarra. Aa, ngulyalku now, ngulyalkurna nyangu, right.

"Nyampu ngulya waja!" Well, kaninjarrarna jitija. Malikijirna ngurungku kangu kujarlulparna kangu, kaninjarrarna jitija.

"You go!" Jitijarna. Ngunajalparlijarra yalirlanya kaninjarra. Ngunajarlijarra, ngunajarlijarra, ngunajarlijarra. Well, walya kujurnu.

"Nyiyarlu ngarra kujurnu walya?" Marntirrji kujurnu. Ngulawarnu nyangurna. Kankarlarrarlijarra warrkarnu, warrkarnu, warrkarnu, warrkarnu, kankarlarrayijala. Palyal-pardijarrarlijarra.

I saw the, you know, wild onions. Then I beat them, shaking out the earth. Indeed, having got them out from the earth, I ate them. I set off again. Then I went towards the west, I went, I went towards the sand-hills. I went in that direction, towards the west. I kept on travelling. I went on. You know, I ate the kanta, from the bloodwood tree, from the bloodwood tree I ate the kanta. After I had split them open, I ate them, sitting in the shade. I hit them with a stick. I travelled again, again westward, I travelled towards the west.

So I went on. I took a dog with me, although later I travelled without the dog. I went on, I went on. I slept one night at Yirlangkurrunya, yes, yes, I slept at Yirlangkurrunya, up on the top. I slept up on the top. Well, you know, rain fell, from the clouds, the rain fell up on the top.

Well, I was sleeping. Later there was thunder where I was sleeping. God had given the rain to me, but at that time I did not know anything about God. I walked about in ignorance.

This is the exact truth I am recounting for you. I am not telling this just to entertain you. So I went on. I became very wet from the rain. The rain went off in the other direction, with the lightning still flashing, that way, to the west. Well, I set off in that direction as well. I went on, to the west, on and on. There the sun appeared.

I was very pleased to see the sun, and that the rain clouds had all gone away. While the sun was out I went into the shade. Then I set off again. I went towards the west, always towards the west. Ah, a hole, I saw a hole, right.

"Here is a hole!" I climbed down into it. The dog which at that time I still had with me also climbed down.

"You go!" It climbed down. We both slept right there inside, we both slept there. Well, something threw earth in on top of us.

"What was that, that threw the earth?" It threw it in little lumps. I looked about. We climbed up, back to the top again. We both got out.

"Ah, it is already late afternoon." I set out, going east. I became frightened. I thought I was going west still, I thought I was still going west. Well, I went east, you know, to a large river bed, I ended up going back to the river bed. You know, that river bed is Wijinpurlurlu, that creek. So, I travelled back there. It was at that place I had lost my mother, there, at that place, Winjinpurlurlu.

Well, I returned east again. I went on and on, in the dark. You know,

"Ah, yuwa, wuraji-wuraji waja nyampuju."
Kakarrarapurdalkurna pardija. Yaliyati, karlarrapurda kujalparna
purda-nyangu, "Karlarrapurdajala ngarrarna yantarla." Well
kakarrarapurda yalirna nganayikirrayijala yangka wulpayi
yalumpukurra pina yanu. Wulpayi yangka yalumpu nganayi
Winjinpurlungu manta.

Ngulakurrarna pina yanu. Yalirla now-rna lose-manurra
ngajunyanguju mother-ju, ngamardiji, yalirla now yalumpurlanya
Winjinpurlungurluju. Well-i pinarna yanu kakarrarayijala. Yanurna,
yanurna, yanurna, yanurna kutukarilki, kutukarilki, kutukarilki,
kutukarilki. Nganayirlarna ngunaja Yarlawarnurla rdakungka.
Ngunajarna. Kujalparnalu, kujalpalu yapangku pangurnu.
Ngulangkarna ngunaja. Yardarna yarnkaja mungalyurrulku. Yuu,
parnkamirra, parnkamirra, parnkamirra. Ngayilparlijarra
yarnunjuku wapaja, maliki and all.

Yanulparlijarra. Well-rna walyirirlalku, yakirirlijarranyanu
pangurnu. Well, ngapa kujalpa wantija. Yakirirlijarranyanu
pangurnu, malikirli, yapangku. Ngunajalparlijarra – yalirlajuku
ngarra. Nyarrpa-jarrija malikiji? Yuwayi. Yalirlajukurlu ngarra
wuruly-manu ngajukuju warnpangkarni. Ngunajalparna warnpa,
ngunajalparna.

Yangkajurnarla nyangu, "Karnuru, maliki nyarrpara waja?"
Warrukirdikirdi wapaja ngantalparna, warrukirdikirdi wapaja-aa.
Nganayiji wardapi, nganayiji wardapiji ngulajulparna
pakarninjinanu, kijirninja-yanu. Pukulyulkulparna kijirninja-yanu.
Yuwayi, no warlu, yuwayi.

And yakajirri, nganayilparna ngarnu kanta. Ngulajukulparna
ngarninja-yanu. Yuwa, pirdaparntajukulparna wapaja. Might-lpaju
wapirrarlu marda nganayi-manu. Yanulparna kakarrarapurdalku
yali jiljakaringirli wurnturungurlu, yali karlumparrangurlu.
Yalingirlirna pina yanu kakarrarapurdalku. Yanulparna-aa.

Well, nganayirlalku, kutukarilkilparna yanu. Wayurnurnarla,
watiyakulparnarla wayurnu, wayurnu. Ngayilparnarla marnpurnu
warru – nganayirla mungangka. Wayurnulparnarla,
wayurnulparnarla. Well-rna rdarri-mardarnu that wakirlpirri,
wakirlpirrirna rdarri-mardarnu.

"Aya, nyampurlajukurna nguna waja."

I slept at Yarlawarnu in a hole. I slept in one which we had, which people had dug. I slept there. In the morning I set off again. Yes, I ran away, I ran away. We were very hungry, the dog as well as I.

We went on. Well, I dug into the soft ground, down into the damp earth, where the rain had fallen. We both dug into the soft ground, the dog and the human. We slept again in the same place. What happened to the dog? Yes. At that very place someone quietly took the dog, while I was deeply asleep. I was very deeply asleep. Later, I saw it was gone.

"Oh, the dear thing! Where is my dog?" I ran around and around, desperately.

I also managed to catch and kill a goanna, but I threw it away. It was not edible because it was raw, so I threw it away. Yes, I had no fire, yes. And I ate yakajirri, I ate kanta. Then I ate those as I went along. I actually walked on quite satisfied. Maybe my father would somehow find me. I went on east, away from those sand-hills I came back east. I went on. Well, I travelled even at night. I was looking, I was looking for a tree. Because it was very dark, I had to feel my way around, looking for a tree. I searched and searched. Well, I managed to grasp hold of a dogwood tree, I grasped hold of a dogwood tree.

"Oh, yes, I can sleep here." To tell the truth, I slept there. I slept propped up against the tree, with my head against it like a pillow, against that tree, the dogwood tree.

Again I travelled on. I travelled a long way, it was from a long distance that I came, in these events I am now recounting. Yes. I went on, east, we both, no, I went on without the dog, without it. Yes. Yes, in that place they had sneakingly taken it. In the place of soft ground.

"Ohh, they have taken it!"

Yes, I kept on going on. Now I was without water, no water, none. I went on, I went towards the east, east. Night fell, there, in that place. I travelled on.

Well, I slept where I was, in the grass, in the dead grass, in the grass. It is dry grass which is found in that place. In that, I lay down. I slept in a place toward the east, no, toward the west. I was lying down, I was lying down. Later when the sun was high in the sky, very late like that I woke up. I set out again. I went away from there, on and on.

"Hey, a dog has brought these here!" A dingo had brought the pups

Jungajukurna ngunajarra. Ngayilparna kuja ngamparl-ngunaja. Rdirrpangkalparna ngunaja, kuja well nyampupiyarla watiyarla, wakirlpirrirlajala.

Yardarna yanu. Wurnturujulparna yanu. Wurnturungurlu nyampuju karna ngari kutu yirri-puralku. Yuwayi. Yanulparna-aa. Kakarraralkurlujarra, no, yanulparna malikiwangulku, lawalku. Yuwayi. Yalirlajukujulu wuruly-manu, walyirirlajala.

"Wa, nyampujulu manu!"

Yuwayi. Yanulparna. Well ngapawangurlalku, no ngapa, walku. Ngayilparna yanu. Yanulparna kakarrara, kakarrara, kakarrara, kakarrara. Kutukari-jarrijaju yalirlajuku. Yanulparna. Well-rna kutu jarda wantija nganayirlalku, now, marnangkalku, yangka liwirrjirla, marnangka. Liwirrji kujaka ngunami. Ngulangkalkulparna ngunaja. Ngunajarna. Nati kakarrarapurda, not kujapurda, kapu kujapurda, no, karlarrapurdarna ngunajalku, ngunajalparna.

Yakarra-pardijarna ngaka kankarlarrarlalku. Kujangupiyarlalkurna yakarra-pardija. Yardarna yarnkaja. Yanurra, yanurra, yanurra.

"Wayi, malikirlijana nyampu kangu – warnaparirli." Kangujana kujapurda, kangujana. Well, yawakiyikirrajana kangu. Ngulangkajukurnajana muku-tardirr-pakarnurnajana. Nyurnulkulpalu ngunaja purdangirliji. Mukurnajana pakarnu. Pakarnurnajana. Nyurnulkulpalu ngunaja. Ngajujurnajana jurnta-yanu. Jurnta yanurnajana.

Yanulparna kakarrara. Yanulparna, yanulparna, yanulparna, yanulparna. Wardapirna pakarnu kirdanyanu. Kangulparna. Nyanungulku now-lparna kangu. Kangulparna, pukulyulkulparna kangu. Well-rna parnti-nyangu. Well-rna kujurnurra, now. Yuwayi, kujurnurrarna kulkurru.

Yardarna yarnkaja. Yanirra, yanirra, yanirra, yanirra, yanirra, yanirra. Kujalkulparna yanu. Wulpayilkirna follow-manu, wulpayilkirna follow-manu, follow-manu, follow-manu, follow-manu. Purajarna, purajarna, purajarna, purajarna. Ngaparna nyangu nganayi Yarrkamardi. That winji kujaka parnka, yali ngapa. Know-manijala karna nyanunguju. Ngulangka ngularna ngarnu, punungkalparna ngarnu. Yuwayi. Ngarnulparna, ngarnu, ngarnu, ngarnu, ngarnu, ngarnu, ngarnu!

there, had brought them. Well, it had brought them to the yawakiyi tree.

Then I hit them all one by one. They all lay dead back there, I hit all of them. I hit them. They all lay dead. Then I left them there. I went away and left them. I went on to the east. I went away. I also caught and killed a big goanna. I carried it along, then I carried this one along with me, I carried it along as it was going rotten. I started to smell it. Well, I threw it away, I threw it away in the middle of my journey.

I went on again. I went away, away. I followed the river bed along, on and on I followed the river bed. I followed it. I saw water at Yarrkamardi. There is a spring there that runs, I know the place, there. There I drank, I bent down and drank. I drank and drank.

"Where? Now a person is coming towards me!" You know, my wantirrirna, my aunt, was coming towards me from over there, Wayikurdu and her family. From that place she followed me.

"Who is that person sitting there?" Well, I saw her, I saw the place.

"Hey, a fire is burning!" I saw it. I went around it, watching it. Yes, I watched it, I watched it.

"Hey, a person is coming." I took off. I climbed right up to the top. I ran off very quickly. Yes, at that point I ran away from that person. I ran and ran. She followed me, all the while crying out to me. My wantirrirna, Wayikurdu, followed me, she kept on after me.

"You can get hold of her there."

I managed to run a long distance, hiding in the spear grass. I had water there to drink, but no food. I was eating yakajirri and kanta, that is what I used to eat.

Well, they continued to search for me. Well, I went around in this direction, around by the east into the mulga trees, I went into the mulga trees. I travelled around this way, I went on. I went on in that direction again. Yes, then I left that place.

That was the place where they had beaten my mother, and left her lying under a pile of firewood, a pile as high as my head. Well, I had turned back again in that direction, to, first, Wijinpurlungu, no, yes, Wijinpurlungu. Well, I was going along back towards there in that direction again. That one had been keeping me safe and good, God perhaps.

Yes, she had been looking for me there, she had been looking for me.

"Nyarrpara? Yapalkuju rdipija!" Nganayilki wantirrina yalinya nganayilki rdipija Wayikurdu. Yalilkiji purajalpaju.

"Yuwa, yalarnimpiji ka nyina." Well-iparna nyangu, ngurulparna nyangu.

"Wayi, warlu ka jankaw!" Nyangulparna. Kulparirlilparna nyangu. Yuwayi. Nyangulparna-aa, nyangurna.

"Wayi, yapa ka yanirni!" Yarnkajarrarna. Warrkarnurrarna kankarlarra. Wajilijikilparna parnkaja. Yuwayi, jurnta-parnkajalparnajana yapaku nyampuju. Parnkajarna, parnkajarna, parnkajarna, parnkajarna. Nyanungurlulpaju liyikarrarlu puraja, wantirrinarluju. Purajalpaju Wayikurdurlu, purajalpaju, purajalpaju.

"Yalumpurla kalakanpa rdarri-mardarni."

Yinya ngarrarna wurnturu wuruly-parnkaja, Yinjirrirlalku. Ngapajurna nyampu ngarnujala, well no miyi. And yakajirri, nganayilki kanta, ngulalparna ngarnu.

Well-lpajulurla wayurnu kujarlu. Ngajurna kujalku yanu. Kakarrumparrarlulku nganayirlalku wardiji-wardijirlalkurna pardija-aa. Yii, kujalkulparna yanu-uu, yanulparna. Aa, yalikirra-again-lparna yanu. Yuwayi, yalingirli kujarna pardija.

Ngajunyangu kujalu ngamardilki yirrarnu warlu, ngiji nyampupiyakurralku. Well, yalikirra-again-lparna kulpari yanu yalumpu, nganayikirra nyiyawiyi, Winjinpurlungu, yuwa, Winjinpurlungurla. Ngulakurranyarna pina yaninja-yanu kujarniyijala, yaninja-yanurnu. Jungarni-manulpaju yali nyanungurlu marda Wapirrarlu.

Yuwa, warrurnulpaju kuja, warrurnulpaju. Yangkajulparna ngunajalku. Yalinyalparna warnpa, warnpalku ngunaja nganayirla yinirntirla wiringka. Nyiyapiya ngarra kirrirdilparna wapaja. Wita, ngari. Ngakalkujalajulu yangka nyampu, nyampulku wirirra manu, nyampurlujala, yuwayi. Ngunajalparna. Nyanungulkuju rdipija. Rdarri-mardarnuju yalirlajuku. Nyanungurluju wantirrinarlu rdarri-mardarnuju. Kujurnulpa. Ngayilparna, ngayilparna, kuruwintiwinti-jurrurnulparlijarranyanu. Kuruwintiwinti-jurrurnu nyanungurluju wantirrirliji waja.

"Yuwa, wantirri waja nyuntunyangu waja ngajujurna. Nyuntunyangu waja!"

Nyanunguju, nyanungujulpa! Well, rdarri-mardarninjarla

Then, I was there soundly asleep, I was deeply asleep beside a big yinirnti tree. I was tall at that time but without breasts, still a girl. It was only later that my breasts developed. I was lying asleep. She came up to me. She grabbed hold of me, my wantirrirna grabbed hold of me. I threw her off, I threw her off. We struggled, she struggled with me, my wantirrirna.

"Hey, I am your wantirri, your aunt, yours. Me, I am your relative, that one, that one!"

Well, taking a firm hold of me, she took me with her. Well, in this way they made a fire for me. They put it around me, to the west, to the south. There was a lot of smoke then. She stayed there, that wantirri, my relative. She sat there, she sat there, in the smoke. We sat there together. I lay down.

And when we slept, I slept like a dog does at their feet. Those people placed me in that position. I used to sleep there like a dog does. I used to sleep there. I did not sleep in their arms. They covered a water-carrier for me. That is where the people, my uncles, put me. Yes, I used to lie there. Well, I started to feel good, I started to mend there, they made me well, those people, in that place, Napangardi and her family. They healed me, they healed me. They made me feel peaceful, they took me with them, they took me along with them then.

The one belonging to who was it, the one without a mother took me, yes, the one belonging to Walyangarnu, the one belonging to that one found me and brought me up, that one. They cooked meat for me there. They made broth for me out of that meat. I used to walk around. I used to eat little yams, I used to eat, you know, that one from the mulga tree, the fruit. I used to walk after him and eat, and the one who maybe had no mother went in front. She used to go along cutting out witchetty grubs. I used to eat everything, yes, everything.

Yes, I had travelled all alone.

That is all.

kangulkujulu. Well, warlujulu kuja yirrarnu, kujajulu yirrarnu, kujajulu karlarra yirrarnu, kurlarrajulu yirrarnu, rduyu-karrijalku. Nyanungulpa wantirri nyinaja ngajuparnta. Nyinajalpa, nyinajalpa. Ngulajuku kunjururlu, kunjururlu. Nyinajalpa well-rlijarra. Ngunajalkulparna.

And malikipiya kalarnajana karlajawana ngunaja. Kalajulu yirrarnu nyampurrarluju. Malikipiya kalarna ngunaja karlajarla. No kalajulu ngamirljirla mardarnu, manu kalajulu parnta-yirrarnu karlajarla —yalumpurrarlunya yapangku ngarraju nganayi, yuwayi. Ngunajalparna. Well-rna, ngurrjulkulparna nyinaja. Ngurrjulkulparna nyinaja yaliji. Ngurrju-manujulu nyanungurluju yapangku yalumparrarluju Napangardimarntarlu. Ngurrju-manu, ngurrju-manujulu, purangi-manujulu. Kanguju, kangulkujulu yalilki.

And nganayikirlangurlulku, wurlkumanu-mardawangurluju manu, yalirli yangka Walyangarnukurlangurlu. Ngulakurlangurlunyaju manu, wiri-manuju yalirlilki wawirrirli nganayirli mijiwirrirli. Yuwayi, ngulangkulpaju nganayi-manu. Kalarna wapaja. Kalarna ngarlajiyi ngarnu, kalarna nganayi yangka wardijiwarnu ngarnu waranjakurlu, kalarna ngarnu ngula pirdangirli-pirdangirlirli. Wurlkumanu-mardawangu kala yanu kamparrumpayi. Wardingirlangu kala pajirninja-yanu. Kalarna everything-iji ngarnu, yuwayi, everything-iji.

Yuwayi, jintarna yanu.
Ngulajuku.

Recorded at Alekarange, 25 October, 1990

Notes on the Plates

Plate 1: WHAT HAPPENED AT THE PLACE OF FIRE
Warlu (fire) dreaming
This painting shows all the activities in the narrative: at the top, the blue-tongue lizard with shields and stick casts his spell, and at the bottom, the flames of the sorcerer's fire pursue the two Jangala men, represented as two horseshoe shapes repeated across the canvas. In the centre are the tracks of the mythical Emu (not in this narrative) which travels across the fire dreaming country eating bush food and laying eggs.

Plate 2: HOW I CAME BACK TO YAJARLU
Pampardu (flying ant) dreaming
This painting shows the travels of the swarming ants in the War-ntunguru area and the ants (Jampijinpa-Jangala) being eaten by the possums (Jakamarra-Jupurrurla). These interrelated dreamings are located in the area around Yajarlu to the south-west of Yuendumu.

Plate 3: THE TRAVELS OF THE WITI POLES
Ngalyipi (vine) dreaming
The witi poles and the ngalyipi vine, used for tying the poles to the dancers' legs, are the main images associated with the initiation of young men. In this painting, the poles are absent but the yellow twisting vine is the central element linking the old men, represented as circles, with the young men they are teaching, represented as horseshoe shapes. The location of the painting, represented by the central circle, is the cave at Yarripilangu, one of the places visited by the men and the initiates in their ritual travels. The red wavy lines framing the vines are creeks and the red horseshoe shape at the bottom right hand corner represents the women watching the ceremony.

Plate 4: ABOUT PATILIRRI
Ngatijirri (budgerigar) dreaming
This painting shows the eggs of the budgerigars in the tree trunks and

191

their birth at a place called Lima from where they travel, represented by the crosses, to arrive eventually at Patilirri.

Plate 5: THE BATTLE AT YUMURRPA
Wapirti (little yam) dreaming
This painting shows the places of Wapurtarli and Yumurrpa, represented by the large circles with Wapurtarli in the middle. The horseshoe shapes with sticks beside them are women seated at holes digging for yams.

Plate 6: THE TWO DOGS
Jarntujarra (two dogs) dreaming
This painting shows the rockhole at Kaljawarnu, at the top of the picture, where the man-dog kills the kadaija man who is then eaten by the two dogs.

Plate 7: THE TWO SNAKES
Kunajarrayi dreaming
The central place of this painting is Kunajarrayi. Japaljarri has painted several dreamings that pass through this country: witchetty grub, budgerigar and women's dreamings. The snakes are associated with witchetty grubs (from which, in the Dreaming, they are born). The witchetty grubs appear down the left of the canvas. The horseshoe shapes in the upper centre and bottom right represent the women looking for bush tucker. The other horseshoe shapes are the two men travelling through the country. The crosses along the top are the tracks of the associated Japaljarri-Jungarrayi dreaming of the budgerigars. The unusual shape centre right is Japaljarri's heart of spirit.

Plate 8: THE MAN FROM WAWARLJA
Jungarrayi dreaming
In this painting the long shape in the middle represents the Jungarrayi, the man with all the wives. He lies sick with boils at Kurra (literally boil) near a soak, seen at the bottom of the picture. Some of the wives, represented by the horseshoe shapes, are tending him and some are fetching water from the soak. As can be seen, the Jungarrayi has many wives, too many – the cause of all the trouble.

Plate 9 (p. 172): TAKING CARE OF MISS PINK
In this photograph Olive Pink is shown at the Granites in 1936. The vehicle behind on which a group of Warlpiri people are seated – a very different mode of transport from the stretcher on which Olive Pink was carried by the Warlpiri men in Ted Egan Jangala's story – belonged to the South Australian Board for Anthropological Research.